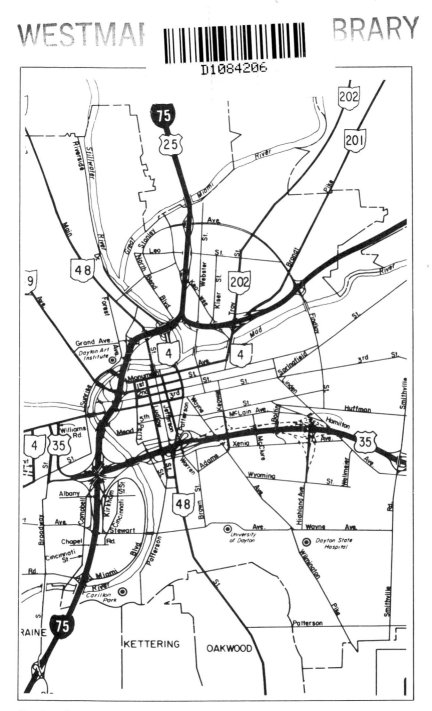

Dayton Area Ohio Highway Map

HIGHWAYS TO NOWHERE

*The Politics of City
Transportation*

BY RICHARD HÉBERT

The life of a city flows along its sidewalks and streets, and the types of transportation employed are the key to the health of that city. When the sidewalks are empty, when getting from here to there requires a private automobile, then life in the city begins to become unbearable.

HIGHWAYS TO NOWHERE diagnoses the condition of city transportation in five representative American cities—Flint, Michigan; Dayton, Ohio; Indianapolis, Indiana; Atlanta, Georgia; and Washington, D.C.—and finds cases of hardening of the arteries. For the past twenty years, city, state, and federal governments have sought in the building of highways in, around, and through cities the panacea for many problems. Instead, their highways have only attracted more cars—and more pollution—into the city and made it easy for the middle class—and thus the cities' tax base—to escape. Mass transit systems have not been given a fair chance to compete, and the poor are trapped in their own neighborhoods.

Flint, a product of General Motors and the automobile, no longer has a public bus system. Almost half of Dayton's downtown area is devoted to moving and storing cars—streets, alleys, and parking lots. Atlanta began work on a rapid transit system only after the city had been riddled and surrounded by interstate highways, expressways, and connectors.

Highways to Nowhere

The Politics of City Transportation

by Richard Hébert

The Bobbs-Merrill Company, Inc.
Indianapolis / New York

The Bobbs-Merrill Company, Inc.
Indianapolis / New York

HIGHWAYS TO NOWHERE focuses on five cities that are typical of many cities in the country. Hébert outlines the history of each city, its economic background, and its power structure. He then relates these factors to the systems of public and private transportation that have developed over the past two decades. He shows how city governments feuded with suburban governments over regional planning issues; how downtown merchants lobbied for highways into the center of a city, then moved to suburban shopping centers when business drastically declined; how expressways sometimes cut off poor neighborhoods from the rest of the city, and how citizens' groups were occasionally able to halt construction of a highway through their city. And he provides thoughtful suggestions for reform, insisting that our cities must start planning for people, not for automobiles.

HIGHWAYS TO NOWHERE is must reading for everyone who wants his city to survive. It is an eloquent plea to citizens and responsible city officials to take everyone's transit needs into account and to save our cities from being strangled by their own highways.

"Hébert is utterly convincing in arguing that faulty transportation decisions are contributing to the decay of our urban centers. He tells, in abundant and interesting detail, the tales of five cities— Flint, Dayton, Indianapolis, Atlanta, and Washington—each plagued by distressingly similar transportation problems. . . . This book is impressively researched, well written, and likely to generate controversy in metropolitan areas."

—*Library Journal*

To Renée and Thérèse,
who will have to live with the cities we leave them.

Table of Contents

Acknowledgments

The information in this book is the result of my own observations and extensive interviews in each of the five subject cities. While the judgments and conclusions are entirely my own, I gratefully acknowledge the patient assistance of and contributions of time by the many public servants, business leaders, news reporters, and others in each of the cities. I particularly thank those at the C. S. Mott Foundation in Flint, Michigan, the Transportation Coordinating Committee of Montgomery and Green Counties, Ohio, the Indianapolis Department of Transportation, the Metropolitan Atlanta Rapid Transit Authority, and the Washington Metropolitan Area Transit Authority.

The cities of Flint, Dayton, and Indianapolis were first researched by me in 1969 as part of the Center City Transportation Study conducted by the Center for Policy Analysis of the National League of Cities and United States Conference of Mayors for the United States Department of Transportation. In this regard, acknowledgment is particularly due Joe Dixon, then a graduate student of business at Indiana University, for his assistance as the untiring other half of my "field team" during that study. Most especially, I am grateful for the help, advice, and moral support of Dr. George Smerk of the Graduate School of Business at Indiana University, without whom this book would not have been written.

R. H.

Introduction

Each morning Jesse Dawson, the black man next door with the raspy voice and the large hands who always says good morning, hoses down the sidewalk in either direction as far as his hose will reach.

Up the street, in front of her row house, a tall, skinny woman with orange hair sprays a mist of water over her small flower garden each evening.

A tiny, dark-skinned woman passes by wearing a pink flowered sari that reveals part of her slender back.

Al, from Millie & Al's about a block and a half away, and his second wife, Louie, come by on bicycles. Al is a heavy mustached New York man with a straw hat on his head and a big cigar poked in his mouth, and his bicycle weaves and wobbles uncertainly.

Nurses in their uniforms come and go from the Visiting Nurses Association across the street, seldom staying long enough for their names to be known.

The homes on the block are turn-of-the-century row houses built when men still took the trouble to decorate eaves and frame windows with arches and gables and gargoyles.

The children play dodge-'em in the street with a soccer ball: the slim young Thai girl, Raveewan, whom some of us call Lovey One, and who has long and shiny black hair and newly budding breasts; a black-skinned boy whose excited shouts have the British accents of a Biafran; some Spanish children whose short and heavy mothers watch from front stoops; a frail and pale Vietnamese child.

In Kalrama Park just beyond the screen of trees and the Visiting Nurses Association a rock combo plays on summer evenings, and of an afternoon the Latins will hold a festival of many colors there and eat a great deal of food from paper plates.

In the basement apartment several doors down there are Buddhist prayer meetings and discussion groups on Thursday nights.

About six houses in the other direction a small group of young people with long, wild hair and beards sit on the stoop and on its black iron railings quietly passing a bottle of apple wine around until late in the evenings.

At night, at Millie & Al's, ten or so Latins gather close about a small table of half-filled beer pitchers and mugs, singing very gustily and out of tune to a guitar while at the back two black dancing couples can somehow still hear the beat of the jukebox's music with their feet and shoulders and elbows and knees.

At the bar you meet a man named Habte Tekeste, who is from Eritrea, and you argue the value of the nation-state system or something else you both know little enough about to make discussion interesting.

On the corner a one-legged man with snowy hair sits on a stool beside his crutches and sells tomorrow morning's *Post*.

Everywhere you go you hear the voices of many nations.

These are the moments of a city's sidewalks, places that are feared by some but loved by those who know that this is where the city displays its special life style most freely and most visibly. The sidewalks are where transportation mixes our peoples without benefit of protection from the walls and closed doors and windows of air-conditioned buildings and cars. On the city sidewalks we can touch, smell, and hear each other. We know sidewalks can be places of ugliness and danger, but we also know them as alive with the sense of our diversity—the true sense of individuality, which, if we remember correctly, was to be a hallmark of our nation.

Would you let all this pass from the American scene?

Sidewalks are urban transportation systems, and if they are not treated as people-moving systems in the best sense of the phrase, they become places of boredom or anxiety, or both. Writing in *Nation's Cities* in April 1971, Robert L. Morris, vice-president of Alan M. Voorhees & Associates, a transportation and planning consultant firm, had this to say about sidewalks:

> An attractive sidewalk conveys the impression that someone has a sense of quality and concern for the environment. On the other hand, a rough, cracked concrete surface, patched with asphalt, says rather clearly that someone doesn't give a damn. It is surprising that a great many businessmen who go to the trouble and expense of providing handsome tile or terrazzo entrances to their buildings will tolerate unsightly sidewalks directly in front of those same buildings. . . .
>
> It is the unusual, the unexpected, the exceptional that so frequently provides life's pleasures. Many cities today are becoming unexceptional, and therefore drab and uninteresting. The sidewalk, where nearly everyone experiences part of the daily urban life, can be used to create a feeling of specialness . . . .

Such scenes as those taken from my neighborhood's sidewalks in Washington, D.C., do not tell me necessarily that the city should be preserved as it is, because I am also painfully aware of the shortcomings of the city—any American city. I also know, however, that in as many ways as there are people these scenes are replicated through much of the continent. As I watch them, they make me believe in the city. They tell me we must not let our cities die, for our cities are—or should be—the springboards of whatever culture and life style history might thank America for. Without them, there would be no suburbs, where, we are told, our literate and well-read affluent increasingly reside.

I am neither an urban planner, an economist, a sociologist, an architect, a demographer, a public administrator, nor a political scientist. I am a lay observer, one who loves the city—or rather, loves how city life can be vibrant, exciting, and multifaceted, not unlike a diamond. As a layman, my attention has tended to wander over many of the city's facets, but usually it has returned to transportation patterns and their influence on and relationships with the urban accouterments: leadership, housing and employment patterns, schools and hospitals, tax structures, the vitality or pallor of cultural and recreational institutions, the conduct of business, hours of liveliness and sleep. This is so because the transportation network a city devises (or allows to grow without design—from sidewalks to subways) is the conduit of its public affairs and, I believe, a key to the design of the city community itself.

Just as sidewalks do not comprise a city's entire transportation network, transportation is admittedly not the only determinant of a city's shape and size. There are many factors that work and interplay in the mind of each person as he makes his individual decisions about his personal or business investments: where and how he will reside, work, study, and employ his leisure; it is the sum of those individual decisions that, in league with public policy decisions and reactions, determines what a city will be. For many families with young children, the quality of schools and play areas will be major factors in choosing a residence; for many retired persons, some semblance of quiet and access to health care, but most importantly, economy, which too often means a lonely room on an obscure side street; for some, regrettably, the racial composition of neighborhoods persists as the major criterion. But for all, access—the availability of good transportation—is one of those factors taken into consideration before choosing the design of life. Perhaps more than any other, transportation plays a major role in shaping the total community, because it affects all of its parts, assembles them, and brings them together into the entity we call the city.

Consequently, while much of the focus of this book is on transportation, the discussion necessarily reaches into each of the facets of urban living to which transportation leads. A corollary is that most of the lessons about planning, economics, and politics to be learned on our city streets and in our subway stations can be applied with equal relevance to city schools and playgrounds, sewer lines, street lighting, police practices, urban renewal tracts, and public housing, each of which is faced with the same obstacle course of shrinking resources and swelling needs.

If our newspapers, magazines, televisions, and radios have driven one consistent message at us during the past ten years, it is that our urban communities are in peril. From our public officials we have had rained upon us an overabundance of promises and programs, which, for lack of commitment, funding, or foresight, have left our cities overcrowded, near bankruptcy, in disrepair, and scarred by poverty, drugs, neglect, and despair. Bewildered by the signs of urban decay all about us, we have not been able to find satisfactory restorative solutions.

We have now entered the second consecutive decade of fear for, and of, our cities—our urban ecology, in the parlance of the 70's. Behind us lie scattered the remnants of the last decade's golden age of hope, when we publicly sent into our city halls a host of new, aggressive, businessman mayors who were going to rebuild our downtowns and succeeded in erecting a handful of glittering new office towers here and there and then privately watched their business leader peers flee to the isolation of suburbia; when we mounted our crusade against blight with urban renewal programs, community action programs, and community-controlled Model Cities programs, and ran blindly into rioting that left still raw scars of destruction and bitterness; when we built great freeway ribbons of concrete that carved up our neighborhoods and dumped new hordes of pollutant-spewing automobiles into our downtowns; when we poured billions of dollars into new classroom buildings and found our youths angry and rebellious and "dropping out" because the dreams we gave them were quashed.

Despite the resources poured into the urban programs of the 1960's, the American city of the 70's is in direr condition than it was ten years before, when it was still somewhat asleep to the full sweep of its problem. For one thing, it is larger than ever. In 1969 alone an estimated 147,000 persons moved from rural areas to our cities. A decade ago, 70 percent of us lived in city areas; by 1970, 74 percent of us did. During the decade all but two of the sixty-six cities and surrounding suburban nooses that the United States Bureau of the Census defines as Standard Metropolitan Statistical Areas had grown in population, Pittsburgh and Jersey City being the exceptions. Yet, while these SMSA's were bursting with new population, the core cities that gave them birth and sustained them were shriveling like overripe fruit: almost half of the nation's seventy-five largest cities lost large portions of their populations—and those almost invariably the more affluent portions—during the decade of urban revitalization. Nor did this happen in only the giant, fearful cities so often associated with crime, drugs, confrontation, and general ugliness. Indeed, the city whose image strikes most fear in the minds of many, New York, lost only about 10,000 of its 8 million dwellers during the decade. True, Chicago lost about 6 percent of its 1960 population of 3.5 million, Detroit about 12 percent of its 1.5 million, and Philadelphia about 4 percent of its 2 million, but the most impressive evacuation rates took place in cities that started out with less than a million: in Boston, where 69,000 (almost 10 percent) left; in Buffalo, where 75,000 (14 percent) left; in Cincinnati, where 54,000 (11 percent) left.

Even cities with some of the last decade's most successful downtown rebuilding programs experienced the flight of taxpayers: Pittsburgh lost an astounding 15 percent of its 604,332 population in the decade—some 92,000—despite the well-publicized glitter of its new downtown Golden Triangle development and the cleansing of its once notorious air. Baltimore, despite its new Charles Center, one of the best downtown developments in the nation, and its ambitious water-front-renewal program, dropped some 45,000 in population, about 5 percent. St. Louis, with its celebrated Gateway Arch and a similar effort at waterfront development, registered the swiftest flight rate of all urban centers during the decade—more than 142,000, almost 19 percent of its 1960 population of 750,000—even while its metropolitan region was recording a net growth of 11 percent, enough of a suburban population explosion, that is, to account for all of the center city's withering and still wind up the decade with a substantial area-wide increase.

The suburban growth tells only part of the story of the center city's dilemma. As the affluent fled the city's troubles and taxes, the poor and the minorities continued to pour in, further taxing the city's dwindling resources for vitally needed services. Newark, Atlanta, and Gary, Indiana, and eleven smaller cities passed the halfway mark in the nonwhites' share of city population, joining Washington, D.C., and Bessemer, Alabama, which had arrived before 1960. By 1970, nonwhites also accounted for more than 40 percent of the populations of Baltimore; Detroit; New Orleans; Washington, Delaware; Birmingham, Alabama; St. Louis, and Richmond, Virginia.

We entered the 1970's embarked on new promises and new programs—each of which seems to ring a note of familiarity with the past. By now we've gotten more than our feet wet in the new decade: we're up to our knees in it and wading further into its unfulfilled promises. The Congress, in its first session of the decade, wrote into its Housing and Urban Development Act a national urban growth policy of sorts, but, as Norman Beckman, deputy director of the Congressional Research Service of the Library of Congress, conceded in the May 1971 issue of the *Journal of the American Institute of Planners,* "Adoption of federal and state urban growth policies does little by itself to make streets cleaner, provide more shelter, enhance the quality of urban life, or even coordinate the actions of federal, state and local governments toward these objectives." In the face of the current and growing proportions of the urban peril (urban "crisis" fails through overuse) the Congress has yet done precious little to implement its overgeneralized urban growth "policy."

Programs abound, of course—as legacies from the 1960's, for the most part. Why do they fail so woefully to measure up to either the dimensions of the needs or the promises of those who formulated the programs? Why did the rebuilding of the 1960's fail to win the hearts of white affluent urban Americans back to their cities? Why are those cities continuing to serve increasingly as concentration camps for the nation's poor, indigent, and outcast? Could it be that we've gone about it all wrong? that the infusion of funds and new programs with high-sounding labels was too simplistic a solution? that something more basic had gone askew?

The five case studies in this book are an attempt to propel forward the rethinking necessary if we are to answer such questions, to examine how the American city came to be what it is, to inspect its structure, its sense of priorities, and the complex weave of its fabric. The five cities were not selected for public chastisement but for the lessons they can teach; they represent neither the worst nor the best the nation has to offer. Almost any other five could have been selected with reasonably similar results. Some of our largest cities—New York, Chicago, Los Angeles, and San Francisco, to name a few—have been discussed at great length by the media, with the net usual reaction being the contention that these cities represent only themselves, that they are not typical and can teach nothing to the broad middle range of American cities. For this reason these cities are avoided, but the case studies selected suggest that there is much common ground between the problems of middle urban America and those of the current or soon-to-become megalopolises.

One of the case cities, Washington, D.C., has also been too much discussed in public, I think, usually by its dominant population of politicians, yet this discussion has tended to cloud rather than illuminate the city's problems. Washington is the political professional's whipping boy—often scolded but seldom properly guided, led, helped, educated, or fed. It is included among the five case studies for that reason.

The selected five run the range of sizes from Washington, at the southern end of the megalopolitan northeast corridor, to junior-sized Flint, hammerlocked into the automotive empire of the upper Midwest. It could be a classical debating game to determine which end of the spectrum has the more severe problems, or which has the best chance of overcoming them. I have chosen not to indulge in the game; its results would hardly prove important or instructive. What is instructive are the lessons these cities might teach about what it is in America that has made such failures of our cities, and what we must do if the destruction of our urban environment—not simply its air and water, but also its people and its sidewalks, its economy, its institutions of learning and culture, its diversity, and its social vitality —is to be reversed.

Washington, D.C.
January 1972

Highways to Nowhere

1
Flint: GM's Mark of Excellence

One of the largest brick buildings in the area stands vacant at the north end of the downtown. Not long ago it was one of the city's major new-car dealerships. Across an expanse of empty parking pavement is another red brick structure, low and long and also vacant, with bare windows across its facade. A sign on one window panel says: "AVAILABLE—99,000 SQ. FT.—AMPLE PARKING." Up above, on the brick face, the discoloration still shows where the "Sears" signature appeared only a year or so ago. The two buildings stand in mute testimony to what has happened to Flint.

More than almost any other city, Flint, Michigan, is a product of transportation and, more specifically, of General Motors. It is neither a large city nor the center of its region on anyone's scale; rather, it seems lost in the vast industrial shadow Detroit throws across most of southeastern Michigan. GM money built it, GM money is destroying it, and, what must seem an irony to Ralph

Nader and corporate stockholders alike, GM money is trying to save it. As a product engineered, styled, and built by General Motors, Flint now bears GM's indelible mark. As such it has its peculiarities that distinguish it from other cities, yet it offers in microcosm vital evidence of where American urban life is going.

Transportation's first decision about Flint, as about almost every other city, was its location. The city straddles the Flint River—not, however, because the river was an important waterway, but because that particular location served as the river crossing of a Saginaw-to-Detroit fur traders' trail. Flint was first plotted in an 1819 treaty as part of a Chippewa reservation that the Indians called "open plain burnt over" and, six years later, was deeded by the United States government to a half-breed. That deeding, and the land sales that followed, marked the beginning of a village in what had once been Indian forest.

The loggers and sawmillers came in the 1830's to carve the surrounding pine and oak forests into houses, sheds, wagons, and furniture for local consumption, but the settlement remained little more than a village until a second transportation decision transformed it into a small industrial center in the 1850's. Michigan Governor H. H. Crapo decided in 1856 to put Michigan's timber in competition with upstate New York's by shipping it to the coast and then over the ocean to an international market. By 1871, the Flint River was clotted with logs and the city had nine sawmills chewing up the once magnificent pine stands. As Flint became one of the major centers of the lumber industry, its population increased almost 83 percent from 1860 to 1870 and another 56 percent in the next decade. Still, the Flint of 1880 was but a town of some 8,400 persons, and by that time the lumbermen were moving westward: only two pine stands remained in the area, and only three sawmills, and Flint was scouting about for a new industry. It found it in a third set of transportation decisions.

In 1870, at the height of the lumber industry, there were five wagon, carriage, and sleigh factories in the city. The decisions made during the 1880's turned that small beginning into an international industry and were to shape the next century's politics, growth, prosperity, and troubles in Flint. One lumber mill turned itself into the Flint Wagon Works, and, more important, a twenty-five-year-old insurance man named William C. Durant decided to get into the carriage-making business after he saw a curious two-wheeled "road cart" churning up the Flint streets one day. Durant and a friend, twenty-five-year-old J. Dallas Dort, borrowed $2,000 from a local bank and bought the patent on the new-style vehicle. At first they contracted with W. A. Paterson, who had been making carriages in Flint since 1869, to produce the simple road carts: two wagon wheels, a springboard seat, footrests, a whip stand, and traces. Quite like today's harness-racing rigs, the new road cart must have been the sports car of its day, inspiring young gentlemen to flashing daredevilry in the streets to beguile young ladies and irritate their parents. Durant soon organized his own company to make the carts and, selling them by the thousands, quickly built his operation into the world's largest carriage company. In 1900 the Durant-Dort Carriage Company, Flint Wagon Works, and the W. A. Paterson Company produced a total of more than 100,000 carriages—and Durant made half of them. With the invention of the motorcar "Billy" Durant was on his way to transforming the world's largest carriage building operation into one of the world's largest manufacturing conglomerates.

It started in 1903 when Flint Wagon Works purchased the new Buick Motor Company and, the following year, talked Durant into running the operation. During those first two years only 60 Buicks were built; in 1905 there were 750, but by 1908 Durant was building 8,000 Buicks and making the Buick the nation's top-selling automobile. Around his factory north of the downtown he gathered together the smaller companies he had brought to Flint to supply him: two axle companies, a spring company, a body company, a varnish works. It was the city's first major industrial complex and today stands as the headquarters for General Motors' Buick Division. A measure of the impact Durant's enterprise had on the city is found in its population boom to supply him with laborers. Population almost tripled between 1900 and 1910—from 13,000 to 38,500.

General Motors was first organized in 1908 from Durant's enormous Buick earnings. In the next two years, the former insurance man bought so many other companies for his new combine that he had to surrender control of GM to a group of bankers in exchange for a loan to meet his debts. He left Flint for five years, but for the interim he installed as GM president Charles W. Nash, who had managed Durant's carriage company; in 1916 Nash left to buy his own company, and it later became today's American Motors. Assisting Nash at Buick during those years was a former railroad man, Walter P. Chrysler, who later formed the Chrysler Corporation. Thus, the origins of three of the nation's "big four" auto makers can be traced to the Durant-Dort Carriage Company and the $2,000 loan in 1886 that made it possible for an insurance man to build road carts.

Durant's fortunes were to seesaw from then on. From 1910 to 1915 he was in Detroit organizing the Chevrolet Motor Company; he moved it to Flint and used it to regain control of General Motors, but a postwar recession caused him to again lose control of GM in 1920. He spent the succeeding years organizing still more automotive factories, including one which ran into difficulty and was sold to GM in 1926; today it is a Fisher Body factory in Flint.

Flint grew rapidly into a city to meet the needs of the new automobile companies. Between 1900 and 1930 its population soared from 13,000 to 156,000, a growth rate seventeen times that of the nation. During the 1930's the growth stopped and Flint actually lost 3 percent of its population, but the advent of World War II and its highway-mobile society aftermath assured Flint of continued prosperity and growth—as long as car production and consumption stayed up. Since General Motors carried out a major program of factory building in Flint between 1939 and 1943, industrial employment—some four-fifths of it directly involved in automobile and automobile-related manufacturing—has consistently outpaced population growth, giving Flint an economy ever more reliant on the vicissitudes of General Motors—its strikes, its layoffs, its wage levels, its employee recruitment, its production quotas, its shift changes, its overtime policies, its materials decisions, its inventory, its plant locations, its investments, its advertising, its model change-overs, even the styling of its models (an "Edsel" at Buick in Flint could have delivered a severe blow to the economy).

Modern Flint is the archetype of the one-company—and one-product—town. In Flint the automobile is not only king, it is a malady. Like tobacco in North Carolina and cotton in the old South, it is bread and butter, recreation, escape, bed and board, politics, life style. Other single-industry towns may be afflicted with some of Flint's problems, but in Flint the choice of the single-industry tenant —along with its requirements for space, the nature of its work force, and its product—has proven particularly disastrous.

The auto makers, thriving and expanding as no other industry has done since World War II, have modernized and economized with a conscious policy of "linear production" that consumes great amounts of room—outward, not upward—that can be found only on the urban fringe. The only facilities in metropolitan Flint that employ 1,000 or more workers are General Motors' plants, and most of those are in the suburbs. A World War II tank facility in Grand Blanc Township some eight miles southwest of downtown Flint has been converted into a Chevrolet auto parts stamping facility that employs some 4,000. A Fisher Body plant also in Grand Blanc employs another 4,000, and Grand Blanc has become one of the area's most rapidly growing townships. Fisher Body has other plants two miles south and six miles north into the suburbs of the city, employing about 7,600 and 4,000 respectively. Three Chevrolet plants some three miles southwest of the city's center employ about 15,000, and another Chevrolet facility a mile west of downtown employs between 9,000 and 10,000. These provide Flint with the world's largest concentration of Chevrolet employees, and Flint GM executives with good reason try to lure Chevrolet Division headquarters back to the city.

Buick, still headquartered in Flint (even the city police cars are Buicks), employs more than 20,000 workers about a mile and a half north of the center of town and has a new division headquarters office building there, a low and flat rectangle of glass, white marble, and black granite that covers three full blocks. AC Spark Plug, born in Flint and bought by GM in its early years, has 12,000 employees two miles northeast of downtown. Topping off the Flint area's major employment are still another forty-five smaller facilities, with a combined work force of 2,300, that supply GM with everything from lacquer and auto waxes to padding for car seats.

This sort of concentration of one industry—and the nature of that industry—in one urban setting presents major complications to the city's attempt to provide a good urban environment. It makes the Flint economy a thermometer of the nation's, reacting mercurially to prosperity and recession. New automobiles have become one of the first items Americans purchase in times of prosperity and postpone in times of recession. Thus, during the early 1950's, when annual Buick production climbed in five years from 500,000 to 750,000, the city recorded enough population growth to reach almost 200,000 by 1960. When pocketbooks are pinched and car-buying declines, however, the auto industry responds with sudden production cuts and worker layoffs; as a result, payment of city tax bills declines sharply.

About 35 percent of Flint's city budget comes from local income taxes. When unemployment runs high, income-tax collections are down and the city is hard pressed to meet increasing citizen demands for public service—be it garbage collection, police protection, or street resurfacing. When a severe slump in the national economy and a protracted strike against General Motors sent the Flint area's unemployment soaring to 8.1 percent in 1970, the city had to adjust its operating budget downward some 10 percent—from 22.1 million dollars to 19.8 million dollars—and curtail services accordingly: one fire station closed, 34 firemen laid off, 24 police positions left vacant, public health nurses dismissed. The city had grown accustomed to better times. During the decade of the 1960's unemployment had hovered around 3 percent most of the time and had even dipped to 2.4 percent in 1965.

The United Auto Workers, without question the most powerful

labor organization in Flint, represents its membership well, however. By the end of the 1960's Flint employers were paying the highest manufacturing wages of all major urban centers in the country: an *average* of $4.56 an hour and $203 a week in 1969. From such affluence, Flint made of itself the American city with the highest per capita ownership of private cars and one of the highest in single-family houses. Practically all of the land developed for housing outside the city limits is in single-family houses (no suburban apartment building boom here for the grown-up postwar babies), and even inside the city limits only about 2 percent of the residentially developed land was in apartments in 1960.

With high wages, cheap federal loans for private homes, high automobile ownership, and major suburban concentrations of General Motors employment, it was little wonder that Flint began feeling the full brunt of suburbanization of its tax base sooner than most cities. As early as 1960 some 56 percent of its urbanized land area was outside the thirty square miles of the city limits, and the suburbs accounted for almost 52 percent of the population in the Standard Metropolitan Statistical Area, already twice the national average in 1960 and setting the pace for other cities to follow during the next decade. Nor did the pace of Flint's suburban growth abate. During the 1960's the city lost a net of some 3,600 in population while its two-county metropolitan area was growing by almost 25 percent and approaching the half-million mark, thanks largely to the decade-long bonanza in auto production and sales brought on by the Interstate Highway program. (In 1955 the president of the Automobile Manufacturers' Association promised Congress that if the nation built the Interstate Highway System, the auto industry could put a net gain of some 23 million cars on the road by 1965—a promise that was kept.) GM's rapidly expanding Flint area work force, as elsewhere, settled in the suburbs, itself taking advantage of the new superhighways built for the cars it manufactured.

Even the socioeconomic status of Flint's population is a product of General Motors. Because it is a one-company and a one-product city, it is also a one-class city. It lacks the diversified population strains that make up most urban areas. Flint's one socioeconomic class may be affluent, but it is decidedly blue-collar, with blue-collar tastes, blue-collar eagerness for the symbols of "making it"—a suburban home, a two-car garage, a private boat, even a backyard swimming pool—and blue-collar distrust of government. It was quite natural that Flint fashion for itself a blue-collar downtown: pool halls, taverns, third-rate restaurants and almost no cultural or recreational activity above the level of the "Adults Only" movie houses and bookstalls on the city's main commercial artery.

Through such a downtown, blight spread easily and quickly in the 1950's and 1960's once the more affluent shoppers and taxpayers had migrated to suburbia. Stores closed and never reopened. Entire blocks of store fronts at the north end of downtown sat vacant and boarded over for years collecting thick gray blankets of dust over windows and the remnants of furnishings, until the city decided in 1971 to tear them out. Between 1958 and 1963 the number of retail establishments in the central business district dropped 22 percent, from 463 to 363; during the same five years the dollar volume of retail sales downtown climbed by only 10 percent, barely keeping pace with inflation, while retail sales throughout the metropolitan area were climbing by 33 percent. In 1958 the downtown accounted for less than a fourth of all retail sales in the metropolitan area, and by 1963 even this had dropped by 19 percent.

As elsewhere, it was the suburban shopping centers that were doing it to downtown, at first shifting downtown shopping from regular daily and weekly purchases to the specialty shopping of heavier merchandise—appliances, clothing, and other once- or twice-a-year items. Then the suburbs even dipped deeply into these sales. By 1968 the small metropolitan area had twenty-six shopping centers either open or under construction outside the central area of Flint—nine of them considered of major size, but not yet quite large enough to be considered "regional."

At that point the largest suburban shopping center in operation was Eastland, an enclosed mall of about sixty stores, including three major department stores, just outside the eastern city limits. Flint was eager to annex the mall. Since it had annexed about two square miles of territory—including another shopping center, South Flint Plaza— in the early 1960's, the city had been unable to expand, owing mostly to a state law passed in 1962 that required separate referenda in *both* the annexing city and the suburban area to be annexed. While most state legislatures continued to be rurally dominated in the 1960's, Michigan's had already passed into suburban control, a phenomenon spreading to other states by the end of the decade. As a suburbia-controlled legislature, Michigan's enacted in the late 1960's yet another law detrimental to center cities seeking expansion. It created a Boundary Commission to review all annexation and incorporation petitions, in effect an added, state-level obstacle on the course toward urban annexation. The commission's first case was that of Flint's attempt to annex Eastland Mall.

The shopping center was in Burton Township, which characterized the city's annexation attempt in a cartoon depicting the "City of Flint politicians" as a fat, pig-snouted man laden with jewelry and dollars dripping from his pockets reaching for the mall and, in the process, stepping on the "people of Burton Township." Captions on the cartoon identified the mall and a plant of GM's AC Spark Plug Division as the township's "only two large taxpayers" and labeled the annexation attempt a "greedy grab [that has] destroyed community relations that have taken years to build."

In fact, there had been no intercommunity relations in the Flint area. In contrast to developments in most other urban areas during the 1960's, no council of local governments had ever been formed. Flint's city manager, Tom Kay, told a United States Conference of Mayors–National League of Cities study team in 1969 that he saw no reason to establish such a forum for intergovernmental cooperation: they were "stupid," they encouraged "fragmentation" of the area (he didn't explain how), they were "powerless," and, whenever controversy arose, dissident members simply quit. The city manager said it was even unlikely that he would ever have occasion to meet or converse with a suburban official unless a major crisis forced a meeting over a specific issue: "I probably would never see him in all likelihood from one year to the next." Subsequently, however, a Genesee County Metropolitan Alliance was formed as a voluntary committee to study possibilities of government reorganization in the area; 20 of the county's 32 local governments belong and pay $100 each in dues, with equal voting power on the committee. But even though Flint is a member, the city manager, by far the most important figure in Flint government (the mayoralty is an honor bestowed on one part-time city commissioner by the others), is "apprehensive that it might be characterized as a Flint program," so he doesn't attend any of its meetings, to prevent "alienating the rest."

On Tom Kay's desk is a pistol mounted above a plaque inscribed with a fitting testimonial to any city governed by such an attitude: "Anyone for Suicide?" With such defeatism and the consequent failure to develop regional intercourse (there isn't even a proper metropolitan-wide planning agency other than the county's customary advisory planning office, itself belatedly organized in 1966 to provide a place to assign federally mandated regional review and planning activities), it was little wonder that Flint suffered badly in its few recent attempts to expand its borders and its tax base. When Flint submitted its annexation petition to the state's new Boundary Commission in 1969, Burton Township submitted its own petition to incorporate itself as a city and place Eastland Mall safely within *its* "city" limits and out of Flint's reach. The state commission ruled in Burton Township's favor; the township was urbanized enough to meet the statistical criteria necessary for incorporation (all the more reason it should have become part of Flint). With the state decision in its favor, the township began the lengthy process toward incorporation: a referendum that approved the concept of incorporation, drafting a city charter, and submission of the charter to the electorate. Eastland Mall was not to pay taxes to Flint.

Burton was not the only township neighbor Flint was having annexation difficulties with in 1969. Several times in recent years Mt. Morris Township had successfully beaten off Flint expansion attempts and now was fighting the city's attempt to annex even a vacant 115-acre tract because it feared that the city would then move to annex a GM factory that made plastic auto accessories. The city also lost that battle before the Boundary Commission, and its borders remained frozen at 32 square miles.

Not only was the city incapable of governing its growth in any orderly pattern, it seemed incapable of even *planning* orderly growth. In the aftermath of World War I, when the city was interested in its unprecedented industrial boom, it organized the Flint Planning Board, which, in 1927, produced the city's first zoning ordinance. After that, planning leadership disappeared and remained dormant through the 1930's and beyond. In 1939 the present City Planning Commission, an appointed and ex officio body, was created, but it was and remains remarkable only for its utter failure to exercise its authority. It has authority to review the city's capital improvements programs and to make its decisions stick unless the City Commission can muster a two-thirds majority to override it, but the planning commission has never used the power in fear of reprisals from the city commissioners who appoint it and determine its funding. It was given zoning powers but has used them ineffectively; zoning decisions are most often made by the City Commission in response to political pressures. The Planning Commission was given control of subdivision development, but by the time it got around to noticing it, there was no land left inside the city limits for subdivision development. The director of the city planning office himself concedes that he would rather switch than fight. Involving himself in the political processes and vigorously advocating acceptance of planning decisions are serious risks to job security, he believes; much better not to allow himself to be upset when decisions "go against you." His strategy appears successful: his tenure with the city has lasted some two decades.

Major decisions have gone "against" him. The state planned an east-west expressway through Flint that did not conform to the city's "master plan" for itself; it was to chomp through part of a golf course and a rugged-terrain park, among other things, and totally alter downtown access and traffic pattern plans. Minor changes were made to save the park and twenty-seven-hole golf course, but still the highway altered the basic downtown-access plan adopted by the city. Planning Director Jerry Childers later recalled, "I ended up supporting the state in opposition to our master plan."

It took three tries and the dubious assistance of New York City's controversial public works chief, Robert Moses, but the city planners did have one notable success that reshaped the south end of downtown. In 1947 they proposed that the city build a new municipal center for city government administration and held a referendum on financing its construction. Officials declined to say just where they would put it, however, so voters turned it down. Again they went to the voters, this time with a general description of the area that the planners had selected for the facility (but not where it was eventually built), and again they were turned down. When New York's Moses came to Detroit in the early 1950's to receive a General Motors award for highway design and construction, Flint officials invited him to visit the city and look over its plans. He sent a few staff members and even came himself for a day or so, and after a few months issued a report supporting a new site selected by the Flint planning office. With the approval of such an auspicious figure as Moses, the city now received the backing of the local press. This and the generally prevalent boom-time optimism of the early 1950's secured voter approval for the project. As a result the city now has a sweeping 6-million-dollar complex of terraced government buildings and spacious lawns at the south end of downtown, and the county government has followed suit with an impressive government office building across the street, complete with plazas and pedestrian walkways and modern sculpture on the roof of a parking deck.

But if the city was to find aggressive leadership for any continuing effort to reverse the blight that was moving through its downtown and out across its neighborhoods, it had to look elsewhere than either City Hall, with its dependence on its conservative blue-collar constituency, or General Motors, with its absentee decision-makers whose interests lay in a worldwide marketplace and not in its native city. Luckily for Flint, it still had the C. S. Mott Foundation. It is no overstatement to say that the foundation has been the single moving force around which all efforts to change the downward course of the city have revolved. Without the Mott Foundation it is unlikely that any other group present in the city would have found commitment to alter the laissez-faire policies that have been responsible for the problems of Flint today.

Charles Stewart Mott was making carriage axles at a factory in Utica, New York, when, on Labor Day weekend of 1905, William C. Durant, then heading the infant Buick operation at Flint Wagon

Works, talked Mott into moving his Weston-Mott Company to Flint and locating it in what was to become the industrial complex Durant was building around Buick. In 1908, the first new company Durant bought into for his just-born General Motors was Mott's axle company. With an exchange of stock, Mott surrendered 49 percent of the company (he was already building it into the world's largest axle factory), and in 1913 Mott sold the remainder of his company for more GM stock. (It remained a separate division of General Motors until 1918, when it was absorbed into the Buick Division.) It has been estimated that Mott's company was worth about 3 million dollars when he sold it to GM for shares then worth about $25 each. It is estimated that each share is worth some $10,000 now and has brought another $10,000 in dividends, according to Mott's biographer, Clarence H. Young. It was with that growing GM-financed fortune that C. S. Mott, concerned about the disposition of his wealth if he should die young, set up a foundation in the mid-1920's and, in 1936, turned it to the building of an extensive program of community school activity—a prototype for the country. As the Urban Land Institute pointed out in a 1967 review of Flint developments:

> Every school building is a community center. For example, whether they have children in the school or not, residents in Central Park may walk to nearby Central High School for a dip in the swimming pool or to pursue hobby or college-credit courses. More than 70,000 adult enrollments are recorded each year in Flint in classes ranging from "Great Books" to cake decorating to millinery to upholstering to calculus. There is hardly a family in Flint whose lives have not been touched by a Mott Program activity and who has not made use of the advantages offered by the community schools, either for cultural enrichment, for personal or family advancement, or for fun.

In its historical cooperation with the Flint Board of Education, the C. S. Mott Foundation sponsors a child health program, a visiting teacher and in-service program, a boys' camp, a training program in homemaking for mothers and daughters, the Flint Youth Bureau for fatherless boys, an interracial program, summer "tot-lots," and teenage groups. For seven years the foundation also has given $50,000 a year in matching funds (the city and school board have to put up another $50,000 each annually) for a school-park program.

During the early 1950's one of the most significant factors in building the community optimism that led to approval of the 6-million-dollar package to finance the new government center was a plan, brought to life by the Mott Foundation, to build a major community college complex just six blocks east of the downtown. The 30-million-dollar college and cultural complex, built on land donated by Mott, now contains some eighteen major buildings, including Flint Junior College, a branch campus of the University of Michigan, elementary and junior high schools, a public school administration building, a planetarium, an art center, a music house, a theater, a library, a five-tiered opera house, and the Sloan Panorama of Transportation.

A stipulation Mott placed on his donation of land for the project was that it be built, not as a resident college, but for commuting local students. To honor the agreement the campus provides no dormitory facilities, but it does include parking space for some 7,000 cars—approximately 5 parking spaces for every 7 college students—a local public decision to subsidize automobile ownership and use in the heart of the city.

A Mott Foundation official estimates that it has spent between 45 and 50 million dollars on Flint education since 1935. It was to protect that investment that the foundation, during the 1950's and 1960's, spread its interest to other community problems—housing, government reform, inner-city redevelopment, public transportation, and a host of other needs. Again, the genesis came during the optimistic first half of the 1950's. Homer Dowdy, now a successful writer and an officer of the Mott Foundation but then a local news reporter, traveled to other cities in the country to study urbanization. Assisted by the Social Science Research Project of the University of Michigan, he wrote a series of articles for the *Flint Journal* entitled "Where's Flint Going?" and determined quite naturally that it was moving to the suburbs. The finding led to a three-year Flint Area Study conducted by a committee that encompassed the city and sixteen outlying local governments. It examined water and sewerage, zoning, taxation, police, parks, the entire range of local government services and needs. It recommended that a uniform county-wide tax assessment schedule be adopted, and it was; that a county planning office be created, and it was, but not until 1966; and that the county halt the construction of a separate sewage-treatment plant, which the county did. But the study's most basic and important recommendation —for a "New Flint"—was scorned as ten years ahead of its time.

"New Flint" was to be a regional government encompassing the city, five adjacent townships, and two suburban municipalities; it was proposed that the City of Flint abolish itself and consolidate with the other local governments. The County Board of Supervisors, composed of the chief executives of each township in the county, reluctant to abolish their jobs, refused to put the question to a referendum. Proponents of the plan took the supervisors to court—and lost; the

state supreme court ruled that the city could not use the state's stat-
utes authorizing consolidation of governments because that would
enable an action by Flint to abolish other municipalities as well.
The court ordered that any expansion of the city would have to
be by annexation—a route the city successfully used in 1962 but
has never used since.

Ten years later, in 1967, the "New Flint" proponents held a
seminar and brought back one of the men who had inspired the effort,
Dr. Basil G. Zimmer, now chairman of the Sociology Department
at Brown University. Zimmer recalled the statements of 1957 that
the concept was ten years ahead of its time and that the situation was
not then "bad enough," but he found only that local officeholders
were even less inclined in 1967 to think of metropolitan approaches
to government than they had been ten years before. The urban area
had rapidly balkanized and become isolationist during the interval.

Not that those with investment in Flint's downtown didn't try to
save it, again under the leadership of the Mott Foundation. Part of
the mid-1950's studies that yielded the "New Flint" proposals was a
1956 review of conditions by a panel from the Urban Land Institute.
Upon its recommendation the Greater Flint Downtown Corporation
was created and a plan devised to revitalize the city's center. President
and guiding force of the new corporation was Harding Mott, son of
C. S. Mott (despite his fears back in the 1920's that his fortune might
be squandered after an early death, the family patriarch is still very
much alive) and president of the foundation. The downtown plan
was incorporated in a 1960 master plan for the city: a traffic ban along
the commercial corridor of Saginaw Street and turning the wide and
cobbled street into a mall with three pedestrian "squares" along its
course, new office buildings and stores, and construction of parking
decks on its periphery. Implementation of the plan, it was hoped,
would generate between 55 and 70 percent more retail business
downtown.

The "master plan" was too ambitious, however. Merchants
were hardly likely to support banning the city's chief product, automobiles, from the main street of the downtown area, no matter how
lovely the drawings of planners. The merchants, bankers, and other
downtown interests did, however, assess themselves 4.8 million dollars
on a graduated-benefit formula to build three parking decks and
assumed management of another acquired by the city in 1957.
Together, the parking facilities offered some twenty thousand spaces
at 5 cents per half hour. By promising to build a pedestrian bridge
from one parking deck they were also able to induce Montgomery

Ward into building a 4-million-dollar store in the heart of the city, the single major retailing investment made downtown in recent decades.

With $300,000 from the assessment funds the Downtown Corporation built attractive canopies over the sidewalks along the four-block retailing corridor and provided the walkways with benches, bulletin boards, telephone booths, planters, and piped music—all tastefully blended to resemble a planned suburban shopping mall. That was exactly the intent: if the city's downtown could not make it as the vital, diversified center of its region, then perhaps it could compete as just another shopping center that provided amenities reasonably similar to those of its suburban counterparts—a clean walking environment, shelter from the more inclement weather conditions, and inexpensive parking. By 1967, upon its return visit, the Urban Land Institute panel found reason for optimism: a nineteen-story office tower was built, a ten-story motel was built, Holiday Inn was interested in building a 250-unit motel (five years later it hadn't gotten around to construction yet), a high-rise senior citizens' public housing apartment tower was under construction, and other buildings were being renovated or added to.

Despite the resurgence, however, the tide of economic decline failed to be turned. The window dressing, the parking garages, and the new buildings succeeded only in slowing the downward trend of retail activity in the downtown area and "lessening the shock" of suburbanization, according to Saul Seigel, then executive director of the Downtown Corporation. Except for shopping, most of Flint's citizens had little reason to come downtown, and now they were also finding fewer and fewer reasons to do their shopping there. Despite the canopied sidewalks, downtown still was not a very pleasant or interesting place to be.

The planning office had never been interested in urban redevelopment, and neither had the city at large. In 1949 City Hall did attempt to create a public housing commission, but when the proposal was submitted to voters, they turned it down. Throughout the 1950's, as other cities were venturing (if somewhat timorously) into public housing development, Flint refused to do so. Only when the National Association for the Advancement of Colored People and the Urban League applied pressure did the city create the office of Urban Renewal Coordinator. It was staffed with one man, a retired commercial and industrial contractor, until his death in 1964.

During the middle 60's the coordinator's office was expanded into the Office of Community Development, appointed by and answerable to the city manager directly, and it became the focal point of urban renewal planning and implementation. More aggressive and imaginative than the semi-autonomous City Planning Commission, it tended to get into political debates, so much so that its director resigned in 1969 when two city commissioners argued whose ward would be selected for low-rent subsidy housing, which neither wanted, and an urban renewal home for the elderly, which each preferred. The debate became so lengthy that the city commissioners, needing a justification for the delay, said they wanted to investigate the Office of Community Development first. The director resigned under a cloud of innuendo and vague charges never publicly specified, much less proved. In contrast with the two-decade incumbency of the city's play-it-safe planning director, the first community development director had lasted only a few years.

The Community Development Office was answerable to the city manager, however, and perhaps for this reason Tom Kay was interested in merging the lackluster City Planning Commission under its leadership in order to consolidate planning. He recognized, however, that he faced reluctance born of the entrenchment of the planning commissioners in their do-little positions. Instead, he has devised a scheme to retain the Planning Commission as an advisory board but consolidate the staffs and functions of the two planning offices under a director appointed by him.

The failure to plan the community's growth and then the failure to begin redevelopment early enough to stem the tide of blight resulted in a community scattered haphazardly over the landscape. Residential areas were squeezed between rail lines and between strips of sidewalk-front stores and major industrial plants. Industrial parking, industrial heavy-truck traffic and industrial fly ash crept through neighborhoods. As if to add insult to injury, the superhighway planners came through with dotted lines on maps that helped speed the sweep of blight, dismembering long-stable neighborhoods and dislocating families. Two basic freeways were plotted: one, a spur I-475 off the major north-south Interstate 75 that bypasses the city on its west side, courses north-south through the city's east side and passes close to downtown; the other is a state-programmed east-west expressway. In its belated attempt to reorder the urban community along some logical lines, the new Office of Community Development was forced to carve up great swatches of the city into Neighborhood Development Program areas; and if they cared to notice, the planners could have seen that in almost every case the targeted zones of deterioration followed the paths of the two expressways. One ran northward from downtown to the city limits and others clustered around the east and south sides of downtown where the two superhighways will approach and intersect once they are completed in 1975. To make way for the interchange alone, just southeast of the new complex of city and county government buildings, some five hundred families had to be uprooted and a long-established black neighborhood destroyed.

In most cases the redevelopment planned in the Office of Community Development entailed construction of new housing, sale of cleared land for Buick and other industrial expansion, and rehabilitation of housing that seemed not to have deteriorated too far. There would be little to alter the basic scatter-pattern of living in Flint, with the exception that higher-density housing—high-rise apartments, perhaps—hopefully would be built in the closer-in areas north of downtown. But, thanks to the new super-roads, the still persistent blue-collar fear of publicly subsidized housing, and City Hall's insensitivity to the needs of close-in neighborhoods, several major blunders were mapped in the planning office.

For one, the north-south expressway would serve effectively as both a physical and a psychological barrier between the dying downtown and its one close-in facility that has a chance of spurring an exciting, active renewal of in-town life: the still expanding college and cultural complex six blocks east of downtown. Closer to the interchange itself, particularly on the north-south route, local streets will be dead-ended, and residents of much of the public housing that the planners are putting in the pockets of cleared land left near the interchange will have a good view of downtown but will be unable to reach it with reasonable ease; the multistory interchange will be in the way.

What appears to be another major mistake is being forced upon residents of a small neighborhood just south of downtown, in the path of the east-west expressway just west of the interchange. Citizens there are having to fight the redevelopment planners to save their neighborhood, not from new housing but from heavy trucks and government construction machinery. The area already includes an asphalt plant, a cement plant, and the heavy-equipment yards of the city's Department of Public Works. The city department wants to expand its facilities, but that would require demolition of the fifty tree-shaded homes that are there and the dislocation of the neighborhood's families. Residents quite accurately point out that their homes are not substandard, that they have been well maintained, and that the city should go ahead and spend the 6 million dollars it is estimated it will cost to move the public works yards elsewhere. Next to downtown is no place for the bulldozers and trucks anyway. But the planners side with the Department of Public Works and against the residents. They point out that the small pocket of homes is caught in a crunch between the transportation paths of the new east-west expressway and two railroad lines. George Ursuy, the new director of the Office of Community Development, remarks, "We think we can convince them to move." Thus, part of another close-in neighborhood is to be sacrificed to an expressway and its remnants will have to leave as well because they will then be *too close* to the expressway.

On the downtown's northern border sits Oak Park, the historic neighborhood that was Buick's birthplace. It is the one redevelopment neighborhood not sliced through by an interstate highway, and one where a major urban renewal effort was attempted, only to be frustrated by the city's dominant population of anti-black, anti-government and anti-tax blue-collar workers. The area is bisected by North Saginaw Street, the major thoroughfare out of downtown, and the long strips of sidewalk shops that clutter the street's frontage. Industrial blight and parking lots are spreading across its unbuffered east side from the Buick complex. The density of homes is three times the city's average. Ninety-three percent of its buildings were substandard or deficient in 1969. Though it had less than 7 percent of the city's population, it accounted for 15 percent of its tuberculosis cases, 30 percent of its venereal disease, 26 percent of its felonies, and 35 percent of its misdemeanors. Its unemployment was at 11 percent. The total cost for rehabilitation and redevelopment, street improvements, tot-lots, and other amenities was estimated at 62 million dollars. The city would get back 10 million dollars from the resale of land it acquired for private redevelopment, and the United States Department of Housing and Urban Development promised to put up 35 million dollars if the city put up the rest: 7 million dollars in non-cash credits for public improvements, 5 million dollars promised by private sources (including the Mott Foundation), and 5 million dollars from a bond issue that needed voter approval. The city was able to muster only a half-hearted campaign that failed to explain adequately what was planned for the area, whereas an all-out effort, well financed and self-labeled a "tax revolt," fought the bond issue with misinformation and racist rumor. The city's voters turned down the project 17,300 to 6,600, even though they were being asked to pay for only one-twelfth of it.

Subsequently, the city included Oak Park in its less ambitious Neighborhood Development Program, a graduated federal-aid effort that will provide new public housing east of Saginaw Street, rehabilitation on the west side, and clustering of the strips of shops along the street itself.

From the northern boundary of Oak Park to the city limits and beyond stretches the 3,500-acre Model Cities neighborhood, 1,100 acres of it within the city limits. The area is to be sliced through by the Interstate Highway. It was proposed that the Interstate be moved to one side to minimize its impact on the area's homes, but that would cost another $304,000 just for the portion inside the city limits, and neither the state nor the city is anxious to spend the money, particularly since the land has already been bought and the families moved out along the original route. Black people account for 60 percent of the neighborhood's population.

Historically the City of Flint has developed two black communities. One dates from the Civil War era's Underground Railroad to Canada. Escaped slaves who left the "railroad" at Flint settled east and south of downtown and produced a stable population that provided the city's affluent society with its domestic workers. Though poor, they took pride in their neighborhood. Nearby, at the end of the 1960's, they could point to "Sugar Hill," where wealthier blacks lived in $25,000 and $30,000 homes. Following World War II, however, the city's reblossoming automobile industry enticed a heavy migration of black workers out of the South. These new blacks settled north of downtown, in the deteriorating houses being abandoned by whites in their flight to the suburbs. At first they lived only east of Saginaw Street, close to the jobs at the Buick complex, but as their numbers swelled they expanded across Saginaw to the northwest side of the city, gradually occupying more and more of the older homes. Though they had better incomes and generally newer and nicer homes, the blacks of the north side were looked down upon as persons of "lower status" by those of the inner city's east and south sides. On the north side they were factory workers; they had dirty factories for neighbors, with blight, ugliness, fly ash and shorter-term residencies. The older families of the close-in neighborhoods had stability, pride, and "Sugar Hill" for a neighbor.

Then the highwaymen came through and purchased the land east and south of downtown for the two expressways and their interchange. Black families who had lived there for generations were forced out. When they could, they took housing close to their old neighborhoods, even though those neighborhoods were now dismembered and would soon be alongside high-speed highways. But for many the only housing options open were in the "lower status" areas north of downtown, mostly in the Model Cities tract, thus aggravating that area's troubles, crowding and public service needs. The Mott Foundation had earlier created a Genesee Community Development Conference to work on housing construction and rehabilitation, but, with the massive dislocation being brought on by the superhighways, it turned its attention instead to assisting relocation of the displaced families. By the end of 1969, when the highway path was cleared, some three thousand families had been moved out of the way, some of them fleeing on their own without assistance or relocation payments. The highway was coming, and in-town neighborhoods had to go. That the highways were to be white suburbia's roads through black inner-city homes was apparent: more than 58 percent of the families displaced by the highways inside Flint's central area were black, even though blacks accounted for only 28 percent of the city's population in 1970 and only 12 percent of the two-county region's, all but about 6,000 (10 percent) of them concentrated inside the city limits.

Perhaps of more concern to the highway builders than the cost to close-in dwellers is the cost in construction dollars, which is being pushed to inordinate heights by inflation. City Manager Tom Kay estimated that the expressways themselves may cost at least half again as much to build as the original estimate of 60 million dollars, and years of inflation ahead in the 1970's may drive that higher still. Included in such figures is neither the estimated 3.5 million dollars that will have to be spent on existing surface streets to widen them enough to carry the traffic loads the freeways are expected to generate (a good bit of that money to be taken from the city's capital improvements fund, which is supported by property taxes, and not from the highway-lobby-defended "highway user" taxes), nor the estimated 2.3 million dollars a year spent by the city on street maintenance, a further subsidy for in-city car travel that is likely to climb as more and more traffic pounds on city streets to and from expressway ramps.

As elsewhere, the superhighways also have hidden costs for Flint —some of them less hidden now that their impact is being felt inside the city tax office. With the coming of the super-roads, suburbanization of major facilities for schooling, shopping, and recreation has quickened its pace. The suburbanization has meant a steady outward flight from downtown, a flight that has left much of the business district in such decay that the downtown itself is marked out on planners' maps as a Neighborhood Development Program target. The worst section of downtown is at its northern end, where the unsightly Flint River and the Chesapeake and Ohio Railroad tracks both cross Saginaw Street, the tracks crossing at grade level. After some seven years of discussion and argument over costs, the city finally reached agreement with the railroad company to have the tracks removed to a by-pass route. The city is also planning major riverfront development and is moving to tear out the rows of shabby commercial buildings long since abandoned and boarded over, including some built on a platform straddling the river itself. Originally the Army Corps of Engineers proposed to develop the river for flood control, but its efforts would have left the river an ugly concrete trough. Planners stepped in to stop the program and redesigned the river frontage as terraced pedestrian parkland. The riverfront program and another part of the downtown renewal plan, a revival of the 1960 "master plan" for a Saginaw Street pedestrian mall, remain but concept drawings, awaiting final decisions on other major developments being considered for downtown by its much more influential private sector leadership—Mott, the bankers, and the auto manufacturers.

While other cities—Atlanta, for example—can still build major sports facilities near the heart of downtown, Flint cannot. The Industrial Mutual Association, a non-taxed organization created in 1901 by the Manufacturers' Association of Flint, has seen to that.

The IMA is an "employee-benefit" organization funded mostly by the loose change employees pay daily into vending machines at the city's factories—most of them, of course, General Motors plants. GM's sheer weight controls the Manufacturers' Association of Flint; and, since a company becomes a member of the Industrial Mutual Association only by being a member of the Manufacturers' Association, GM also controls the IMA. During the middle and late 1960's there were repeated pressures to remove tax-exempt status from the IMA, and the association found itself with an embarrassingly large surplus of funds needing to be spent quickly if it was to avoid taxes on them. It decided to build an ice hockey arena. (Hockey is to the Flint area what football is to the Southeast and the West Coast.)

A private site evaluation was conducted by a local bank, including analysis of accessibility for both a downtown location near the IMA's riverside auditorium and a suburban setting. One thing urged for *all* site options was that the selection be near expressway entrance and exit ramps. About ten or twelve acres would be needed, it was estimated. Enough land could have been found downtown for the original arena planned, but not enough to provide major parking for it as well, it was believed, nor enough for the low, flat monster that the IMA eventually built. The city's planning director correctly believed the arena should be located downtown to lure new activity to the city's center, and when the IMA instead came forward with a rezoning petition for a site on the city's eastern border conveniently near the east-west expressway, he tried to talk city commissioners into turning it down. It was a losing battle. The planning director was not invited to neighborhood meetings on the planned facility, and when the actual rezoning hearing was held he found hundreds in the chamber to support it but no residents expressing the customary concern for preservation of the character of their community. A self-styled non-fighter and non-meddler in politics, the chief officer responsible for orderly growth in the city did not protest too much.

GM and the IMA had ample reason for insisting on a suburban site. Downtown land was more expensive, and the IMA, wary of impending taxation on its funds, was anxious to spend them without the time-consuming inconvenience and complexities of assembling a large enough plot of near-downtown property.

The IMA, meanwhile, had expanded its plan and has now opened a 5.5-million-dollar complex that includes two ice rinks, one with three times the floor space of the riverside IMA auditorium near downtown. The facility sprawls over 25 acres and provides 1,000 parking spaces and seating for 1,500 in the junior arena and 4,200 in the larger. The main ice rink, which can accommodate up to 800 skaters at one time, opened to professional hockey in 1969, and Buick is thinking of relocating its annual new-model preview from the considerably older IMA facility downtown to the suburban arena. The new-model show is one of the few major events each year that still bring large numbers of visitors to the city. When the Urban Land Institute panel that visited the city in 1967 learned about the IMA decision to build the skating rink on the edge of the city, it included a stern warning in its report:

> Every effort should be made to provide attractions and amenities downtown other than shopping facilities. Have something to attract the youngsters so they will bring their parents to the central business district. For example, the I.M.A. Skating Ring [*sic*] should have been downtown. *Do not ever miss a bet like that again.* (Emphasis added.)

The Urban Land Institute had one other caution for downtown Flint that in later years would ring like a prophecy of doom. It said that it was "vitally important" that downtown stay strong enough to attract major new retail investment. "You can ill afford to let it get away from downtown," the panel said in its report. "Today Flint has no modern regional shopping center. The core area could quickly become a 'dead duck' even if the beginnings of a strong outside center is [*sic*] allowed. If inducements are necessary to prevent this, they should be seriously considered."

Flint not only did not heed the warning, it acted on the reverse principle. J. L. Hudson, owner of Michigan's largest department-store chain, expressed interest in locating a major store in downtown Flint and began seeking an appropriate site. Downtown retailers, jealous of their hold on what retailing business downtown was able to retain, repeatedly frustrated his attempts. Subsequently, Hudson announced that he was abandoning his downtown plans. Instead he would build the area's first regional shopping center some five and a half miles west of downtown, beyond the city limits and beside the east-west expressway. Downtown Flint merchants and allied interests reportedly approached Hudson about changing his mind again and selecting a downtown site; it is reported that Hudson declined with a reminder of the obstacles they had placed before him earlier when he had been interested in Flint's downtown.

Not only did Hudson build a giant 25-million-dollar 1-million-square-foot mall outside the city, complete with drive-up banking, but he also talked Sears Roebuck into moving out of what had been downtown's largest store and relocating on the mall as well. The downtown Sears store stood abandoned, and a sign in its window advised prospective tenants to contact the Piper Realty Company.

The suburban Genesee Valley mall dealt a severe blow to downtown retail sales. Sometime during the mid-1960's the merchants had stopped letting downtown and comparative retail sales volumes be known publicly, perhaps because the numbers offered little food for optimism, but Saul Seigel, administrator of the Downtown Corporation, estimates that on the basis of parking statistics at the corporation's four garages, downtown sales are down between 10 and 20 percent since the mid-1970 opening of the new regional mall. The Urban Land Institute's warning is coming true.

In a June 1971 report to the members of the Greater Flint Downtown Corporation, Seigel pointed out that Hudson's new mall had spent more than $100,000 on promotion even though it had been open less than one year, while merchants downtown had spent less than $20,000 a year over the past five years. He told the corporation's members that he had seen one measure of the effects of this imbalance the previous Saturday, when he had visited both Genesee Valley and Eastland Mall for two hours before coming downtown. "The malls were absolutely jammed with people and activity. Although the downtown retail stores were busier than usual, there was no comparison between the two." Almost as a gratuitous footnote he added, "White people are most dominant at the malls, while the blacks continue to shop downtown."

In fact, it seemed that for all downtown's efforts to save itself, each step it took forward was countered by a doubly powerful lure to the suburbs: the Buick decision to build a giant headquarters building next to its plants rather than build a landmark downtown skyscraper for the city of its birth; the freeways that uprooted long-stable neighborhoods of the close-in city; the ice rink and Hudson's mall; the manager of Chevrolet manufacturing in Flint seeking a suburban site to offer should Chevrolet Division headquarters be enticed to the city; and a decision to close the only two high schools left near the city's center and relocate them in new facilities at the city's outer limits.

The early-starting and still accelerating movement to the suburbs; the far-flung dispersal of housing, jobs, schooling, shopping, and recreation; the affluence bred of car production and consumption; the society's need to demonstrate allegiance to Buick, to GM, and to the auto industry in general by espousing wholesale the status-consciousness obsessions undergirding automobile advertisement; the blue-collar mentality that distrusts government inroads into "private" enterprise regardless of private enterprise's impact on land use, tax collections, and vital public services—all contributed inevitably to the death of public transportation in Flint.

For an entire generation and more, riding a bus in Flint has been considered beneath human dignity; buses are considered no more than a poor man's product (much the same as in other cities, but sooner and to a much greater degree in Flint), and a bad one at that. In such an environment survival is impossible for any form of transportation other than the private automobile and its superhighways. At least one federal transportation official privately commented once (if not more often) that if there were a single city where a demonstration program to save and improve bus service was doomed to failure, it would have to be Flint, Michigan, "the most hostile environment you can find" for public transit.

Before 1936 the city was served by street railways; that year removal of tracks from the streets was started and Flint Trolley Coach began operating a combination of trolley and bus service. In 1944 its ridership peaked at 25 million, many of the riders forced into public transit by wartime gas rationing and lack of automobiles and parts, but during the first year after the war, ridership still stood above 23 million. By the mid-1950's, however, increasing car ownership and use in the city was cutting severely into the trolley company's operations; foreseeing deficits ahead, it was sold in 1956 to City Coach Lines, Inc., a Delaware corporation home-based in Jacksonville, Florida.

In 1957, years before bus operations in most other cities were to face the same plight, Flint City Coach Lines, Inc., realized its last profits. In that year its net profit from bus operations was but $13,342 —down 90 percent from its income level in 1946, when even the same amount of income would have been worth considerably more. By 1958, the first of an unbroken string of years in which the company operated at a loss despite repeated service cuts and fare increases, ridership had collapsed to little more than 5 million a year, a drop of 78 percent since 1946; only four years later even this had fallen another 44 percent from the 1957 level and stood at a bare 19 percent of 1946 ridership. In 1962 the City of Flint contracted with a transportation engineering firm, Simpson and Curtin, to study the system and find a solution. The consultants urged the city to create a public transportation authority, purchase the company from its private owner, and operate it as a public enterprise. Flint City Coach Lines, Inc., was all for the idea. Authorizing legislation was adopted by the Michigan legislature in 1963, the Flint Transportation Authority was incorporated the following year, and on May 1, 1965, public transit in Flint passed into public hands. By that year, ridership was down 55 percent from 1957 and more than 85 percent from 1946.

The Flint Transportation Authority was headed by an appointed, part-time, three-man board: the city manager acting as chairman, the school board's business manager as vice-chairman, and a private attorney as secretary-treasurer. The board contracted with the previous operators of the bus lines, Flint City Coach Lines, Inc., to continue operations. Thus, the only immediate saving to bus operations was the $40,000 a year the company had been paying in taxes. (The next year the FTA had to raise fares to 35 cents.) Under the new arrangement the first 5 percent of fare-box revenues went to Flint City Coach Lines for its management services; after that, fare-box revenues were used for wages, maintenance, and other operating costs. Third priority from fare-box revenue was to pay the 4 percent interest on the transportation authority's 1.07 million dollars in bonds acquired by Flint City Coach Lines in exchange for its buses, yard, and buildings; twice in 1968 the authority failed to take enough money in fares to meet its interest payments on the bonds. Should any revenue be left over, it was then to be used to pay principal on the bonds, establish a depreciation reserve for equipment replacement, and provide working capital reserves, in that order. Seldom was enough money available from fares to meet the last three needs. Ridership in 1967 was down to 2.5 million and by 1969 to 2.2 million—less than half the number of riders in 1960 and less than 10 percent of the number of riders in 1946.

As if the bus operation hadn't headaches enough, it was chronically plagued with employee difficulties. It was experiencing an annual turnover of about 88 percent among its drivers and maintenance crews, owing largely to the high wages being paid by manufacturers in the city, wages with which the ailing bus company could hardly afford to compete. Consequently, it was reduced to hiring the least skilled and least dependable from the work force. Because drivers often failed to appear for work, City Coach Lines had to keep ten extra drivers on the payroll to be certain it would have drivers enough to meet its schedule; still bus schedules became notoriously undependable. As turnover increased and the quality of its drivers dropped, its accident rate rose. During a typical six-month period late in the 1960's, 33 of its 48 traffic collisions involved bus drivers who had had less than a year of experience. Because manufacturers in the city were attracting the best mechanics, the quality of City Coach Lines' maintenance crews also fell, and with them the quality of bus rides, the appearance of buses, and the image of the bus service.

About half of the bus riders were schoolchildren, riding at reduced fares. Officials of Flint City Coach Lines estimated that the students did $30,000 worth of damage to buses during 1968, but when they asked the Flint Board of Education for an annual subsidy of $100,000 to preserve school bus service, they were turned down without negotiation. School officials contended that transportation of students was not the responsibility of the school board (the state authorized funds for school bus service only in its smallest cities and in rural areas), and when the Flint Transportation Authority cited damage to buses done by students, school officials contended that it was done when buses were late arriving at the schools or when too few buses came to pick up students—forcing undue waiting and overcrowding.

There had been a few scattered attempts to lure more riders to public transit, and without exception they had failed. On some routes drivers were occasionally instructed to put their uniform caps over the fare box and give all boarders a free ride, but there was no advance notice of the free samples. A downtown shuttle service was tried along the commercial corridor to the Sears store then at the northern end of downtown, but it was not widely advertised and was soon found unprofitable. The Greater Flint Downtown Corporation paid a charter fee of $50 a bus to provide a free shuttle service between a parking lot on the edge of the college and cultural complex and downtown stores on Fridays and Saturdays during the 1967 Christmas shopping season, but discontinued it for lack of ridership; at the same time, however, the corporation was also promoting its 5-cents-a-half-hour parking decks close to the stores, and the garages were staying filled, and as an added subsidy for auto users, merchants were paying between $70,000 and $100,000 a year for free parking stamps in a "Park and Shop" program.

City Manager Tom Kay, serving as chairman of the transportation authority, demonstrated his attitude toward innovative public transit thinking by his reaction to a proposal by Model Cities planners that they jointly study the economic feasibility of a "micro-bus" feeder system or a special jitney-like service to be provided by driver-owned vehicles. Though Model Cities officials thought their idea was getting consideration by the transportation authority, Kay privately called it "patently ridiculous" and dismissed out of hand an economic feasibility study of it as "not based on any economic considerations." Kay added, "I don't want to associate myself with that plan."

In 1966 the Flint Transportation Authority, with public and private funds that included a substantial grant from the Mott Foundation, contracted with the American Academy of Transportation, a private organization based at the University of Michigan in Ann Arbor, to examine the system again and recommend changes that might reverse the slow dying of the transit. The study produced the single significant innovation in public transit's history in Flint. The academy's report, issued later that year, recognized that fare increases had been only short-term financial answers because in the long run they were followed by even steeper declines in ridership. Similarly it recognized that something more basic than the bus system's pattern of routes was to blame: "It is quite clear that any further modifications to this basic route structure and operational method show little promise of effecting an increase in the number of passengers. . . ." What it offered, instead, was "a new kind of bus service tailored to compete effectively for private automobile oriented passengers."

The newly added bus service was dubbed "Maxi-Cab." It offered a new bus with a distinctive look, taped music, coffee and doughnuts on board, and door-to-door service. To institute the service, pay for its planning and initial costs, and buy a fleet of twenty-six new buses, the Flint Transportation Authority applied for and received almost a million dollars in federal aid from the Department of Housing and Urban Development; the Mott Foundation contributed $100,000 toward the city government's local share. The federal grant authorized a three-year demonstration program, officially beginning in January 1968.

The American Academy of Transportation and the Flint Transportation Authority conducted a study of Maxi-Cab's likely market: the major GM plants and their 42,000 GM employees who worked and lived within the service area. (The state limited the Flint Transportation Authority to service not farther than two miles outside the city limits.) Interviews in a preliminary market study showed that 26 percent of the workers would use the service and another 33 percent were interested but wanted to be shown how it would work. It was optimistically estimated Maxi-Cab might draw some

23,000 commuters out of their cars. In August 1968 a two-week teaser campaign saturated the area with radio announcements (especially on Country and Western stations), postcards, billboards, and even an airplane-towed message: "Max Is Coming." On August 18 a press preview and radio and newspaper advertisements announced the start of service, and on September 9 the first Maxi-Cab buses ran.

Maxi-Cab parties were held in GM plant cafeterias with mini-dressed "bus bunnies" on hand to distribute information, establish personal contact with riders, and sign up new riders. Sometimes the young girls rode the buses also, but eventually they remained at Flint City Coach Lines offices handling complaints, signing new riders, monitoring the Maxi-Cab routes and instructing drivers on their route changes to meet the fluctuating demand. On each run the bus driver was to stop by the front door of every "commuter club" member signed up for his route. The system was a model of flexibility. Routes changed each time new riders were added or old riders lost; most commuters were picked up at home, and only a few had to walk as much as half a block to meet the buses. Fares, billed monthly, ranged from $9 to $18, depending on the home-to-work trip length.

Service began with two routes and expanded to thirty by the end of the first full year of service, but it wasn't long before the nature of Maxi-Cab's market made itself known. Some complained that they wanted music "with a real beat" instead of the music "to sleep by" that was being played on the buses. Also, after only a few months, on-board coffee and doughnut service in the morning was discontinued because of its lack of appeal: only curious members of the press and bus bunnies and other transportation authority employees made use of it.

But there were also more serious problems. Maxi-Cab was drawing commuters out of their cars, but not nearly enough of them, and, more significantly, it was not holding those it had signed up. In the first year it signed some 520 "commuter club" members for varying lengths of time, but at the end of that year it was only carrying 230 riders a day. Four out of five of those who had quit riding the Maxi-Cabs said they had left for unavoidable reasons. Those reasons were imbedded in the nature of the automobile industry: frequent shift and plant reassignments that moved riders to times and places not served by Maxi-Cab; unannounced overtime work that meant riders would miss their return ride home; layoffs and other erratic employment patterns that didn't coincide with any bus schedule. Often workers who reported to work at the same plant at the same time didn't end their work day at the same time. For instance, at one Chevrolet plant 86 percent of the hourly-rated employees on the first shift began their work day at 6 A.M., but for 29 percent the shift ended at 2:30 P.M. and for 57 percent it ended at 3:30 P.M. Workers aware of the fact that they might be shifted to an unserved plant at mid-month or who knew they were often subject to unscheduled overtime work were unlikely to commit themselves to a monthly bus schedule contract. Additionally, Maxi-Cab could not count on holding its ridership during summer months, when GM plants laid off workers for the annual model changeover.

And there were the strikes. As early as two months after Maxi-Cab had started its regular runs, a two-and-a-half-week strike at the Buick plants took the steam out of Maxi-Cab's initial advertising campaign. There were more and bigger strikes to follow.

Personal problems also got in Maxi-Cab's way. Many of the blue-collar workers liked to stop off for a few beers on the way home from work each day, something they couldn't do on a Maxi-Cab. Still others quietly let it be known they didn't want to leave their family cars at home because their wives would be tempted to indiscriminate shopping trips.

Despite the setbacks and problems, Maxi-Cab continued to lure new riders out of their cars, but only in a very discouragingly slow growth until it reached a high of 310 daily passengers in October 1969—a little more than a year after the inception of service. From there it leveled off for the remainder of the year and into 1970. The transportation authority theorized that it was because the city was debating whether or not to keep the Maxi-Cab service or let it go under with the rest of bus service and that the debate, featured in the news, convinced potential riders that the city would never spend money to keep the service alive. On top of that, some four thousand GM workers were on strike from September to the end of 1969 at one of the Fisher Body plants.

Maxi-Cab received a small but unforeseen helping hand, however, when the national economy slowed down late in 1969. With the drop in auto buying and auto production, GM was making less use of overtime and Maxi-Cabs had to make fewer special runs to pick up overtime workers at the plants.

In November and December of 1969 the city at last took dramatic action to prolong the life of bus service: it made wholesale cuts in nighttime service on regular bus routes, received an additional $482,817 in federal aid and matched it with $241,409 in local funds, and vowed to keep bus service going, accepting new recommendations from the American Academy of Transportation that it study the possibilty of providing specialty bus service only—Maxi-Cabs, taxi-like "dial-a-bus" operation for off-peak-hour service, and special school-bus runs. It also promised to keep applying for federal assistance, hoping eventually to replace all its buses with new equipment. Without such action it seemed certain that all bus service would end with the decade. Maxi-Cab funds had all been drained away by the failing regular bus routes; while Maxi-Cab fares were paying the special bus service's operating costs, they were hardly bringing in sufficient funds to rescue the chronically ill city bus system as well. As early as midsummer 1969 it had been obvious that all bus service, Maxi-Cab included, would run out of funds by the end of November if such major action wasn't taken. Only the new federal grant, a thinly veiled operating subsidy (federal law did not permit direct-subsidy federal aid for transit operating costs), kept bus service alive another year.

In February 1970 the city broadened the Flint Transportation Authority's board to ten members, replaced City Manager Tom Kay as chairman with Stephen L. Miller, a Chamber of Commerce employee who later went to work for the Mott Foundation, and hired a new director. The transformed Flint Transportation Authority began a technical study of the feasibility of broadening the service county-wide—a move that would have brought under its fold more GM plants, more potential riders, and, most important, more potential sources of local government appropriations. Such a plan would also have allowed the transportation authority to absorb outlying school-bus systems one at a time, sell off their buses, and provide school-bus service with regular transit vehicles. The local governments they consulted agreed, as long as there would be no cost to them—and no local subsidy of bus operations. Public transit was still private enterprise, as it had always been, and it had to pay its own way out of the fare box.

Despite the efforts, it was far too late. There wasn't time enough to implement the plan. Month by month even Maxi-Cab was now losing its public: down 2 riders in March 1970, 7 in April, 12 in May, 20 in June, 1 in July, and 2 in August, when it canceled four of its runs to combine them with others. In September the United Auto Workers struck General Motors in a corporation-wide shutdown that was to last almost to the end of the year. All Maxi-Cab runs were terminated except those to the city-owned hospital and the AC Spark Plug plant. After the strike, at year's end, only 95 subscribers were riding on 12 runs. The remainder of the twenty-six new buses bought with the federal aid were being used for charter service and on regular bus routes, and they were faring no better: the bus system that had carried 25 million passengers in 1944 carried only 1.5 million in 1970. To make matters worse, the city government invoked its austerity program to ward off the effects of drastically cut income tax collections expected after the strike and ordered a general cutback on spending, bus service included.

On January 15, 1971, the expiration date of the federal demonstration project that had made Maxi-Cab possible, the Flint Transportation Authority made a 25 percent across-the-board cut in service and personnel. It tried to keep Maxi-Cab alive for a few weeks more by raising all fares $5 but found only 28 riders still willing to use it. Deficits that had been running about $25,000 a month were cut to $17,000 a month, where they stood on February 22, when bus drivers, unable to reach agreement on a contract with the transportation authority, went out on strike. All public bus service came to an end in Flint, Michigan.

It was estimated that about 6,000 persons had been using the bus service daily—about half of them students and half of them too poor, too old, or too infirm to own or drive automobiles. With the death of the bus system they were left stranded—immobilized by the most mobile society ever devised by man. Because the 6,000 daily riders represented only about 3 percent of the city's population of almost 200,000, city officials decided that it wasn't politically worth an operating subsidy that would cost an estimated $250,000 a year, even though eight other cities in Michigan already were directly subsidizing bus operations.

As early as December 1970 the director of the Flint Transportation Authority, Sydney W. Barkman, wrote into his monthly report, "It completely escapes me as to what logic they (city officials) are trying to apply in solving this latest crisis," and in his next and final monthly report he added, "The community proved that under its present structure . . . no project could be run successfully in the City of Flint."

When the buses had stopped running, there was only the mopping up to do. Flint City Coach Lines got back its original buses, its land, and its buildings, and the Flint Transportation Authority got back its worthless bonds. The school buses continued to run under a special city appropriation.

The shutdown of public transit service continued for a year and a half before bus drivers agreed to return to work for the public authority and the city agreed at last to provide a meager subsidy for a shoestring operation. Using only the 26 former Maxi-Cabs, a reconstituted public transportation authority continued transporting school children and reopened a few basic routes providing widely spaced service. Thus it joined the swelling ranks of small and middle-sized cities whose bus operations are either dead or providing skeleton service that is "hanging on by a thread," as one federal transit official remarked. "After all," he added, "who really cares? You're talking about such a small minority of people."

The mayor, meanwhile, named his own citizens' task force to help seek a public transit solution, and it was faring no better. On its shopping list of ideas was a revival of the small-bus "broker" concept whereby a driver would own or earn a commission from his "bus," similar to taxicab operations and not much unlike the "micro-bus" plan advanced by Model Cities officials earlier and discarded in scorn by the city manager.

Whatever Flint decides to do, its surrender of fixed facilities back to Flint City Coach Lines means it will have to start from scratch on any new transit venture. Flint City Coach Lines isn't likely to treat too kindly any offers to start up again in a city that has publicly vilified it and whose city commissioners have administered repeated verbal abuse over an extended period of time; not that the company's management doesn't deserve the verbal abuse, but the community at large and the social and economic structure its leadership urged upon the region also deserve their majority share of the blame for the collapse of public transit. Flint City Coach Lines did little enough to alter that, but there probably was little it could do to change the course of its own destruction in such an environment.

Flint's closely knit private power structure, meanwhile, is preoccupied with much more grandiose plans and projects than the saving of public transit. In early April 1970, when winter was blowing its last across Michigan, twenty-nine of the city's leading private figures responded to an invitation by Harding Mott, president of the foundation, and gathered for three days at a lodge owned by Consumers Power Company at Tippy Dam. They were the top executives of the city's major banks, real estate dealers, Editor Glen A. Boissonneault of the *Flint Journal,* active and retired GM executives and leaders of such parallel and overlapping "civic" groups as the Mott Foundation, Industrial Mutual Association, Manufacturers' Association of Flint, and the Greater Flint Downtown Corporation.

According to a later account in the *Journal,* much of the three days was spent in discussion of "local government, race relations, unemployment, health, culture, civic leadership, community pride, federal programs, and renovation of downtown." After the three days the men continued to meet informally but regularly as the Flint Coordinating Committee, and by September they had incorporated a tax-exempt Flint Area Conference, Inc., described in a vague but verbose stream by one of its originators and its first president, Saul

Seigel, formerly of the Downtown Corporation, as "an exciting new
organizational concept for private sector community participation, a
catalyst for a renaissance of spirit, pride and progress in the area,
an action-oriented civic process. . . ." (Seigel now describes himself
as an "urban philosopher" and is an "urban affairs consultant" to the
Mott Foundation as well as the operating head of the Flint Area
Conference, Inc.)

In mid-1971 the new coalition of private leadership officially
opened for business by naming its board. Harding Mott became
chairman, and Homer Dowdy, the journalist-turned-author-turned-
Mott-Foundation-vice-president, became treasurer. Heavily represented on the other twenty-four board seats are bankers and top
GM executives, including the general manager of GM's parts division,
both the retired and current general managers of AC Spark Plug, and
the retired general manager of Chevrolet Manufacturing. Others included Arthur E. Summerfield, Jr., a former United States Postmaster
General and the city's leading Chevrolet dealer, William C. Crick,
managing director of the Industrial Mutual Association, and W.
Osmund Kelley, executive director of the Manufacturers' Association
of Flint.

The conference steers clear of assigning itself any social-develop-
ment tasks; its only concern is for physical and economic development,
patterned after the Allegheny Conference of private industrial and
financial leadership, which worked closely with local government in
creating the dramatic "Golden Triangle" renewal in downtown Pittsburgh.

Three top-priority items, all interrelated, are at the forefront of
the Flint Area Conference's development formula for the city. One
of these, development of a new cargo airport large enough to
accommodate the largest and newest of the jumbo jets, such as Lock-
heed's C-5A, is under study by the American Academy of Transportation and will be ten years in the making, assuming the state
provides enabling legislation. Heading the conference's airport development program is Ronald O. Warner, retired manager of Chevrolet Manufacturing in Flint. The airport is needed to lure in the
second of the conference's objectives—more industry and, in particular, still *more* GM plants. Without new job opportunities it is feared
that the young will abandon Flint as they did in the 1930's. Thus,
according to the Mott Foundation's Homer Dowdy, it is hoped that
GM will locate its new catalytic muffler plant in Flint, a plant that
it hopes will produce a product—developed by the Flint-based AC
Spark Plug Division—capable of satisfying the anti-pollution movement in Washington, D.C. (A major blow to Flint's pride as the

world's largest concentration of Chevrolet employees was GM's decision to locate its new mini-car Vega plant in Lordstown, Ohio, instead of in Flint.)

But the most ambitious and dramatic of the conference's announced goals is Centric 80. Its objective is to rebuild downtown Flint, tying together its government center on the south, the college and cultural complex at the southeast and east, the central commercial corridor, and the IMA Auditorium and hotels on the north. Plans to develop a Saginaw Street mall have been revived. There are to be new office buildings, hotels and convention facilities, apartments, a climate-controlled central shopping mall, landscaped plazas, and vistas of fountains and sculpture—all targeted to be in place by 1980 and estimated to cost up to 110 million dollars.

A key feature of the plan is yet another new expressway, slicing north-south across the west side of downtown and tying in at either end with the north-south Interstate under construction on the east side. (The cost of the freeway isn't included in the 110-million-dollar estimate.)

The development of the entire Centric 80 plan into actual construction is to be handled by a corporation the Flint Area Conference plans to "spin off." That corporation, though not bound to the plan by law, hopefully will see to it that private developers build only in accordance with it.

The conference has retained a wide range of consultants to work on every preparatory aspect of the development dream, but the most auspicious of these by far is architect Minoru Yamasaki, designer of the Pacific Science Center at the Seattle World's Fair and, more recently, of the monumental World Trade Center in Manhattan. (Flint leadership is still awed by Moses-like builders from New York.) Yamasaki's task is to design what the conference and even the city's director of Community Development believes will be the launching pad for all of the other downtown development—an automobile hall of fame.

The idea of a hall of fame to the automobile seemed to fit nicely into the Office of Community Development's plans to redevelop the Flint riverfront instead of letting the Army Corps of Engineers turn it into a concrete trough. In 1965 consultants offered three alternate plans of river redevelopment to the city: create an island and parklike environment, create a waterfall and parklike environment, or cover it over with concrete. The city planners liked the island idea best and in 1969 passed it on to another consulting firm which also came up with three alternatives: a 13-million-dollar plan to back up the river, create an island near the Saginaw Street crossing, and provide riverfront walks, a 10-million-dollar no-island plan with a lower water table and riverfront walkways, and a 6.4-million-dollar plan of flood-control work and minimal riverfront landscaping. Increasingly cost-conscious city officials chose the no-island 10-million-dollar option.

At about that time the Flint Area Conference surfaced with its plans, and Yamasaki is now drawing preliminary designs for a downtown memorial to the automobile to be built by the National Automotive Hall of Fame, Inc., an incorporated nonprofit organization being staffed by the Flint Area Conference. The memorial is to be built on a man-made island in the river—in effect resurrecting the proposal dropped by city officials. The concept behind the hall of fame is to tell, in three-dimensional forms, the complete story of the automobile's impact on American society: the development of suburbia, far-flung regional shopping malls, superhighways, and vacation-time mobility; the unprecedented growth it gave, not only to the small wagon makers' shops of the 1880's, but also to the steel, rubber, glass, aluminum, asphalt, concrete, petroleum, and insurance industries; the effect it has had on air pollution and the efforts being made by the automobile industry to combat it.

One is led to wonder whether this monument to the automobile will also tell the stories of the millions maimed and thousands killed each year by automobiles; of the waste of natural resources represented in junkyards that lie languorously over rural hills in most parts of the country; of the legacy of immobility it is leaving to those too young, too old, too invalid, or too poor to drive; of the thousands of families that have been uprooted by highways; of the neighborhoods that have been split apart by urban expressways; of the traffic strangulation taking over many American cities whose downtowns were never meant to absorb the superhighway-sized traffic jams poured into them; of the tax-starvation diet the suburbs have forced on cities off which they live and breed parasitically; of the oil spills off the continent's coast; of the pressing domestic needs that have gone begging while highway builders and auto makers have grown ever more prosperous off the 5-billion-dollar-a-year for-highways-only federal trust fund; of the wasting of the land by highways, subdivisions, and the suburbanization of a society that never had a full opportunity to first become urbanized.

Whether or not all these stories are told in the proposed National Automotive Hall of Fame, there is probably no more fitting monument for Flint. The automobile made the city, and the automobile has been breaking it. It is proper that automobile money attempt to put it back together again. One has doubts, but it may be that a hall of fame, rising on a man-made island in a rechanneled river in downtown Flint, spanned on either side by freeway lanes of the new proposed expressway and undergirded by a huge underground parking lot, may be what it will take to revitalize downtown Flint into an active, exciting place of multiple activities—conventions, theaters, good restaurants, other entertainment, and pleasant places to walk— the sort of place we are told it was during its boom of the "Roaring Twenties" but has never been since.

There was one cautionary note in 1971, and one the city's leadership did not seem prepared to hear. At the first, board-selection meeting of the Flint Area Conference, a letter was read from Ward McCallister, the Model Cities' planning supervisor, and William J. Meyer, a political science professor at the Flint branch of the University of Michigan, which they said represented only their personal views, not their institutions'. It said in part: "We would suggest that the general public has the right to review such goals, considering the broad public impact of the proposed Centric 80 plan. We would question the wisdom and intent of developing a plan of broad public impact such as Centric 80 in relative secrecy. . . . [It is] not responsible to develop a physical and economic plan and fail to address the social implications of that plan."

It was the sort of advice which the private power structures of many other cities had failed to hear when they earlier set out to rebuild their cities. Flint's power structure may well be advised to do better.

2
Dayton: New Freeways, Old Trolleys

They call it "Action City," but:

1. In 1958 the *Dayton Daily News* published a highly acclaimed series of "Metropolitan Heartbeat" articles urging Dayton to take note of its withering downtown and to do something about it. In 1970, Cox Enterprises, owner of the *News* and its sister daily, the *Journal Herald,* topped off a 3-million-dollar 100,000-square-foot six-story office tower complete with 400-car parking, and was prepared to duplicate the venture with an adjacent tower for a total 6-million-dollar investment—not downtown, but in suburban Kettering.

2. In 1960 the editor of the *Journal Herald,* Glenn Thompson, sat down with the city's industrial leaders and, by the following year, persuaded them to organize formally into an Area Progress Council dedicated to the revitalization of the city, its heart, and its fractionalized urban region. A decade later, by now retired editor Thompson was calling the Area Progress Council "a quicksand for ideas."

3. Early in 1968 the Dayton Chamber of Commerce formed the Area Response Council, a congregation of representatives from more than 320 schools, community clubs, civic associations, churches, industry, labor unions, and other organizations, on call to meet whenever an issue required a public decision. On such occasions the delegates were given all available information and points of view—both pro and con—on the issue at hand, be it the need for metropolitan government or a tax increase, and then were dispatched to disseminate the information among their respective group memberships, to poll the members, and to send the results back to the chamber. While admittedly of little value as a scientific public opinion–sampling mechanism, the Area Response Council was a major contribution to the arsenal of electorate education. Properly used, it could go a long way toward assuring that a knowledgeable public would act responsibly in referenda. As late as mid-1969 Chamber of Commerce officials were describing it as an "important" tool for "building a needed cohesiveness in our communities" and boasting that the United States chamber was monitoring the experiment closely. By the end of 1970 the Area Response Council was phased out of existence in favor of a foundation-funded Public Opinion Center, which does a considerably more scientific job of sampling public opinion but can do nothing to educate the public or drum up voter support for such locally distasteful medicine as tax increases and regional government.

These and similar developments, and the urban undercurrents they illustrate, are propelling the city and region of Dayton into its own "urban crisis," ironically born—like Flint's—of the very industrial wealth that gave the city its early vitality and leadership.

Economic activity in Dayton, Ohio, born and raised at the confluence of the Miami River and three of its tributaries from the north, was limited in 1800 to that of a marketplace for nearby farmers. Manufacturing and industrial growth did not begin until the 1829 opening of a barge canal to Cincinnati and, soon afterward, the railroads. The manufacturing investments that followed these transport ventures were convincing evidence that transportation was a key to growth—and growth patterns. An "industrial crescent" emerged along the rail lines and the river. National Cash Register was born in Dayton. So were Dayton Tire and Rubber, and Dayton Computing Scale Co., later merged into International Business Machines. All were settled in by 1885 and all remain today, including the transportation system-oriented crescent shape of the industrial corridor.

The American inventive genius that spawned the national industrial revolution also brought on Dayton's: Charles Kettering invented the electric cash register, which pushed National Cash Register into leadership of a national market. Kettering also invented the electric starter, which brought the automobile industry to the banks of the Miami River. Other large home-grown industries of Dayton include the Mead Corporation, McCall Corporation, and Huffman Manufacturing. The Wright brothers conducted their early aviation experiments there, and now aviation is big business in Dayton, allowing the city to promote itself as the home of sprawling Wright-Patterson Air Force Base and the United States Air Force Museum.

As a vital part of its industrial expansion Dayton developed early a strong, manufacturer-based leadership. When a 1913 flood killed 400 and wrought 100 million dollars' worth of damage, the founder of National Cash Register, John H. Patterson, stood on the courthouse steps and personally began a community campaign that rapidly collected 2.5 million dollars, created a regional flood control conservancy district, and built five dams on the Miami River. That same year he headed a city charter commission which made of Dayton one of the first cities to operate under a self-governing charter and the commission-manager form of city government persisting in Dayton today. When World War II established the military as a major national employer, it was Patterson's son who donated much of the suburban acreage that assured continued expansion of Wright-Patterson Air Force Base to its present 7,888 acres.

The Air Force's expansive move to suburbia was but the start of the war-spawned shift in the economy and appearance of the Dayton area, a shift still inexorably in progress. Dayton's secure manufacturing base meant that wages ran well ahead of the national average as war production turned to peacetime production. Dayton built what has become the third largest concentration of General Motors employees anywhere, some 33,000 workers in mid-1971 spread over a landscape of four GM divisions headquartered in the area: Frigidaire, Delco-Moraine, Delco Products, and Inland Manufacturing. Spurred by such industrial growth and the unions representing this growing population of skilled workers, the average hourly wage in Dayton manufacturing climbed to $2.73 by 1960 and to $3.95 by 1969, an increase of almost 45 percent in the nine years.

GI loans and, beginning earlier, FHA loans made surburban home buying easier for returning World War II and Korean Conflict soldiers and their new families, and the population growth outside the city began to outstrip that of Dayton. Kettering, on Dayton's southern exposure, was a village of chuckholes and cornfields in 1954. By the 1970 census it was a sprawling suburb devoting 1 percent of its land to manufacturing and numbering almost 70,000 residents. Wayne

Township's twenty-two square miles in the 1950 census counted 1,900 persons, most of them farmers, but that was before Charles H. Huber arrived in 1956 to build his first house. Since then his wholly owned C. H. Huber Enterprises, Inc., has built some nine thousand homes and effectively altered the township's name to the unofficial "Huber Heights." (Huber also built a water and sewer system for the area and sold it to the Chicago-based Ohio Suburban Water Company, which pays him a $750 subsidy for each new house.) In the process of building a sizable fortune Huber, along with other developers, has turned the township into one of the fastest-growing suburbs in the nation—numbering some thirty thousand residents by 1970.

Kettering and Huber Heights are not so exceptional as they may seem. In 1940 the three-county Dayton area encompassed 383,975 persons; by 1950 this had climbed to 518,642, and by 1960 it reached 694,623—an area-wide increase of 81 percent in the twenty years, 34 percent in the latter ten years. The city itself, meanwhile, recorded only a 9 percent increase from 1950 to 1960 (from 243,872 to 262,-332); and despite projections of continued growth in city population, the city actually had lost a net of 7 percent of its 1960 population by the 1970 census. Meanwhile, the Standard Metropolitan Statistical Area had grown to four counties and had registered a 15 percent population increase, to 850,266. That the city dwellers were fleeing to the suburbs in part to escape the waves of job-seeking blacks from the Southeast and, during the 1960's, poor whites from Appalachia was also increasingly evident in the statistics. As the suburbs grew more crowded, they also became more homogeneously white. In 1970, 11 percent of the population in the metropolitan area was black, but nearly four-fifths of that group lived within the Dayton city limits. The suburban towns, which had registered the most impressive population gains during the preceding decades, were almost entirely white by 1970. For example, only 7 of Oakwood's 10,000 population were listed as Negro, only 15 of Centerville's 10,000, and only 136 of Kettering's almost 70,000. In Dayton itself, meanwhile, blacks accounted for more than 30 percent of the total population of 243,601.

Though the blacks had come looking for jobs, they were confined economically to the city, while the newest and best jobs were moving to the suburbs. Not only in Flint has General Motors been on a course to the suburbs, anxious to reap the economies of single-story linear production, which does not require movement of materials, men, and equipment up and down elevator shafts but does require large acreage, both for plants and for employee parking. Additionally, the giant corporation believes in keeping its administrative services and management-level personnel near the plants, not in a downtown skyscraper.

Thus, in 1952, Delco Products opened a plant in Kettering, a city that effectively barricades Dayton's southern border, and in the mid-1960's moved its executive offices and engineering facilities out of downtown Dayton to new multimillion-dollar facilities at its Kettering plant. (It still maintains one plant on the edge of downtown Dayton and another on a peninsula of incorporated land that juts far north of the city's main area.) Though GM's Frigidaire Division maintains headquarters and one factory downtown, its largest plant facility, employing some 10,000 in early 1970, is spread over the village of Moraine, also on Dayton's southern border—a village of only 2,283 acres, 41 percent of which is devoted to manufacturing and service to manufacturers.

GM has not been alone in the exodus. When National Cash Register decided to expand, it began a ten-year building program including a fourteen-building, 8-million-dollar Technical Services Education Center on eighty-five acres of land some twelve miles south of downtown and a 1.5-million-dollar five-story sales and service building in Kettering.

Once the suburbanite settled in with his garaged transportation ready to take him wherever and whenever he wanted, it took little more to entice retail merchants out of downtown in pursuit of Dayton's high level of disposable income. In the downtown Dayton of the mid-1940's there were three department stores of roughly equal size and sales volume. By the early 1950's, a former tie salesman in one of the stores, the late Arthur Beerman, had launched a campaign of personal competition against his former employer. He bought the two other stores and began building and opening small suburban shopping centers at a passionate pace during the 1950's and early 1960's. (He also closed one of his two downtown outlets.) His former employer, Rike's, continued to expand downtown operations and corner most of the downtown department store market, but while Beerman's share of downtown profits declined, his income soared in the suburbs, and he succeeded in driving his competition to the outlying neighborhoods as well.

To ensure further expansion, Rike's passed into the chain ownership of Federated Stores in the mid-1960's, and a new wave of Rike's expansion swelled—this time much of it also in the suburbs. In 1965 Salem Mall opened, the city's first regional shopping center, more than six miles northwest of the Dayton downtown. It has a Rike's and a Sears Roebuck, and across the street two smaller discount-house shopping centers have been opened. By the beginning of the 1970's an even larger suburban regional shopping center, Dayton Mall, was opening about nine miles south of the Dayton downtown, including large outlets for Sears Roebuck, Rike's, and J. C. Penney. The Dayton Mall was strategically located with immediate access to Interstate 75 northward to Dayton. With Cincinnati, an urban complex twice the size of Dayton, only a thirty-five-mile drive southward, Dayton Mall's developers, Sears Roebuck, wisely calculated that the mall would attract shoppers not only from Dayton's populous southern tier of suburbs but from Cincinnati's northern suburbs as well. Arthur Beerman, contending that he was excluded from the new project, immediately drew up plans to build his own adjacent center. (Beerman had built and opened eight suburban shopping centers in the region by 1969, a year before he died.) Though statistical information on the relative volume of retail sales in downtown Dayton is not available, it is acknowledged by most that downtown Dayton's economy suffered a severe blow from the suburbanization of shopping, with a commensurate loss of potential tax dollars to the financially strangled city government.

Understandably, merchants and other commercial interests were alarmed by the developments of the late 1950's. They looked to transportation, to "easy access," for their answer. At that time, that meant the Interstate. But I-75 was being built *toward* Dayton, from the north and the south, not *through* its downtown. Not surprisingly, it was the general manager of a General Motors division, Vincent Blaire of Delco Products, who stepped in to make sure the in-town superhighway would be built quickly. He personally intervened with the Ohio highway director and officials of the United States Bureau of Public Roads and found that delays in through-Dayton construction were the result of a "communication lag" among the geographically scattered—and quarreling—officials involved. Once he offered his services as "communicator," the eight-lane freeway was built, consuming some fifty acres of valuable downtown property along the Miami River. While it eased access into the downtown area, it also eased access to the outside, spawning such substantial out-of-city investments and spending futures as the Dayton Mall and an office park being developed by Huffman Manufacturing, maker of lawnmowers, service station equipment, and bicycles, near I-75 south of the city.

Once the highways were built, the suburban subdivisions filled with families, the new plants firmly fixed as taxpaying suburbanites, and the choicest intersections blanketed with shopping centers and asphalt acres of parking, it was only natural that other facilities would emigrate—branch banks with drive-up teller booths, schools, and recreation facilities. When the community's power structure organization, the Area Progress Council, decided the city needed a local state university, it collected 3 million dollars in local donations, got another 3 million dollars in matching funds from the state, and began building Wright State University as a commuter campus northeast of the city, near Wright-Patterson Air Force Base. Its enrollment climbed to 10,000 during its first few years' operation; without bus service, most of the student body arrives by car—an average of 1.3 students in each —consuming 6,000 parking spaces daily. When the University of Dayton, the nation's ninth largest Catholic campus, decided to build a sports arena, it built a 13,000-seat basketball center at a safe distance from downtown—just off Interstate 75. When the city decided to build a multipurpose sports arena, it went ten miles north of the downtown area; the facility is used almost exclusively for professional hockey.

With their education, sports, shopping, entertainment, jobs, and housing in the suburbs, and freeways in place should they ever have to travel to or through the city, the residents of suburbia prepared to defend what they had against any city attempt to win back some of its lost economic vitality. The city's most available tool was annexation, but on its southern border it was hemmed in by the already incorporated areas of Oakwood, Kettering, and Moraine. Northward it attempted in 1969 to annex Salem Mall, but another suburban commuter community, Trotwood, annexed it instead, to the applause of Trotwood's residents and a peevish response from Dayton city commissioners.

The peevishness was directed at suburbia and failed to acknowledge the fact that the city had done little to save itself. Its almost Flint-like, wholesale elevation of the private automobile to supremacy over all urban transportation assured that the exodus to suburbia of all facets of community life—from swimming pools and movie houses to taxable private homes and factories—would proceed at a freeway pace. It also guaranteed that downtown Dayton would have to serve the automobile and not the people. Thus, Dayton has dedicated 45 percent of its downtown land area to movement and storage of motor vehicles—streets (many of them eight lanes wide), alleys, and parking. The central business district counts 16,327 parking spaces; during the summer of 1968, the last time anyone made an official count, a total of 219,098 trips were made into and out of the downtown area during the 7 A.M. to 7 P.M. period of an average workday. This means about 1 parking place for every 13 trips; but of course, with all of the activity relocated to the suburbs, most of the vehicles only passed through downtown, finding little reason to stop and park, probably to the chagrin of the downtown merchants who had so anxiously sought the Interstate.

On December 5, 1968, fully ten years after the *Dayton Daily News* had urged the community to pay heed to its "metropolitan heartbeat," a local Center City Task Force was presented with an ambitious downtown rebuilding plan by its consultants, architect-planners Rogers, Taliaferro, Kostritsky, and Lamb of Baltimore, who had been instrumental in the downtown renewal planning in that city, economic and market analysts Arthur D. Little, Inc., and transportation planners Wilbur Smith and Associates. The task force, created in 1967, was a thirty-five-member group of industry leaders and government officials named by the City Commission. It prominently included the bankers —those "who had an economic stake in the outcome" of the planning process, rather than planners, who might work only in the "abstract," as was pointed out later by William Ingler, an executive of National Cash Register. The chairman of the task force was Norm Gebhart, the general manager of General Motors' Delco Moraine Division.

By the turning of planning decisions over to nonplanners, the consultants were faced with numerous debates over their work. The plan finally adopted called for an investment of 215 million dollars over a ten-year period—150 million dollars of it in private funds—compared to only 55 million dollars which had been invested in downtown construction during the preceding ten years. The task force decided that these private and government investors would build four concentrations of downtown activity, located a block or two from the Third and Main Street heart of the downtown, one at each cardinal point of the compass: a retail and high-fashion center northward, where Rike's store was already located; a government and education center west, where the county government was already preparing to build a 4-million-dollar administration building and had opened a new 4-million-dollar jail and courthouse, and where twenty-one acres were already cleared for a 17-million-dollar Sinclair Community College, scheduled to open in September 1972, with an eventual enrollment of some eight thousand students; major office tower construction to the east, and a Mid-Town Mart south.

The Mid-Town Mart project, assigned top priority, is to cover four blocks with office and retail space, a convention center, a hotel, parking decks, a multipurpose transportation center, and a multipurpose civic and sports facility. The multipurposefulness of the civic center has been frustrated by the development of the suburban basketball facility by the University of Dayton and of the suburban hockey arena by the city. The multipurposefulness of the transportation center, now under construction, has been reduced to a 4-million-dollar 1,000-car parking garage capable of handling helicopter landings on its roof and bus turnarounds at street level, with between 30,000 and 40,000 square feet on the first floor assigned to car rental, and possibly—but not likely—a downtown terminal for air passenger and baggage check-ins. (Under the latter scheme, air passengers and baggage would be shuttled to the municipal airport by helicopter.) One city commissioner, Thomas B. Andrews, suggested that the design of the center also allow for a future rail rapid transit terminal, should the city decide on a rail commuter system someday. His idea to hold open an alternative to automobile travel received short shrift and no action. Instead the "multipurpose" transportation center is to be little more than another example of public subsidy for private automobiles.

The city built its 5.6-million-dollar convention center at Mid-Town Mart with bonds backed by general city revenues and expected to open both it and the parking-transportation building in 1972, to coincide with the opening of the downtown commuter campus of Sinclair Community College. The private investments in Mid-Town Mart are lagging behind public investments. The city has selected the single "mega-structure" plan of a local joint venture, Landeau Corporation, to include limited office space, a hotel, luxury apartments, and two floors of commercial space. Rejected was a Cincinnati developer's proposal for separate office and hotel towers to be linked by a low commercial and theater building. Construction on the project, to cost an estimated 18 million dollars, has yet to begin.

The ambitious downtown rebuilding plans did have one significant by-product: they launched a spate of private office and other buildings scattered over the downtown area that had little resemblance to the adopted plan. One example: Holiday Inn built a twelve-story hotel at the northwest corner of downtown that was widely touted by the Chamber of Commerce in 1969, when it was approaching its topping-off ceremonies. In 1971 the 2.5-million-dollar hotel was backed up against a spaghetti bowl of noisome eight-lane freeways and rampways, complete with Gulf Oil service station, and fronted on an alley; the only access to its entrance was through a network of alleys and parking yards.

The most precedent-setting proposal in the Task Force plan is the one least likely to be implemented in the foreseeable future: narrowing the inordinately wide downtown streets, widening sidewalks and permanently closing four blocks of Main Street to traffic for a pedestrian mall or transitway. The city did close Main Street (except for cross-street traffic) for Dayton's 175th birthday party weekend in June 1971 to see how it would work, but then loaded it with special events, such as concerts and a boat show, in a calculated move to attract large numbers of suburbanites to town. The party did succeed in luring in higher levels of shopping, and sequel celebrations were planned, but when all the analyzing of such one-shot experiments are completed, it is unlikely that the city will decide to take that much land away from the automobile. The retail merchants of downtown Dayton have logged a consistent record of opposition to any alterations of street-use patterns that they feel will reduce the amount of automobile traffic passing their store fronts. (They have, however, banded together to institute a downtown "mini-bus" loop and underwrite its costs.)

The adoption of the privately operated automobile as the sole means of transportation in the city by all except public transit's captive riders, those too poor, too young, or too feeble to drive; and the corresponding commitment to subsidize the automobile with wide streets, ample parking, taxes to build massive freeways, and still more taxes to replace the taxes on lands and buildings chomped out of the tax rolls to make way for the highways, virtually assured disperal of population and urban activity, the resultant collapse of the city budget, and the deterioration of its environment. The urban excitement is largely gone from Dayton's downtown now. The city has become a tangle of streets and cars belching noxious pollutants and a visual cacophony of service stations and drive-in stands lined up along major corridors. The urban core has become a welfare recipient, largely abandoned to the poor and the black, to society's outcasts who require large amounts of public help to maintain even a subsistence level of life and are unable to pay the taxes required to supply those services. Dayton's "metropolitan heartbeat" is sounding hollow.

Racism, the urge for a green lawn, and the desire for space and quiet and undisturbing homogeneity may have sent America's urban dwellers to the suburbs, but cars and highways took them there, made the trip easy, and continue to permit those who made the trip the luxury of living off the withering fruits of the city without the annoying expense of nurturing it. No amount of downtown investment, no number of renewal plans, housing construction, improved schools, or improved police protection can redress that unless they include two high-priority commitments: the development of a truly balanced transportation system that moves people instead of vehicles without destroying all in its path, and a logical assignment of urban governmental jurisdiction—regional government capable of embracing the entire urban community. Belatedly, and perhaps with considerably less conviction than is required, Dayton's leadership has begun to address itself to both questions.

The regionalization of planning is well established, in Dayton as elsewhere. Almost predictably, it was the need to coordinate highway planning by various local governments that led to the modern-day regional planning agencies of Dayton. For years local governments argued with the state highway department about which bank of the Miami River should receive Interstate 75. At a meeting with state officials in 1959, the local officials were advised to sit down and put together their various "master" plans. In doing so, they discovered how each jurisdiction's planning map failed to mesh with that of the government next door. Out of the effort a two-county Regional Transportation Committee was formed, and in 1963 and 1965 it published the two volumes of its report verifying what anyone could see for himself —that automobile travel was the dominant mode and was likely to remain so. Apparently untroubled by this, the committee urged that forty more miles of expressway be added to the region's then existing seventy-five miles of committed expressway to meet 1975 needs.

Two years later, in 1967, Montgomery County formed the Montgomery-Greene County Transportation Planning Program group, dubbed the Transportation Coordinating Committee (TCC), a name that stuck. The TCC, assigned the task of comprehensive regional planning for *balanced* transportation, is in fact a highway planning and building agency that reflects all too vividly the auto's domination of the area. It supervises construction of some 60 million dollars' worth of major highways a year in the two counties. Not until 1969 posed a crisis in public transit did TCC enter into public transportation planning as well, despite the fact that the reports of the original Regional Transportation Committee had pointedly observed that improved public transit was vital for the improvement of currently wasteful land-use patterns, for strengthening the urban core, for minimizing sprawl, for preserving highway capacities and for reducing rush-hour highway demands. The study recommended express bus services, park-and-ride facilities, and several local service improvements. What happened to public transit in Dayton in the years following that report was almost the direct reverse of the recommendations.

A second regional planning outgrowth of the Regional Transportation Committee's work was the MVRPC, the Miami Valley Regional Planning Commission, which does general land-use and development planning for the four counties of the Standard Metropolitan Statistical Area plus one other. Two counties, however, intended to pull out at the end of 1971. One of them did.

Regional *government,* as opposed to regional planning, has had quite a different and more troubled history, one that began as early as 1957 with the formation of Community Research, Inc., an agency geared to perform basic research for local community agencies and funded by the industrial leaders of the city. Community Research participated heavily in the fact-gathering for the *Dayton Daily News* "Metropolitan Heartbeat" stories, and one of the agency's first efforts was directed at the need for reorganizing the Montgomery County government into one capable of providing city-like governance county-wide. Its report was published in 1959, and when the power structure formed itself into the Area Progress Council in 1961, it took this on as one of its first priorities. Sweeping changes in county government, in effect consolidation of city and county governments, were proposed, and the community relations director of National Cash Register, William Ingler, took on the chore of leading a campaign to win voter approval of the plan. Though financed with a war chest provided in large part by the manufacturing leadership of the city, Ingler received only lip-service support from locally elected officials. The measure failed in its 1961 referendum.

A second attempt was made, but this time the proposed changes were so modest that they failed to attract much interest—and still received only superficial backing from the Montgomery County Commission. "Bill Ingler was so punchy from the two failures he wasn't there the third time," recalled Dr. Jeptha J. Carrell, the director of Community Research, several years later. The third attempt never reached the ballot box.

The best that local officials were able to achieve was the formation of the Miami Region Council of Governments (COG) in 1968, after two years of study spearheaded by Community Research. However, only one local government outside Montgomery County elected to join and pay its membership fee. Under state law the Council of Governments was given action—instead of merely planning—agency powers, but in its first year devoted its energies to planning instead. It was able to get private foundation funds of $35,000 to help its first-year operations, but by mid-1969, because of its heavy emphasis on planning instead of action, the foundations withdrew their support and COG was threatened with collapse. To save it, a move was begun to merge the several regional planning and action agencies and, possibly, to build for a future regional government. The merger would have involved TCC, MVRPC, COG, and the Health Planning Council of the Greater Miami Valley.

Until talk of a merger began, rivalries and jealousies and personality conflicts had been largely confined to those between local governments. Now they surfaced between two of the agencies themselves, TCC and MVRPC, and their directors. The director of TCC was Martin Kask, a tall, slender, erect blond man from Seattle with a distinctive mid-European accent. "You can't miss spotting Mart, he's all one color," one of the women who work for TCC once remarked. The director of the MVRPC was Dale F. Bertsch, a more aggressive and less formal man—he is prone to prop his feet on his desk, something Kask might never do—with a political background. He describes his general strategy this way: "If I wanted to pry loose a decision, if I had the time, I'd try to get the business leaders to put pressure on. Or I'd get a city official who was running for office, a guy who could benefit. In our last county elections, I wrote policy papers for two county commissioners and their two opponents, often on opposite sides of an issue. This is like establishing communications. You set yourself up in a supportive role." (The two incumbents lost.)

Bertsch's MVRPC offered a merger plan whereby both it and COG would abolish themselves and then reconstitute themselves as a Regional Council of Governments given action agency powers, with TCC and HPC acting as policy advisory committees on their specialties of transportation and health. Enter the personalities: which agency's board chairman would chair the new council, which agency's operating director would direct the new council's staff. The two more rural counties under MVRPC's umbrella, which had chosen not to take part in COG, feared the new council would be getting too much into "action agency" activity instead of planning. They rejected the idea as too close to a regional government threat to their autonomy. Bertsch privately accused Kask of lobbying behind the scenes and getting COG to similarly reject the MVRPC plan, even though he watered the proposal down by eliminating the granting of COG-like action powers to his planning agency. COG came up with its own plan, merger with TCC, whose board then rejected the idea—whereupon Kask privately accused Bertsch of lobbying behind the scenes with his own TCC board members. Also moving somewhere indistinctly in the background of the various merger bickerings was an attorney, Mrs. Lillian Kern, an assistant Montgomery County prosecutor who serves as attorney for TCC, COG, a newly formed Regional Transit Authority, COG's Law Enforcement Committee, the County Commission, and, among others in her private practice, the moving van company owned in part by Charles M. Lewis, a Montgomery County commissioner and president of the COG board. Apparently the only agency involved that she did not represent was Bertsch's MVRPC.

Thickening and stirring the alphabet soup of the merger movement was a nationally publicized, poorly veiled racist controversy erupting over MVRPC's precedent-setting housing plan, made public by MVRPC during the summer of 1970. The plan assigned quotas of low- and moderate-income housing to communities throughout its jurisdiction, thus scattering through the area badly needed housing for those trapped in the inner city. It was the first of its kind in the nation and drew front-page attention from the *New York Times* and high praise from Secretary George Romney of the United States Department of Housing and Urban Development. Contributing to the furor, perhaps, was the fact that the MVRPC also had muscle with which to implement its plan: it had review powers over all federally assisted housing in the region, including both FHA and VA loans. Full implementation of the plan, however, still required active approval and the proper zoning actions by the member local governments.

To secure official adoption of the plan by local governments, MVRPC staged a series of public hearings during 1970 and let the storms of the white suburbs erupt. That the storms did erupt was a measure of the racial intent which, at least in part, undergirded the flight to suburbia in the first place. In the Greene County community of Bellbrook, east of Dayton, the school superintendent sent students home with a warning to parents that property taxes could be raised ten mills if black and other poor children went to their schools. Bertsch recalls that the hearing that ensued was "extremely malicious at best." In Trotwood, northwest of the city, there was an attempt to impeach the mayor when the local council adopted the MVRPC's plan. In Oakwood, south of the city, the city council rejected the plan, but after a scathing editorial by James E. Fain, editor of the *Dayton Daily News,* reminding the town that "the opportunity to live in Oakwood is a burden that should be shared without regard to race, creed, color, religion, national origin or draft status," the town reconsidered. On its first go-round, the town of Moraine also rejected out of hand the idea of rezoning for public housing.

The flow of threatening telephone calls from suburbia came so heavily at one point that four MVRPC staff members switched to unlisted telephone numbers. There were bomb threats and " the whole bit," Bertsch recalls. Still, when the dust settled, every political jurisdiction involved had taken some action in support of the plan— about two-thirds of them adopting resolutions of endorsement, the remainder simply directing their representatives on the MVRPC board to vote in favor of it.

It was little wonder, then, that local governments balked at handing any additional action agency powers over to MVRPC. By the time the regional agency merger movement had subsided, the Health Planning Council had decided to go its own way, TCC had done the same, and COG had divested itself of its staff and handed over to MVRPC its one remaining function, a modest regional law-enforcement program for which the State of Ohio was willing to pay $45,000. The best of the residue was an effort to locate all of the agencies (excluding the Health Planning Council) in offices on one floor of one building. Since COG was bereft of staff, this meant getting the two warring offices, TCC and MVRPC, to at least try to be neighborly by virtue of proximity. Though Bertsch felt that the space had been found by mid-June 1971, TCC board chairman Charles Simms, a builder and city councilman in Oakwood, was remarking to the TCC staff at a going-away party for Mart Kask that no such place had been found and "I kind of like it where we are." By the following year the several agencies were at last sharing office space and secretaries. Kask, meanwhile, was director of Seattle's COG, and his merger rival, Bertsch, who had tried for more than a year to embrace Dayton's COG within his own agency, was complaining that his own staff member heading up COG's one activity, regional law enforcement, seemed to be more answerable to local area police chiefs than to him: "I probably couldn't fire him if I wanted to." The history of regional agencies in Dayton has made it clear that a proliferation of special-purpose offices is hardly an ideal way to build a cohesive regional effort.

The latest of the special-purpose regional ventures in Dayton, and at once its most ambitious, most timid, and perhaps most essential, is in public transit. It is an action agency born during the height of the anti-regionalism housing and merger controversies, a notable achievement in its own right. But Dayton had little choice: by 1969 its public transit was headed for bankruptcy. The regional authority was created for the rescue mission.

City Transit Company carried 59 million fare-paying passengers in 1943, its record year, when bus operations in most American cities were reaping profits from the war economy that had shut down most private automobile production and use. By 1968 this had plummeted to 17 million passengers, a drop to little more than a quarter of its peak-year performance. During 1968 the company recorded its first deficit operation since a transit strike in 1961—losing $26,000 on operations. It came as no surprise: while fare-box revenues were falling, operating costs had climbed by 25 percent since 1959.

City Transit President W. W. Owen and Board Chairman George W. Shaw detailed their grievances in a letter to the Dayton City Commission on June 29, 1969:

> For the past 20 years, and more emphatically for the past 10 or 12 years, government at all levels has shown the utmost anxiety for the

convenience and comfort of the auto driver and his expeditious movement on the streets, with little or no regard for the bus rider. . . . Whenever there was a conflict between the interests of the auto driver and [the] interests of the bus rider, the issue was resolved in favor of the automobile.

The bus company executives detailed examples, from the location of bus stops at mid-blocks to rerouting requirements to make way for expressways, from the one-way-street program which "deprives buses of 50 percent of their potential use since there is only one right curb lane on a one-way street" to urban renewal, which permits the use of cleared land for excessively low-cost parking and dislocates transit's riding public.

> This was not, of course, done on purpose, but the penalties to the bus riders were by-products of the moves to transport people in private automobiles. Each move compounded the problem, traffic-wise, air pollution-wise, and transit-wise. About five years ago this attitude began to change, but the changing attitude has heretofore not been sufficiently implemented.

City Transit Company was not without fault. To meet rising costs it had cut service and raised fares. It used trackless trolley coaches it purchased from other cities as they abandoned their trolleys; by cannibalizing the old coaches, City Transit was able to keep them rattling on the streets long past their recommended life span of twelve years. Of its 133 trolleys operating in 1971, one was a 1951 model and the remainder were 1947, 1948, and 1949 models. It also was running forty-six diesel buses on the streets, twenty-five of them 1965 and 1968 models, two of them 1957 models, and the remainder dating between 1947 and 1955. (City Transit did dip into its 3.8-million-dollar depreciation fund in 1971 to purchase one new trolley from a Canadian builder and was rotating the $35,000 machine through its route system in search of rider reaction.)

Tied to overhead trolley wires as they are, Dayton transit system's coaches lose the one major advantage that buses have over other existing public transit—route flexibility. Thus the trolleys still follow the same age-old routes and turn around at the same no-longer-outlying points as they have always done, despite drastically shifted housing, employment, and shopping patterns. One trolley runs down a quiet and thinly populated residential street where the sidewalks remain as empty as the trolley itself, while three blocks away a parallel street bustles with commerce and pedestrian traffic—and no trolleys. It is not an isolated case.

Nor did City Transit improve its service or market its product as actively as it might have done. When a suburban bus line discontinued its service to the outlying Wright State University campus, City Transit agreed to provide sixteen trips daily to the campus under a subsidy agreement, but after a brief attempt the service was discontinued. The company had no person specifically assigned to promotional and marketing activities and no expert promotional counsel. As in Flint, on several occasions company officials instructed drivers to put their uniform caps over the fare box and allow all riders to board free, but never deployed any advance or follow-up publicity, thus rendering the free-sample approach of little value in building patronage.

At the start of 1969, City Transit raised fares to 30 cents (25-cent tokens) and by the end of the first three months found another 9 percent of its ridership shaved away; the fare increase helped it hold operating losses to $4,192 for the calendar year. In 1970, however, it logged an operating loss of $284,140, despite a mid-year fare increase to 35 cents that transit officials said cut ridership by a phenomenal 30 percent—to less than 14 million riders, under 23 percent of its 1943 ridership. Despite losses netting a reported deficit of $29,762 for the five years ending in 1970, the company distributed more than a million dollars in dividends to its stockholders during the same period, including $383,732 in 1968 and $382,536 in 1969, taken, the company officials said, "out of retained earnings."

On January 1, 1971, City Transit's franchise agreements with the cities of Dayton, Oakwood, and Kettering expired. The approach of this expiration deadline caused the bi-county Transportation Coordinating Committee to institute a study of alternative countermeasures in 1969. Upon TCC's recommendation, and under new enabling state legislation, the cities of Dayton, Oakwood, and Kettering created the Miami Valley Regional Transit Authority in 1970 and assigned the TCC staff as its office force, but they declined to give it any authority beyond negotiation of a new franchise with City Transit Company.

No new franchise was negotiated. Instead, beginning January 1, 1971, City Transit continued operation without a franchise, drastically reduced service by eliminating late-night, Sunday, and holiday runs, and raised fares to 40 cents (less than four months after the preceding fare increase). Drivers soon afterward continued to work without a union contract. In May the company declared its intention of dropping three suburban routes in Kettering and Oakwood and agreed to keep the runs operating only when the Kettering run's bus riders successfully petitioned their city council and the Regional Transit Authority to keep the buses running—with a subsidy if that was what it would take. "Very possibly a lot of people could lose their jobs because of this. . . . Some people would be totally sunk," according to Mrs. Mary Marshall, organizer of the petition drive.

The two cities of Oakwood and Kettering agreed to guarantee City Transit an $11 hourly fare box take on the three routes, and at the start of June 1971 the Regional Transit Authority agreed to help by contributing up to $2,500 for the subsidy for forty-five days —to end in mid-July, when subsidizers backed out. The Regional Transit Authority action came after several months of continued bickering among its member cities. As originally constituted, the authority's board of trustees included six members from Dayton and only two from Kettering and one from Oakwood. Kettering wanted Dayton's strength pared to three so that it would not have a controlling majority. By the spring of 1971 Dayton agreed to the membership change, provided it could get additional representation up to six as other jurisdictions decided to join, and the way was cleared for increasing the authority's powers, this time giving it permission to subsidize or purchase City Transit—if it could raise the funds. The difficulty was that the authority had a miniscule operating budget in comparison with the 60 million dollars a year being spent for highway building in the two-county area: about $16,000 from a five-cents-per-capita levy against the three city governments—with Dayton paying $12,000 of it.

Only two avenues were open for maintaining any public transit: a subsidy for City Transit and outright acquisition by the Regional Transit Authority. TCC urged that the transit authority opt for public ownership because it felt that the rapidly deteriorating image of the City Transit Company would not hold up long enough to secure a favorable vote for a subsidy. Once the Regional Transit Authority decided to seek funds to buy the company, again it had two legal options: general fund appropriations from its three member governments, or a referendum for a special tax increase, which could generate an annual 1.3 million dollars in revenue for the authority.

While Kettering and Oakwood might have been able to squeeze enough from their general funds to meet their obligations to the transit authority without a referendum, Dayton was in no such position. In 1971 the city was threatened with bankruptcy. In 1969 it had sought a graduated increase in its local income tax from 1 percent to 1.5 percent but ran headlong into a tax rebellion that stopped it in a two-to-one ballot rejection. A few months later the city did secure voter permission to continue the income tax at its 1 percent level but warned that this could finance city operations only for another two years. It did not even reach that far. The nationwide United Auto Workers' strike against General Motors that ran from September to

December in 1970 severely cut into the city's income-tax collections and, in the words of Dayton Finance Director Winton Parent, "cut us down to our knees." The income tax represented about half of the city's budget. An austerity program was launched; services were cut and departments were ordered not to fill vacancies. Still, with the economic recession severely reducing job opportunities outside of government, the expected attrition within government failed to take place. By the end of 1971 the city had been forced to lop up to 500 employees from its work force of 2,300. It had no room in its budget for any increase in payments to the Regional Transit Authority.

The second option, a special ten-year, 1-mill property tax referendum, offered quite a different problem: Dayton and Oakwood were willing to try despite the general taxpayer rebellion and the need to get at least 55 percent voter approval, but Kettering declined, in an obstinate refusal of regional cooperation. Kettering city officials insisted on seeking an income tax instead—in a referendum almost sure to fail. Kettering's action seemed to conceal a subtle racism, one inextricably intertwined with the regional plan for dispersed public housing; without public transit service the suburban city would probably be rejected by the United States Department of Housing and Urban Development as unsuitable for publicly assisted low-income housing.

To effect the split in financing methods, Kettering resigned from the transit authority, and the "regional" agency was reconstituted as a two-city venture. Kettering promised that if its income tax referendum succeeded, it would rejoin the agency. Dayton, meanwhile, had its own dilemma. As elsewhere, taxpayers were in no mood for tax increases. Not only had every Dayton ward rejected the income tax increase in 1969, the city voters also had turned down a levy for building the new downtown convention center at Mid-Town Mart and, beginning in late 1969, rejected four times running any increase in school taxes—not for construction of new schools but simply for continuing public school operations. In December 1969 the Dayton Board of Education asked for a 7.5-mill property tax increase; 60 percent of the voters rejected it. The Board of Education launched a heavy voter registration drive and in May 1970 again went to the polls, this time for a 10.5-mill levy; 54 percent of the voters said no. In September 1970, asked again for a 10.5-mill levy, 54 percent of the voters again said no. Two months later the school board trimmed its request back to 8.5 mills and still faced rejection, this time by 62 percent of those voting.

Still, Dayton and Oakwood were willing to try for the special transit tax. They cited a January 1971 referendum in upstate Toledo where voters approved by a three-to-one margin a ten-year, 1-mill tax for public acquisition of its transit company, but it was hardly likely that Dayton's business leadership would mount a vigorous public education campaign comparable to that which had been so successful in Toledo. The leaders of Dayton's manufacturing back-bone were in a pessimistic mood generally. At the McCall Corporation, strikes had temporarily driven away seventy-two of the major national magazines it had been printing in Dayton, including the *Reader's Digest, Newsweek,* and *U.S. News & World Report.* Though they did return, it was generally conceded that employee problems at the Dayton plant were so recurrent they made the future too uncertain to keep such major customers happy for very much longer; many feared that corporate decision-makers outside Dayton would close the facility should it be threatened with the loss of too many customers.

At Frigidaire, layoffs had reduced the work force from 15,000 to about 11,500 after the General Motors strike forced wages so high that the GM division's household appliances were being priced out of the market. City leaders feared that GM would phase out its refrigerator plant in Moraine and maintain only its smaller auto air-conditioning facility, which employs about five thousand just northeast of the central business district. In a delayed reaction the Chamber of Commerce formed a committee in mid-1971 to "Save Frigidaire for the Community." (The trouble eventually was resolved by renegotiation between management and labor.)

National Cash Register was down to 16,000 employees in 1971, a 25 percent drop from 1969 employment, in a corporate attempt to switch to electronic products—which required fewer parts, and thus fewer workers.

Wright-Patterson Air Force Base, the area's largest single employer, had a military and civilian work force of 28,000 in 1969, before recession swept the country. By mid-1971 it was down to about 26,000.

Layoffs, job cuts and attrition in the two-year period ended March 31, 1971, had reduced the four-county area's manufacturing work force by 17,700, and unemployment in the area had climbed to 5.4 percent from its March 1970 level of 3 percent. By June 1971 it was up to 7.2 percent. It was little wonder, then, that the leadership of Dayton's industry was not particularly excited about mounting an aggressive tax-increase campaign for transportation's stepchild transit company.

City Transit agreed to keep its buses running without a franchise until the October referendum, and the bus drivers' union agreed to stay on the job until then without a labor contract, but it was unlikely they would continue much beyond that, except with a severely cutback system of bus routes.

In July 1971 public subsidy for City Transit's three routes in Oakwood and Kettering ended, the company decided not to pay its $4-per-seat tax to the state Public Utilities Commission and thereby dropped its service on two routes in an unincorporated area just west of the Dayton city limits, and City Transit Chairman Shaw described continuance of bus service for Dayton as a "nip and tuck" question. Operating without a franchise, he was free to continue cutting service to a bare minimum and raising fares at will. He had noticed little if any decline in ridership since the service cuts and fare increase of January 1971, but that was probably due to the fact that his ridership had "bottomed out." It now consisted only of its captive ridership of the non-mobile dwellers of the inner city; regardless of the fares and service levels, his riders had no other option except to stay home, and most of their trolley rides were probably "necessity" trips.

Public transit should not be reduced to a service for the mobile society's outcasts alone. As author Helen Leavitt pointed out at a transportation conference in Washington, D.C., in June 1971, when a public service is not used by those who can most afford to maintain it, it deteriorates. This has happened to the cities' public schools, public hospitals, and public transit. It had most assuredly happened to Dayton's bus and trolley system when Dayton and Oakwood taxpayers were asked to bail it out of bankruptcy.

Whether it was service cutbacks, the realization that people needed more than automobiles for movement around cities, or the fact that, as one Dayton city commissioner put it, "people are fed up with negativism," the voters of Dayton and Oakwood did what even the most optimistic were afraid to expect them to do: by more than a three-to-one margin (26,556 to 7,784) they copied Toledo and approved the 1-mill property tax increase—the first new tax approved in Dayton in almost four years—to give the regional transit agency 1.1 million dollars a year for ten years. The authority was at last in position to try to save public transportation—hopefully, eventually, for more than an impoverished, captive few. With bus service cut to a "bare bones" system, including elimination of all weekend and after-8 P.M. runs, the bus company and transit agency entered into what promised to be a year or more of disagreement over terms for switching to publicly owned transit. Meanwhile, to keep fares from climbing above 40 cents, the transit authority agreed to kick in a $10,000-a-month subsidy, funded from the new transit tax.

The TCC and the Regional Transit Authority have as their top priority mission the mere salvaging of City Transit for Dayton's poor and non-mobile, but they also have one noteworthy project aimed at attracting the middle classes back to transit, an urban corridor demonstration program entirely funded by the United States Department of Transportation. They plan to run express buses along a buses-only paved roadbed to be built alongside the Penn Central railroad tracks from downtown Dayton to Kettering, and eventually beyond. The agencies received $158,000 in federal aid to plan the project and $405,000 for purchase of the right-of-way from the railroad. They anticipate a cost of 2.5 million dollars to build the roadway, a project that could involve some eighteen months following purchase of the land. At times TCC staff members even discuss the possibility of a future downtown shuttle service, probably by "minibus," for distributing suburbanite commuters who choose to ride the "busway."

A three-man citizens' committee has gone even further. It proposes that, instead of a busway, a lightweight, electrically powered rapid transit line be built along the Penn Central right-of-way. The rail system would run at surface level between Centerville on Dayton's urban fringe and the Dayton downtown "transportation center" in the Mid-Town Mart project, then dive underground as a short subway route underneath Main Street, which, under the committee's plan, would be turned into a traffic-free pedestrian mall covered by a transparent skylight. The plan takes into account the fact that the city may eventually want to build an entire radial system of rail rapid transit routes.

It is probably the boldest plan yet advanced to bring harmony back to the urban region of Dayton and the transportation that ties it together; yet, with the low level of public transit service now available in that area, it is unlikely that one express bus route or one rapid transit line will entice enough Kettering or Centerville commuters out of their cars to make the project a success in the public mind of Dayton. The rail transit scheme has the better chance by virtue of its glamor and its sharp departure from older, uninspiring modes of urban transit, but Dayton taxpayers are likely to continue insisting that, rail rapid transit or not, the fare box pay for public transit's operating expenses—unlike public police and fire departments, public garbage collection, public schools, and public parks. What is more probable is that Dayton will consider the demonstration project proof positive that the city was right to choose the private automobile as its dominant mode of movement, since that, obviously, is what the people "want." Such thinking fails to recognize that for more than two decades the American public has been given only one choice, has had a barrage of automobile and highway propaganda thrown at it, and has been forced by permissive, scattered land-use policies to rely on the only vehicles that could take it where it wants, when it wants. With this sort of attitude training behind them, Kettering residents are hardly likely to swarm to a new one-route bus or rail service overnight.

If Dayton continues its policy of population and urban activity dispersal, and concomitantly, if it continues its almost total reliance on the automobile for mobility, it is inviting urban chaos. Its downtown rebuilding schemes notwithstanding, it may find in its future a self-portrait much like that of Los Angeles: freeways, wasted lands, no readily identifiable downtown, and a pollution-laden atmosphere.

Population projections by the Miami Valley Regional Planning Commission show that by 1980 the four-county area will probably pass the 1-million mark, with the Dayton city population continuing its descent, down to only 21 percent of the Standard Metropolitan Statistical Area's 1980 population. By 1995, the MVRPC estimates, the four counties will have a population approaching 1.5 million, with slightly over 15 percent of that population living within Dayton itself. Without a healthy public transit alternative to the automobile, the City of Dayton can expect a population boom in cars that demand ever-increasing highway space, which in turn will generate further suburban sprawl, further auto usage, further highway construction.

Within this dismal fabric, however, there exist a few threads that warrant qualified optimism, if they are grasped, strengthened and utilized aggressively. The current levels of investment in new downtown construction may help keep the core of the metropolitan area economically alive, at least for daytime use in office space for services for Dayton's manufacturers. Still, attempts thus far by civic leaders to lure the area's major home-grown manufacturers themselves into building downtown headquarters has failed to produce any significant change in manufacturing's inexorable exodus to the suburbs, the result in large part of the absentee corporate structure that has grown up in American industry in the postwar economy.

A second and perhaps more significant shift is in the public's response to highways. Since 1969, residents in southeast Dayton have fought vigorously against a proposed 7-million-dollar connector-freeway to run south from the city's east-side expressway, U.S. Route 35. They insisted, not that the highway be rerouted, but that it be eliminated altogether as destructive of their neighborhoods—and they succeeded. Opposition has also effectively stopped further planning for a freeway which was to be routed through the city's northwest residential areas, and extension of the east-west freeway westward from downtown through Dayton's Model Cities area may also be a decade away, if it is ever built; Model Cities representatives objected to the highway's land-gobbling and neighborhood-blighting effects and won agreement that the highway be replanned as a "joint development," including provision for community facilities or housing to be built above the freeway. Planning was to be carried on by the TCC staff and Model Cities representatives, but by mid-1971 the state highway department was interested in getting into the project on an active basis. State highway departments have had notoriously poor relations with inner-city dwellers, and Ohio's has been no exception; it is likely to run into heavier opposition and to be forced to admit someday that the highway may never be built through Dayton's Model Cities neighborhoods.

North of the city, in Butler Township, the TCC wants to build an access freeway to its municipal airport in Vandalia, but township residents have now tangled the project in court. Ironically, Mart Kask's last official act before leaving his post as TCC director in June 1971 was a six-hour stint on the witness stand in the Federal District Court defending that highway project.

Such anti-highway sentiment is born of resentment against freeways that have callously divided and destroyed neighborhoods, barricaded communities behind high embankments, and brought blight to their flanks. Should the resentment continue to mount, the Dayton area may be on its way to providing decent, safe, efficient, and comfortable alternatives to the scatterized life style of its present automobile society.

The effects of the highway-building realities of the past and present—the widespread dispersal of the city to regional dimensions —must also be dealt with. It makes little public policy sense to plan regionally and implement locally through a hodgepodge of bickering governments. As a *Dayton Daily News* editorial pointed out during the 1969 Salem Mall annexation dispute, "Sink or swim, we are all in the same choppy urban waters and washed by the same problems." Dayton's transportation needs do not stop at the city limits, though Dayton's government must. The same could be said for its housing needs, for its educational needs, for its police, sewage, and recreation needs. Dayton no longer has city limits; only its government does. This is why a Regional Transit Authority had to be created to attempt solutions to the public transit crisis, and why the MVRPC wisely drew up its public housing plan as a plan for the entire region, not only the inner city.

It is little wonder that at each crisis in city financing or annexation the specter of regional government has raised its head, though only to be driven underground again. Regional government in Dayton probably offers the only sound foundation from which to respond to the urban region's needs—for economy in government, for efficiency, for uniformity in taxation, and for the equitable distribution both of urban government's services and of the burdens of paying for those services by the entire population, which is, in fact, being sustained by the metropolitan heartbeat.

In both the MVRPC housing plan and the Regional Transit Authority's activities the seeds are sown for a future regional government in Dayton. They must be fostered, not feared. They must be allowed to grow. Whether they will be is very much in question. Not very long before his office was abolished, the director of the Miami Valley Council of Governments, Charles B. Hetrick, wrote in a newsletter to his members: "Governments are to serve their citizens, not their own corporate needs, but that's not the case here. There is much too much 'My town against your town' instead of 'How can we help our people?' "

Less than two years later, in a letter to the editor of the *Dayton Daily News,* private citizen Hetrick declared the effort to merge COG and other regional agencies "a total failure" and added: "It is clear that the conflicting special interests of local governments and regional agencies have been placed far ahead of overall public control and popular judgment."

The public, civic, and industrial leadership of Dayton has its task carved out for it: it must pull these pieces together and vigorously begin a public education drive aimed at creating a regional government which can cope with Dayton's problems. It must see to it that such a regional organism is equipped to lead, not merely to make of its actions simple reflex responses to the dispersal patterns the automobile has spread across the urban landscape, but to halt that trend and to protect the urban environment by a wiser blend of land use and transportation, both directed at service to people rather than to their machines.

3
Indianapolis: A City Whose Time Is Coming

Indianapolis is one of the seven cities of the United States that do have regional government. Introduced at the opening of the 1970's, its Unified Government (popularly contracted to "Uni-Gov") is an innovative attempt to make sense out of the often bickering, almost always overlapping local governments and agencies that preceded it. Yet, if anything, Indianapolis is even more wedded to service for its automobile population than is Dayton, Ohio. It is a marriage that will, in the long run, frustrate the city's attempt at a more logical framework for local government as the city is forever forced to follow outward the automobile's propensity for dispersal. Not surprisingly, it was transportation, and specifically the automobile and its insatiable appetite for space and funds, that prompted Indianapolis to institute Unified Government.

Transportation has always been a major force in the shaping of Indianapolis. As the federally mandated regional transportation study for Indianapolis points out in the introduction of its report, "Transportation figured strongly in the Indiana legislature's decision in 1820 to move the state capital from Corydon to what is now Indianapolis. . . . The subsequent failure to develop the White River into a navigable waterway severely handicapped the early growth and development of Indianapolis. It was not until 1847, when the western extension of the railroad reached Indianapolis, that transportation began to exert its strong and ultimate influence upon the city's growth. By 1885, seven separate railway systems radiated outward from Indianapolis, and it began to develop as a major regional market center."

Ironically, it is the same number—seven—of expressways that the city hopes eventually to build to replace the railroads and produce what the regional study, published in 1968, said will be "a degree of access to the national highway network that is virtually unsurpassed by any other city." Yet, the report admits, probably less than 10 percent of the traffic that will use the freeways in the city will be the national highway network's long-distance through travel, thus effectively putting aside contentions that the city freeways in any way resemble the "interstate" nature of the system first envisioned by Congress in adopting the national freeway package in 1956.

As in Dayton and elsewhere, the adoption of automobiles and expressways as a single-mode urban transport system has been as much encouragement to the post–World War II population dispersal as a reflection of any well-thought-out attempt to serve that dispersal. In Indianapolis there was little to discourage the urban population from sprawling across the landscape. Looking down on the center of the city from a helicopter, one is immediately impressed by two facts: how expansive and flat is the belly of the nation, reaching farther than the eye can see in every direction, and how much of this heartland city's downtown is paved over for the single task of storing the cars that daily come across those flatlands to reach it.

At the city's very center stands the Soldiers' and Sailors' Monument, a 285-foot spire decked out with spread eagles and fighting men on its sides, fountains and pools and walkways at its base, and a museum in its bowels. The monument and its circle are the hub of the city's densest growth, the "Mile Square" that, despite an impressive array of high-rise structures, still devotes a full two-thirds of its land to streets, alleys, and parking lots where cars can waste away the day for as little as 75 cents; the immediate periphery of the area is paved over with even more and larger parking yards, driving considerably higher the percentage of valuable in-town land allowed to lie barren for the automobile. It is little wonder that Indianapolitans bestow upon themselves the luxury of in-town automobile usage, a luxury relatively easy to afford now, but one likely to run up a considerably higher bill in direct and indirect cost in the not too distant future.

Indianapolis is a regional center city, serving as a hub for the ring of larger, home-office cities of the industrial Midwest—Chicago, Detroit, Cincinnati, St. Louis—and its downtown is a reflection of the financial and branch office functions it serves: quiet, restrained, respectful, businesslike, without bustle. Its dominant fashion is the white collar. It houses four major banks with combined deposits of some 2.5 billion dollars, the headquarters for the city's major utilities, a wide range of branch offices for national corporations, the gold-domed state capitol and expanse of state office buildings, national and state headquarters for the American Legion, a memorial to the American flag (from the roof of any Indianapolis skyscraper it appears that the city displays more United States flags from its office building rooftops than any other city, with the possible exception of the federal office district of Washington, D.C.), and 20 of the city's 71 home-based insurance companies. In more ways than one the insurance industry has long been a backbone of Indianapolis: as an economic and wage stabilizer, as a member in good standing of the civic power structure, and as a geographic spinal column. Fully 42 of the 51 home-based insurance companies not anchored downtown are housed in a two-mile strip on either side of North Meridian Street, the city's arrow-straight thoroughfare that divides its northeast quadrant from its northwest.

Combined with high levels of white-collar employment in keeping Indianapolis wage levels high is the city's manufacturing, which employs one-third of the metropolitan region's nonagricultural work force, but the diversified nature of both manufacturing and total employment gives Indianapolis an economic stability that would make a city like Flint, or even Dayton, envious. In late 1968, before the national recession, unemployment in Indianapolis was at a stable 2.2 percent, and between 1950 and 1970 it held to an average of 4 percent. Even with the national recession of the early 1970's, most of the city did not feel the pinch felt in Flint and Dayton, though in the summer of 1970 unemployment did reach above 5 percent.

On such long-term affluence the suburbs could expand rapidly, and did. Until the start of World War II there were approximately 5,500 persons in Indianapolis for every square mile of urbanized land, but with the end of the war and the arrival of large-scale FHA and VA housing, the urban density dropped to below 5,000 per square mile by 1960 and to an estimated 4,500 per square mile in 1970, owing almost exclusively, admits the Indianapolis regional transportation report, to "the *auto* and the greater land requirements of single-story industrial and commercial buildings"—in other words, the sprawling suburban plants and shopping centers that serve the auto-mobile society.

While the number of persons per square mile was dropping, the urban region's population was climbing, most remarkably during the 1960's, and reaching farther and farther away to consume the land. During the last decade the eight-county Standard Metropolitan Statistical Area's population grew 18 percent and topped the million mark, while Center Township, which includes most of the land inside the pre-Uni-Gov city limits, declined by almost 18 percent, from a population of 333,351 to 273,598. Meanwhile, the whole of Marion County, seat of Indianapolis, was growing by 14 percent, and five of the seven outlying counties of the region were registering population increases of more than 30 percent, one of them marking a phenomenal 40 percent jump in the ten years.

Not all of the new suburbanites moved into one-family homes. During the 1960's, as the national population grew younger, apartment building for singles and young marrieds boomed beyond the city's fringes. In Indianapolis, as in other cities, it happened where the concrete noose of the I-465 beltway was being built. Apartment conglomerates now stand like hedgerows along Post Road just outside the superbeltway on the east side of the city, disgorging thousands of automobiles each morning and swallowing them back each evening. It is a scene duplicated daily throughout the beltway system. With the opening of the 1970's, however, the building boom switched back to its earlier bent—suburban single-family homes with going prices now ranging upward from a low of about $20,000.

Not everyone could take advantage of the prosperity and corresponding mobility. As in other cities, Indianapolis's population became increasingly black—and poor—while suburban areas remained white and affluent. In the 1960 census, blacks accounted for 16 percent of the Marion County population—but for 40 percent of its dilapidated housing, 29 percent of its population dependent on public transportation for work trips, 22 percent of its dwellings with more than one person per room, and 29 percent of its unemployed population. By the 1970 census, if its racial count can be believed, blacks represented almost 17 percent of Marion County's population, while in the less crowded surrounding counties only 28 of 31,000 residents in Boone County were black; only 272 of 54,000 in Hamilton County; only 42 of 35,000 in Hancock County; only 348 of 54,000 in Hendricks County, and only 7 of 44,000 in Morgan County.

Two-thirds of the black population of Marion County in 1970

was confined to only 27 of the city's 180 census tracts, almost entirely segregated into the northern third of Center Township within the old city limits. Each of those 27 tracts numbered more than 75 percent of its population black, many of them well above 90 percent black. When matched against a map of this sort of racial distribution, most of the acreage in the city used for industrial jobs are found across town from the concentrated black residential areas. Partly as a result of poor transportation to these work sites, unemployment has soared in the inner city. In the seven antipoverty target areas mapped in Indianapolis, the unemployment during June 1970 was at 9.5 percent, compared to the 3.5 percent "recession" unemployment rate throughout the region.

Historically the industrial plants of Indianapolis have been located along the radial railroad corridors that slice the city into wedges. While a few of these are found in or alongside the black residential neighborhoods, they do not represent the largest concentration of employment, especially not the newest, highest-skilled, and highest-paying industrial jobs. Those which do are also in white suburbia: Detroit Diesel–Allison Division of General Motors, the area's largest single employer, with a work force of some 13,500, is in Speedway, about seven miles west of downtown. The native-born pharmaceuticals firm, Eli Lilly and Company, which plays historic economic and leadership roles in Indianapolis similar to those of National Cash Register in Dayton, has its major plant, employing 7,400, relatively close in—about a mile south of downtown—but still two bus rides from where most blacks live. Radio Corporation of America, with 7,000 employees, is at three sites—two miles east of downtown, seven miles east of downtown, and nine miles west of downtown. Western Electric, with 6,500 employees, and Chrysler Corporation's electrical plant, with 2,800, are with one of RCA's plants seven miles east of downtown. Ford Motor Company, with 4,200, and International Harvester, with 3,000, are some seven miles southeast of downtown. Naval Avionics, employing almost 3,000, is six miles east of downtown. The United States Army's Finance Center at Fort Harrison, employing 5,000, is some twelve miles northeast of downtown. Link-Belt division of Food Machinery Chemical Corporation, with 4,300 employees, is a neighbor of RCA's west-side plant about nine miles from downtown.

Suburbanization of shopping was, of course, keeping pace with suburbanization of good jobs and good housing. By the end of the 1960's the Indianapolis downtown area accounted for only 24 percent of all retail service floor space in Marion County, while new suburban shopping centers and malls accounted for 28 percent and the remain-

ing 48 percent was located in ribbon strips alongside the city's major
streets, a product of the stop-and-shop automobile way of life that
occupied Indianapolis and most other cities before the advent of
expressways, exit-ramp clusters, and shopping centers. One of Indianapolis's regional shopping centers, Lafayette Square northwest of the
city, now occupies more than a million square feet of floor space.
The regional transportation study group of the 1960's calculated that
suburban shopping center activity consumed about 250 acres of land
by mid-decade and that this would triple to 750 acres by 1985.

In the process the downtown is losing sizable chunks of the region's
purchasing dollar. In 1960 it was estimated that the Indianapolis central business district did 260 million dollars' worth of business in retail
sales; by 1967 the United States Department of Commerce said that
this had fallen to 214 million dollars and represented only about one-
fifth of the region's more than 1 billion dollars in retail activity; by
1970 the Indiana National Bank estimated that the downtown's retail
business had slipped another 12 percent in only three years—down to
$188 million—but the bank had no 1970 estimate of region-wide sales
on which to base relative comparisons.

The building of expressways not only scattered the city's economy
and tax base far beyond the city limits; it also put a heavy and direct
tax burden on local governments. With so many freeways destined
to arrive in the city, it became evident early in the 1960's that the
city's surface streets would have to be widened and their routing jug-
gled just to handle the traffic loads the expressways would pour upon
them. It was becoming obvious that expressways were doing more
than carry traffic: they were also generating traffic, by encouraging
development at their exit ramps and by inducing frustrated and unconsulted commuters to switch to automobile travel. Indianapolis officials have estimated that the task of preparing their local streets to
receive these new expressway-bred traffic loads will cost the city and
county governments at least 35 million dollars—more than 3 million
dollars above what the State of Indiana will be paying on its share of
all Interstate construction inside Marion County. Stated another way,
local governments will have to pay about 10 percent *more* for the
supposedly gratis (to local governments) Interstates than the state
will spend on its 10 percent share of the total program. No one questioned the wisdom of entering into such a massive local road-building
commitment. The only question considered was the method of raising
the money, and that became one of the prime issues that led to the
"unification" of local government in Indianapolis—but not without
some years of road-money headaches first.

The first attempt to raise the road-building funds was through creation of a county-wide Metropolitan Thoroughfare Authority in 1963. It was a technique the city had used often to circumvent a state law that forbids municipal corporations from issuing bonds in excess of 2 percent of the assessed valuation of all properties on its tax rolls. By creating special-purpose corporations, each could be given its own 2 percent bonding capability. Thus, to try to keep up with the service needs of their spreading population, the city and county had given birth to county-wide authorities for health care and hospitals, the airport, flood control, and the public library system, each with its own 2 percent bonding allowance. In addition, a City Redevelopment Commission was created and given 1 percent bonding, a Parks Authority was created and given .75 percent bonding, and a Sanitation District was created and given an exception-making 10 percent bonding. With the creation of the Metropolitan Thoroughfare Authority— and its own 2 percent bonding allowance—the state also authorized a $10 wheel tax on all vehicles, which would have given the new authority an estimated 4 million dollars annually to begin its road improvements program. A successful court challenge by irate citizens produced a ruling that the new tax applied only to commercial trucks—and cut the 4 million dollars down to half a million annually.

Another attempt was made in 1967, this time broadening the thoroughfare authority to a highway-focused Mass Transportation Authority with jurisdiction over traffic control—already being governed by the county and the city's traffic engineer—and assigning to the authority two more tax sources: about 1.5 million dollars annually in cigarette taxes diverted from the city government and 7.5 million dollars in local rebates of 92 percent of state-collected inheritance taxes. Yet again the lion's share of the new funds became tangled in legal trouble. The governor attempted a pocket veto of the inheritance-tax rebate but was overruled in court, whereupon the legislature in 1968 tried to repeal it retroactively for the governor. It was now the city's turn to go to court; and it was not until 1970 that the authority collected its full share of the inheritance-tax rebate for the period between enactment and repeal. Meanwhile the authority had to limp along on a total annual budget of 2.45 million dollars, far short of meeting the needs of its four-year program to spend 15 million dollars a year on paving, extending, widening, or otherwise altering its system of roads (most of it to satisfy expressway-generated traffic) and 1.5 million dollars a year simply for administrative and traffic-control costs.

A key group in drafting the thoroughfare and transportation authority legislation had been young Republicans who spent the mid-1960's in a successful move to unseat the old guard of their party and then set about challenging the long-entrenched Democratic control of City Hall. In 1967, backed by the city's power structure of insurance, banking, and some industrial interests, and led by mayoralty candidate Richard Lugar, a candidate carved in the handsome, wealthy, and young image of John Lindsay of New York, the Republicans took over the city administration, despite the overwhelmingly Democratic voter registration within the city limits. It was then time to unveil the Uni-Gov legislation which the Republicans had been preparing privately in concert with their transportation measures. (The Democrats had made a similar attempt in 1965 and had failed when the news media labeled them "power-hungry.")

Uni-Gov was patterned after the city-county consolidation that had been implemented successfully in Jacksonville, Florida. It merged the two governments and their revenue sources, but not without compromises. The county government remained as a token entity, principally to collect its property taxes and to operate the sheriff's department and courts. Three incorporated towns, including tax-rich Speedway west of the city with its "Indy 500" raceway and its massive plant for GM's Detroit Diesel–Allison Division, were allowed to exclude themselves from the Unified Government. Also compromised away was a home-rule provision which would have freed Indianapolis from the severe state-imposed prohibition against taxation by cities. Indianapolis, as a city, is still forbidden to tax anything—from income to sales—and can, under Unified Government, make use of property taxes only because the county can collect them.

Uni-Gov's mayor is elected county-wide, including those three areas excluded from its government, and names his own cabinet of departmental directors. The combined City-County Council consists of twenty-nine seats, twenty-five filled by district election, four by county-wide election.

Once Unified Government came into being, the city almost immediately began to realize significant economies. Offices were consolidated and communications channels were opened. The city's bond rating, which had slipped during the 1960's owing to the proliferation of separate, special-purpose bonding authorities and a flooding of the market with the maximum allowance of bonds, climbed to an AAA. Despite major new bond issues for sanitation facilities, roads, a stadium, parks, and a jail, Uni-Gov is still considerably below its new maximum allowed indebtedness.

Uni-Gov was also able to bring back into the fold of urban government major industries that had been beyond its reach, not only for bond-allowance setting but for a special county-collected tax as well. Under provisions of the Unified Government legislation the more rural areas of the county were permitted to remain "outside" the Uni-Gov system for purposes of fire and police protection; their fire protection would continue to be provided by part-time and volunteer fire departments, their police protection by the county sheriff's office. For this service they paid a fire and police property tax at a rate of 21 cents for every $100 of assessed valuation. Those areas that met certain criteria of population density and land use and had such essentials as local fire hydrants could get city-style police and fire protection by merely petitioning the City-County Council and agreeing to pay the higher Uni-Gov police and fire tax: $2 for every $100 of assessed valuation. Through such petitions Uni-Gov "annexed" to full urban citizenship during its first year and a half such valuable outlying properties as the Western Electric plant, the Chrysler plant, the Ford plant, other industrial sites, and a recently built regional shopping center and about 250 of its residential neighbors. In this way Uni-Gov has proved unusually capable of following its tax base out to the suburbs (but not beyond the Marion County borders, where future city dispersal is sure to continue going.)

The new government has also been able to shave pennies from its overall property tax rate without pinching its budget—by increasing instead its service and license fees.

Despite these assets designed to please the conservative and budget-minded dominant population of Marion County, Unified Government has one birth defect: unlike its model, the Jacksonville consolidation, Uni-Gov was designed and came to Indianapolis with neither a public vote, local public hearings, nor other significant, broad-based public involvement designed to give it a foundation of popular support. Considerable pressure was mounted in the state legislature by suburbanites, many of whom felt that a referendum requirement might subject the "super-government" to popular defeat, but with the compromises and almost daily lunches and conversations between Mayor Lugar and state legislators, the referendum provision was defeated. Unified Government was not to get its first ballot-box test until more than a year and a half after its creation, in the 1971 election, when Mayor Lugar himself faced his first county-wide campaign. He had Democratic opposition from the attorney who had successfully sued the state for the city's past-due inheritance-tax rebate. Lugar could be expected to get little more than 10 percent of the usually Democratic black vote, and his own supporters were forecasting early in the political season that he would lose a significant amount of Republican support from conservative suburbanites opposed to the way the new consolidated government had come to office. To the latter, Uni-Gov seemed a liberal attempt to inundate their votes with the more liberal-minded city vote; to many blacks it was an attempt to inundate *their* vote with *white suburban votes*. Lugar, rather than shy away from the issues, ran his 1971 campaign touting Uni-Gov's achievements; Indianapolis, his campaign slogan proclaimed, was "a city whose time has come." His forthrightness paid off. Lugar —and Uni-Gov—won healthy endorsement.

Two of Uni-Gov's departments merit special consideration. Both were designed as intermodal agencies for greater balance of interests and efficiency of operation. One is the Department of Metropolitan Development. Its predecessor, the Metropolitan Planning Department of Marion County, created in 1955 by the State of Indiana, was in a real sense a precursor of Uni-Gov: a county-wide agency with city-sized powers. It was granted jurisdiction not only over the usual county-wide planning activities but also over county-wide zoning decisions—authority usually given only to planning and zoning offices confined to city limits.

The county's Planning Commission was also given a strong structural base from which to work. If a zoning petition was rejected by the appointed nine-member commission, there was no appeal except through the courts; if the zoning petition was approved, it then also needed approval of the County Council, but if that council amended or reversed the commission's decision, it was sent back to the commission for concurrence. If the Planning Commission still insisted on its earlier decision, the County Council could call it back but had to muster four out of five votes within thirty days to override the commission's position. Such authority vested in the commission was bound to give it considerable power over the shaping of the urban county's development.

The Planning Commission and its staff used its power to some advantage—though most notably it was to the advantage of the local government's favorite public works projects: building roads. Beginning in 1968, the commission told those seeking rezoning for major developments that they would have to dedicate to the Mass Transportation Authority any land that agency would need for its four-year road-building program as outlined in the 1968 regional transportation study. In the summer of 1969, for the first time a developer refused to comply. The commission, previously unopposed to his request for permission to build a service station, voted unanimously against it.

Perhaps a more significant test of the commission's freedom of action was in a zoning request to allow the developer of the Lafayette Square shopping center to build another giant shopping mall east of the city. The planning staff calculated that some 3 million dollars' worth of major road improvements would have to be made in the area because of the traffic the shopping center would generate. Despite the fact that the developer was represented by a law firm which included the state's National Republican Committeeman, the commission, appointed by city and county administrations of the same party, insisted that the developer pay half the costs for the road improvements, including the widening of one road to at least a mile away from his shopping-center site. According to Uni-Gov planning officials, the developer has since put his project on "the back burner" for a combination of reasons: the road improvement costs, the failure to construct an expected housing development in the area, and the fact that he "caught hell" from competitors at another major east-side shopping center. Apart from this and a precious few other exceptions, according to one of the city's leading real estate attorneys, Indianapolis has failed to use its considerable zoning powers to effect orderly development of its urban area. Its zoning actions have been more on the side of permissiveness for developers, regardless of where or what they wanted to build.

With the advent of Unified Government, the planning agency maintained its nine-member board appointed by the mayor, the City-County Council, and the County Commission and retained all of its powers; but Deputy Director Michael Carroll is unable to come up with any new, post-Uni-Gov examples of political freedom exercised by Uni-Gov's Department of Metropolitan Development. Yet, from the perspective of a year and a half's testing, it appeared that the department was at least functioning at the hoped-for streamlined pace. By mid-1971 ground had been broken for Operation Breakthrough's experiment with mass-production housing, some 2,500 housing units had been refurbished under its Operation Rehab, its concentrated enforcement of building codes in the central part of the city had been completed, and it was annually increasing its production of public housing. Carroll said the agency would never have been able to bring all of the administrative and regulatory pieces together had Uni-Gov not concentrated in the one department all of the necessary machinery, not only the previous planning and zoning functions of the old county planning department, but also the programs of urban renewal, property acquisition and disbursal, tenant relocation, and housing construction.

The new government's planning and zoning arm has meant a significant change for downtown Indianapolis in the adoption—at last—of a plan to develop Market Square, a run-down area surrounding the City-County Building and the old City Market at the

east pole of downtown. Until 1971, the area included a few badly
deteriorated buildings and—like the kitchen floor on which a child
has erected a few widely dispersed, rickety stacks of building blocks—
parking lots. In 1971, construction started.

The original plans for Indianapolis in 1821 dedicated a site
on the east side of downtown to be set aside as open land for an
"internationale" marketplace. The market's first building was erected
a decade later and was replaced in 1867 by the present structure, a
great chamber roofed with an "iron casted," vaulted dome. In succeeding decades it became the major focal point of civic, community,
and cultural affairs in the city and earned a place in local history: in
1877 a new Marion County Courthouse was built across the street;
in 1888 Tomlinson Hall was built next door and became the city's
first cultural center for operas, concerts, plays, and athletic events;
in 1910 Indianapolis built a new City Hall half a block away.

In the second and third quarters of the twentieth century, as
Indianapolis turned its attention to the suburbs, the area fell into
disrepair. The market became a major tax burden; authorities tried
to close it as a health hazard and would have succeeded but for a
lengthy legal battle that ended with appropriation of local funds in the
mid-1960's to restore and preserve the market. Tomlinson Hall was
razed by a fire in 1958 and only its cellar remains, with paved parking
above. The courthouse became a nesting place for rats, roaches, and
pigeons, and local government functions overflowed the limited space
in the once magnificent City Hall.

Efforts to redevelop the area actually began in 1959 with the
demolition of the old courthouse and construction in its place of a
twenty-eight-story City-County Building. The old City Hall now
houses the Indiana State Museum. For the next decade a succession of
plans were aimed at renewing the area and redeveloping it as a dependable east-side anchor capable of balancing the west side's gold-domed
capitol and expanse of state office buildings; in succession the plans
were drafted, read, discussed, and shelved.

Getting similar treatment were alternative plans for location of a
multipurpose sports facility. In 1966 the county planning office suggested the southeast corner of downtown, by then fallen into misuse
and abuse by rail spurs, an unfenced junkyard, decaying structures,
and—of course—parking yards. In 1968 the same planners suggested
twenty-three acres southwest of downtown, being vacated by the Hy-
Grade meat processors whose slaughterhouse there had been destroyed
by fire the year before.

It is likely that both the arena and Market Square projects would
have borne fruit without Unified Government, but it is a fact that the

newly consolidated Department of Metropolitan Development was able to put them together into one package in 1970, suggesting that the arena be located within Market Square. In 1971 Mayor Lugar announced a 32.5-million-dollar project to include a two-block, eighteen-story, domed sports arena sitting atop parking-deck pedestals and straddling Market Street (so as not to interfere with automobiles bound for a future expressway "inner loop" five blocks away); twin twelve-story office towers behind the city market, linked by a five-story parking garage; a "pocket" park on either side of the market, and a rathskeller in the still-preserved basement of Tomlinson Hall under one of the parks. For the arena, rathskeller, and park development the city is putting up 12 million dollars in general obligation bonds, the principal of which it hopes will be paid out of the rent that private investors will be charged for the arena and rathskeller, and the interest of which it plans to pay out of the increased property taxes it will collect from the private developments in the area. Present property taxes on the sites amount to less than $70,000; once developed, the area is expected to bring more than $425,000 a year.

A group of private investors will be spending 20.5 million dollars to construct the office towers and parking facilities and will lease the arena from the city. They, in turn, will rent the arena to the home-town professional basketball team, the Indiana Pacers—who had to reschedule a league championship playoff one year recently: there had been a scheduling conflict with a circus at the local coliseum. The basketball team was planning to develop an arena complex for itself on the far northwest side of Marion County, but at the 1971 unveiling of the Market Square Development plan, the president of the Pacers, L. Charles DeVoe, announced, "We have become convinced that there are compelling reasons for locating downtown, and we are abandoning our northwest-side location." Officials hope to have the arena ready for the 1973 basketball season. Meanwhile, they were scouting for a professional hockey team that might also like to occupy the arena.

The downtown location is expected to spin off other close-in development, including Lockerbie Fair, a long-hoped-for project to construct a picturesque in-town neighborhood of nineteenth-century buildings around the still-existing home of Hoosier poet James Whitcomb Riley, and the central business district has also seen other major investment in recent years as part of the general attempt in the 1960's to save downtowns by building office towers: Indiana National Bank has relocated in a 20-million-dollar, thirty-seven-story headquarters building; a new main post office has been opened; Blue Cross–Blue Shield has a new eighteen-story, 20-million-dollar tower; American Fletcher National Bank opened a new head-office building on Monument Circle in the mid-1960's. But what the city is counting on most to spur downtown development is the combination of the Arena–Market Square project on its east side and a 16-million-dollar Indiana Exposition-Convention Center at the southwest edge of downtown, a low and long suburban-styled structure designed to accommodate heavy equipment trade shows and large conventions and being financed by a special 3 percent tax on hotel and motel accommodations.

With such revitalization of downtown expected and planned for, it is remarkable that planners can so unquestioningly espouse population and development dispersal as a way of urban life, and automobiles and highways as the way to get there. Yet that is exactly what is occurring in Indianapolis. While consultants churn out reports repeatedly urging both wiser use of downtown space now wasting away in low-tax-yield parking lots and more attention to people-moving transit and pedestrian traffic, the city eagerly awaits completion of its in-town freeway system, including an inner loop designed to pour a maximum stream of automobile traffic into downtown streets. Merchants and planners alike insist that this will save the downtown from its retailing doldrums and its nighttime barrenness. They fail to foresee that those are exactly the conditions their highways are inviting. They have not studied the experiences of cities that have gone before them. They fail to understand the effects that will surely come as automobiles gobble up more and more valuable space for streets and parking (the region's transportation study showed an expected need to almost double the number of downtown parking spaces by 1985), pollute the air, corrode buildings, gulp more and more tax base from maximum-use development, kill and maim pedestrians, carve up in-town neighborhoods, and assault the eyes, ears, and taste of those who know and enjoy the city life. Many of the planners of Indianapolis frequently cite congested eastern seaboard cities and their troubles with blight, congestion, crime, filth, and slum ugliness as the option they are avoiding by their policy of population dispersal via automobile. They steadfastly refuse to recognize that, at least in part, it was the adoption of the automobile for city travel that bred much of the very urban decay they seek to escape by car.

Accordingly, what shortcomings existed in the pre-Uni-Gov county planning office and still exist in the new Department of Metropolitan Development are not in the structure or the assigned powers, but in the attitudes of the commissioners and staff planners. Their contradictory, simultaneous devotion to automobiles and to a strong, active, and concentrated downtown is one example of policy blindness. Another is that for a full decade the county planning department resolutely refused to request *any* federal aid rather than accept federal controls, guidelines, and review requirements. This is endemic not only among the county planners but among Indiana officials generally; until 1965 state legislation did not even permit the city or county to seek federal funds—with the unused exception of planning grants. Just as the insatiable automobile inexorably led Indianapolis toward regionalism, it also led the city to accept federal planning funds: the first federal planning grant sought by county planners, in 1965, was for the Indianapolis Regional Transportation and Development Study, the "comprehensive transportation plan" Congress decided in 1962 to make a prerequisite—effective in mid-1965—for all federal highway funds in any urban region of more than 50,000 population. Since that time Indianapolis and Uni-Gov planners, and local officials generally, have been less reluctant to seek federal aid, but have remained adamantly convinced that federal funds should come to local governments without controls. As the now assistant director for planning and zoning, Donald Spaid, commented in mid-1969, "Give us the dollars, we'll figure out how to spend them. We'll do it a hell of a lot better than the feds ever dreamed of doing it . . . . We want the right to squander on our own mistakes."

It is hardly surprising that Indianapolis Mayor Richard Lugar, despite the election-year need to secure political fences at home, helped shape President Richard Nixon's revenue-sharing legislation and then spent much of 1971 campaigning for its support in cities across the country. In essence, the measure would distribute federal funds back to states and cities without "strings" tied to either programs, matching funds, or other controls—exactly what Indianapolis officials have been demanding all along.

One of the "mistakes" Indianapolis planners and administrators undoubtedly would make with the no-strings federal money would be continued subservience to automobile travel to satisfy a prime tenet in their own brand of American urban dogma. In the mid-1960's, would Indianapolis or similar cities have entered into comprehensive transportation studies if the federal government had not placed such a vitally needed "control" on its highway money?

Indianapolis's study produced at least a meager start toward acknowledging the need for an urban transportation alternative to the private automobile. It recommended express bus service along five freeways, two paved routes for buses only, outlying park-and-ride stations for the freeways and busways, turning of the downtown's Monument Circle into a pedestrian mall, closing of the downtown section of Washington Street to all but bus and emergency vehicle traffic (Washington Street is the city's major east-west thoroughfare,

spanning Marion County and crossing downtown just a block south
of its monument), and feeder and local bus service lines. Next to
nothing has been done with these recommendations for people-serving
transportation since they were advanced in the mid-1960's. Instead,
almost everything has been done to make city life easier for automobiles.

The creation of Uni-Gov's Department of Transportation as a
multimodal agency, patterned after the United States Department of
Transportation and similarly acronymized into DOT, was a deception.
In any other time it would have been more honestly called a department of highways. In 1969 the then chairman of the Mass Transportation Authority (also a euphemism, since the only "mass" it was
dedicated to moving was the city's growing mass of automobiles) and
a close advisor to Mayor Lugar, William K. Byrum, said transportation would be the "Achilles' heel" of Uni-Gov: if the new consolidated government failed to solve present and coming transportation
problems, it would probably face public and political rebuke. By 1971
it was clear that Uni-Gov's DOT would be using nothing but pavement
to resolve these transportation troubles.

The DOT and its appointed Transportation Board are headed by
a highway engineer named Richard B. Wetzel, who dismisses the
public transit recommendations of the regional transportation study—
particularly the ideas for a downtown mall, a transitway, and commuter busways—as a "whore's dream." Both he and his director of
traffic engineering, a former State Highway staff man named James
H. Cox, believe that any detailed transportation planning should be
done by *their* department and that, if anything, planners in the Department of Metropolitan Development do *too much* transportation
planning. The clear implication is that the planners are responsible
for the "whore's dream" of future mass transit.

Wetzel takes a special pleasure in recounting how, in July 1970,
the National Shrine held its convention in Indianapolis and got the
city to close Monument Circle to traffic for three days. Retail merchants complained that their retail sales fell sharply. Someone who
came through downtown during that period said later that he could
have fired a shotgun down the sidewalk and not wounded anyone.
Leaders of the downtown's retailing, utilities, and financial circles
met and decided to register a protest demanding that nothing of the
sort happen again. As a result, the project—apparently along with
turning the downtown portion of Washington Street into a transitway—was put "officially in limbo" to await "an opportunity," according to Cox. No one wanted to consider the possibility that Indianapolis

shoppers stayed away from downtown *not* because Monument Circle was closed to traffic (knowledgeable local drivers try to steer clear of the circle, anyway) but because the newspapers had adequately warned their public that something on the order of a million Shriners were to be in town—so many, in fact, that they had to be housed in hotels throughout the county. Who wanted to come downtown to do battle with the Shriners? (The fact was that most of the Shriners themselves were not downtown.)

One significant, albeit timid, step was taken in the direction of implementing at least part of the regional transportation study's transit plans for downtown. A prerequisite to turning downtown Washington Street into a buses-only route was reversal of traffic flows on a parallel pair of one-way streets to provide for through-town automobile traffic now using Washington Street. When first attempted in the late 1960's, downtown merchants successfully opposed the proposal before the City Council; they feared this would eventually lead to eliminating automobile traffic from in front of their stores and would hurt sales. Once the City Council voted down the one-way change, planners returned to the merchants, held numerous meetings to explain the plan and its benefits for the downtown generally, and managed at least to silence the opposition the next time it came to a vote in the City Council. The one-way pair reversal was adopted and, almost simultaneously with Uni-Gov in January 1970, put into effect. It represented the only change in downtown traffic patterns in Indianapolis since 1953. While it might be described as an attempt to recognize public transit needs, its only effect thus far—and for the foreseeable future, considering the downtown interests' adamant defense of freedom for automobiles—is to make automobile travel downtown easier still.

On paper, of course, the DOT is multimodal, responsible for all forms of transportation in the county. In reality, air travel is excluded, left with the Airport Authority because that agency had too high a level of bonds outstanding to be safely absorbed into DOT's massive need for road-building bonds. In reality, also, public transit is excluded because Indianapolis remains the only city in the state that is forbidden by law from spending public funds on public transit construction or operation. (The DOT is permitted to spend money for transit *planning* only.) The smallest cities of Indiana were granted the right to own and operate public transit as long ago as 1957; middle-sized cities received the same permission from the state legislature in 1965, to allow Fort Wayne to buy its failing transit company. Indianapolis, the only Indiana city that meets the legal criteria of a "first-class" city, has no such enabling legislation.

That leaves the DOT with highways; and highways—or roadways by a variety of other names—are exactly what they build at DOT. Wetzel, and highway builders generally in this country, insist that roads are being paid for through "use" taxes, in the form of tolls and, most often, state and federal gasoline taxes. A breakdown of the 15-million-dollar annual budget of Uni-Gov's DOT belies the statement. A state cigarette tax gave it about 1.75 million dollars in 1971, the inheritance-tax rebate added another quarter-million, and a "Cumulative Bridge Fund," collecting a ten-cent property tax on each $100 of assessed valuation, put another 1.8 million dollars on top of the overall budget. The bridge fund earmarks those property taxes for bridges only; if unused, they remain in the fund until spent on building bridges. The fact is that in 1971 almost one-quarter of the DOT's total budget of some 17 million dollars, including the bridge fund, came from non-highway-use taxes, and these figures do not even consider the peripheral costs of highway building borne by non-highway-use taxes—neighborhood deterioration that makes urban renewal necessary; air pollution programs; traffic policing services; the costs of clogged court dockets arising from traffic collisions and violations; the personal sacrifices of injury, death, and property damage, and of relocation due to highway routing; the property-tax burden caused by removal of highway acres from tax rolls, to recite only part of the litany of highway-caused woes.

With its powers and responsibilities amplified to include all those previously distributed among the city's Board of Works, Civil Engineer, and Street Engineer, the county's Highway Department, and the county-wide Parks Department's boulevard responsibilities, and with its budget expanded to some 17 million dollars a year, the DOT should have been happily on its way to greet the coming of the Interstates. It wasn't. Wetzel would like to spend some 75 million dollars by 1978 to build roads—"and that won't completely do the job we'd like to see done"—but his department's 2 percent bond allowance limits him to about 33 million dollars. As Wetzel says, "That's why revenue sharing is so important."

Under the Nixon proposal a separate revenue-sharing pot would be set up for transportation, and Wetzel estimates it would give him about 3 million dollars in direct funding annually for any transportation project he wishes—"more than enough" to retire the added road-building bonds Wetzel wants. What is of prime importance to him is to receive the federal revenue-sharing funds directly, without the strings of either the federal or the state government in his way, a protection the Nixon package would give him. "Those guys have been building highways through cornfields so damn long I don't need their fingers in the pie," Wetzel says of both state and federal highway officials, and by way of example he adds, "You don't have to relocate cornfields." One is led to wonder just how ruthless Wetzel would have an administrator be in dislocating hundreds of families and small businesses for the sake of a city expressway.

Another part of the Nixon package for transportation revenue sharing would earmark funds for public transit, of which Wetzel estimates Indianapolis would get about 1.8 million dollars; if the for-transit-only "control" were not placed on those funds, it is a fairly safe bet that Wetzel's DOT would spend that, too, on roads. He may yet, and try to justify the move by saying that roadways help buses as well as cars.

The roads that occupy the local DOT most are those tied to the Interstates, of course. The Interstate network scheduled for Indianapolis is to be completed and opened by 1976, two years before Wetzel expects to be fully ready for them. "We may have set too high a goal," he confides. "We haven't gone far enough fast enough." The Interstates, when completed, will look like a wheel with an outer beltway rim, I-465, an "inner-loop" hub around three sides of the downtown, and the "spokes" of I-65 and I-70 running northwest-southeast and east-west respectively. Two other Interstates are not scheduled to penetrate within the outer beltway—I-74 west to Peoria and southeast to Cincinnati, and I-69 northeast to Detroit.

To these ambitious plans local highway officials have been wanting for at least a decade to add two more freeways: an 8-mile Harding Street Expressway as a north-south span on the west side of the city, with a 2-mile spur to the inner loop to close its west side and make it a full noose of concrete around the downtown, and a 9-mile Northeast Expressway to slash diagonally across the city from the inner loop to where I-69 now will dead-end at the beltway. The Federal Highway Administration has repeatedly refused to put either one of them on its Interstate Highway System maps, so the local DOT hired New York consulting engineers Coverdale & Colpitts to do a feasibility study on making the two routes toll roads to be run by the state's profitable Toll Road Commission. The consultants' report was issued in April 1971.

Coverdale & Colpitts estimated the total cost for the Harding Street Expressway, including toll-collection facilities, at more than 63 million dollars and said that tolls from anticipated traffic, including what the consultants said would be an additional 10 percent traffic load "induced" by the expressway's presence, would not be enough to retire the expressway-building bonds.

Once the route was declared unfeasible as a superhighway, the

DOT immediately switched gears and entered into design work for constructing a grade-level pair of one-way streets to substitute for a west-side connection for the inner loop. This, Wetzel and Cox say, is essential to take the burden off other local streets that began to be felt at the close of 1971, when Interstate 65 from the northwest arrived at the inner loop, which was not yet built. Local government was too slow in recognizing the problems ahead, Wetzel says, and as a result construction of a special pressure-relieving link between the one-way pair and the I-65 interchange with the inner loop is not to be completed until the end of 1974, about the same time that the inner loop freeway will be completed and the cross-downtown traffic pressure somewhat reduced.

Before considering the Northeast Expressway project, which the consulting engineers did find feasible (though under somewhat strange circumstances), it is worthwhile to take note of some of the more remarkable statements committed to writing by the consultants. One was that their study of the economic feasibility of the two toll expressways used data "more than six years old" and therefore they had to place "more reliance . . . on statistics of subsequent growth and development than is fully warranted by the available statistics." They used guesswork *they* didn't even trust!

Another set of remarkable statements in their report came in answer to the DOT's request that they also look into the "potential for rail or bus rapid transit in the corridors traversed by each project." The consultants said some bus rerouting might be done, and that the possibility of providing express bus routes on the Northeast Expressway should be studied. The consultants cautioned, however, "It is obvious that such a study, if undertaken as part of the expressway planning, would have to weigh the effect of such a bus operation on the passenger-car toll collections of the expressway." In other words, express public transit service might have to be sacrificed in order to get enough cars to use the expressway and pay for its construction with their tolls!

The most astounding twists of logic contained in the Coverdale & Colpitts report, however, concern the feasibility of the Northeast Expressway. That route had been a dotted line on planners' maps of Indianapolis since 1960, and land for the outer half of it had actually been purchased as early as 1956, the inaugural year of the Interstate Highway program. Though enough land was acquired on the outer half of the route to make it a four-lane expressway, it was only built as a two-lane state highway that opened in 1958. The remainder of the land remains idly in government's hands. When it was proposed that I-69 be continued from the beltway to the inner loop, highway planners asked that the outer half simply have its other two lanes paved, and that land be acquired for the inner-city half—including more than two miles bisecting what has now become Indianapolis's Model Cities neighborhood. The Federal Bureau of Public Roads refused to consider the Northeast Expressway project as part of its basic Interstate system and said it would not consider this project until it prepared its post-1972 plans. (At the time, the Interstate program was to be completed in 1972; it has since been extended to 1977.) Yet the dotted line remained on the maps of the area, and wary owners of property along its route, many of them absentee landlords, were kept ignorant of just when the highway would come through and take their homes and businesses away; as a result, structures in the area fell into disrepair. DOT's traffic engineer, James Cox, says the property owners used the highway routing as "an excuse" not to keep their property in good repair. In 1968 the expressway was officially taken off the thoroughfare plan for the city, but it still showed up as a dotted line in the regional transportation study's map released that year, and as a set of arrows in a Comprehensive General Land Use Plan released in November 1969 by Marion County's Metropolitan Planning Department.

In the meantime, that northeastern neighborhood of Indianapolis had been one of the original areas chosen for the new Model Cities program. The 4.5-square-mile area has a population of about 53,000, four-fifths of its homes have housing-code deficiencies, of which over half are rated as serious, more than one-third of the families receive welfare, and almost one-third subsist on less than $3,000 a year. Its southern boundary is already traced by the concrete trough of I-70 out of the east. Charles Martin Sevilla, in a doctoral thesis on highways and Model Cities submitted in 1971 to the Urban Law Institute of George Washington University, states that the City Demonstration Agency, the local model city coordinator of various federal offices contributing to the program, and local residents did not learn of the Northeast Expressway plans until "a group of architects performing a land use study for the Model City planners discovered the plan during the course of their work and relayed it to Model City people."

A major concern in the neighborhood was the too-recent history of I-65 construction in the northwest part of the city. Even Wetzel and Cox concede that the design of that Interstate was a community tragedy: as it sliced through the neighborhoods it turned local streets into dead-ends, alleys, and cul-de-sacs, with little cross-access. Residents of the Model Cities area did not want a repeat. James Cox recalls that when he went to meet with Model Cities representatives, "I ducked the subject over and over until I had to face the issue and talk about the Northeast Expressway. I told them if we didn't build it, we'd have to find nine more lanes of surface streets inside Model Cities" to handle the traffic the six-lane expressway would handle. He didn't say whether he was including expressway-"induced" traffic in his estimate of need.

In 1969 Indianapolis again asked the federal government to include the freeway in its Interstate schedule, and again the Bureau of Public Roads rejected the idea. The Bureau was getting nothing but trouble from anti-highway citizens along its inner-city Interstate routes and was apparently in no mental frame to accept another thorny route. Undaunted, the Indianapolis DOT turned to its New York consultants to see if the highway could make it on tolls.

Coverdale & Colpitts determined that the project was "probably financially feasible . . . subject to the limitations of the data used and with the interjection of certain assumptions beyond the basic assumptions of our study."

Those "certain assumptions" were astounding. Finding that the route would not support itself on tolls alone, even with the added 10 percent "induced" traffic load, they recalculated, this time charging estimated operating and maintenance expenses to unidentified "sources other than toll revenues." This showed only a marginal likelihood of producing sale-worthy revenue bonds, so they tried again, this time assuming that one-fourth of the total project cost would be charged to some unspecified source other than tollgate revenue bonds. Again the results were only marginally hopeful for DOT. In other words, there probably would *not* be enough traffic on the highway to pay for even three-fourths of its construction! On their fourth attempt the consultants assumed that once I-69 out of the northeast is completed to the beltway it will produce "substantially higher" traffic demands for the toll expressway, so they estimated traffic loads at a full 50 percent higher than they had originally estimated might be diverted from other streets. (It is somewhat noteworthy that they defended this assumption with the same argument that anti-freeway forces have been using, that "the history" of the Interstates shows that expressways always generate for themselves more traffic than was planned for in an ever-growing vicious circle.) Coverdale & Colpitts added, however, that "we have not . . . been able to find factual support for such an assumption in the 1964 basic data which we have used." Factual data or not, the assumption was made, and bond consultants happily declared such a proposal "highly feasible."

Model Cities planners and residents, apparently cowed by highway engineers' statements that many more local streets would have to be widened and their speed limits raised if the expressway wasn't built, were ready to give in. If the toll expressway is built, it will be a lasting concrete memorial to the highway engineers' callous disregard of human and community values—as well as of honest cost-benefit accounting. The consultants' report and the DOT's unconscionable insistence that a northeast expressway be built regardless of the evidence against it will live as testimonials to the reputation of highway builders: they build white men's highways through black men's homes. There are many examples of such urban highway-building intransigence, but few are so clear-cut as the case of Indianapolis's Northeast Expressway.

The dotted line across northeast Indianapolis did not go back on the official map in 1971 because that was an election year and, according to Wetzel, the mayor didn't want citizen antagonism stirred awake. Instead, Wetzel's department devoted much of its energies in the time-honored election-year practice of resealing with asphalt about 150 miles of the county's 800 miles of "unimproved" roads, even though Wetzel admitted that it was just "an aspirin" approach and "not the way I like to do business." The unimproved roads consist of chipped stone sealed with a thin layer of asphalt, almost guaranteed to break apart and collapse into chuckholes when spring thaw follows the winter freeze. With elections out of the way, it is likely that the dotted line of the Northeast Expressway will be reentered on the official DOT highway plans in 1972.

Model Cities, meanwhile, also had its transportation plans and was trying to carry them out, without the assistance of (but with private scoffing from) the local DOT. With some $70,000 in federal funds from the Department of Housing and Urban Development, the Model Cities agency was able to buy and operate two small Ford Econoline vans as a local public transit service. Lacking technical experience, the locally organized corporation was unable to maintain schedules or routes and ran the service almost as an on-call, taxi-like operation. In 1971 it was seeking professional transit management and $196,000 in federal aid to expand to six buses and improve service.

Another poor people's public transport project never left the starting gate. The Employment Task Force of the Greater Indianapolis Progress Committee, a group of leading businessmen from the community appointed by the mayor, proposed in 1969 to use surplus buses of the privately owned Indianapolis Transit System on three special crosstown routes to provide door-to-door service between the city's three worst inner-city poverty neighborhoods and outlying employment centers. Employment immediately alongside the three proposed routes totaled some 40,000, and another 20,000 employees worked within five blocks of the routes, all in areas not served by the regular bus service in the city. To operate the project for fourteen months the Mass Transportation Authority in 1969 was seeking, in behalf of the task force, $62,536 in aid from the United States Department of Transportation's Urban Mass Transportation Administration, to which the authority was to add $7,348. Despite repeated assurance from Washington that the grant was being processed, Indianapolis never received the aid, and the program was never started. It must seem strange to Model Cities residents that so much energy and logic-contortion could have been used to assure that a 50-million-dollar toll expressway would be built through their yards and homes but that less than $70,000 could not be spent to provide reverse commuter bus transportation between the inner city and suburban jobs.

That has been the history of bus transportation in Indianapolis for more than a decade. Largely the result of far-flung population, employment, and shopping dispersal, the Chicago-owned Indianapolis Transit System experienced a ridership decline quite similar to that of Dayton's bus company and city bus companies generally. The Indianapolis Transit System boasts that it has been carrying passengers for hire since 1864—but it may not have many more years to add to its century of private-enterprise transit (and in Indianapolis *public* transit is considered the province of only *private* enterprise). In 1961, by no means a record year, the bus system carried almost 23 million passengers, but by 1970 this had fallen to just under 18 million, a decline of almost 22 percent for the decade. To keep its fare-box take high enough to pay for the bus service, the company raised fares from 20 to 22 cents in 1963, to 25 cents in 1965, to 30 cents in 1968, and to 40 cents at the end of 1970.

With the exception of a three-year period in the mid-1960's when its ridership seemed temporarily to stabilize itself, each fare increase brought a corresponding drop in the number of passengers carried. To its credit, during the three-year period of stability the company used its income to buy new, air-conditioned buses. Its 233-bus fleet includes 77 new coaches bought since 1965.

Not to its credit is the fact that the company was especially anxious to rid itself of special fares offered to school children. Since 1961 it had provided rides at a 15-cent fare to elementary school students and at a 20-cent fare to high school students. When it raised fares in December 1970, it also raised school fares to 20 and 25 cents, but claimed it could not continue to police student mischief and vandalism on the buses for such reduced fares. As of the end of the 1970-71 school year, the company altogether dropped its special student rates. Ironically, the student population represented the only growing market for bus rides—a growth of about 23 percent from 1961 to 1970. At the start of the decade students represented about 12 percent of the company's ridership; by the end of the decade, thanks in part to the decline of non-student ridership, they accounted for about 19 percent of the total.

The Indianapolis Transit System told the state's Public Service Commission in mid-1971 that its operations lost a net of $104,960 during 1970 and expected that the full effect of new wage levels written into a three-year contract with the Amalgamated Transit Union late that year would drive costs up another $561,477 for the next calendar year. While company president Edgar Claffey told the state agency that he recognized the hardship higher bus fares imposed on the parents of students, senior citizens, the poor, and the unemployed, "The principle objective of an urban transit company is to obtain sufficient income to stay in operation." The Public Service Commission agreed and granted him the requested fare increase to 40 cents. Claffey said the 1970's had opened for him with severe declines in ridership: "The decline became obvious as 1970 became older. Even before the fare increase [in December 1970] we were off 6 to 7 percent."

Claffey, a veteran of bus transit, heads a management team with an average length of service of about thirty years. He and his top staff are hardly inclined to look favorably on new suggestions for expanding or improving bus service. The net result is that, strangely enough, Claffey and the DOT's Wetzel are together: both think little of any scheme to close Washington Street to everything but buses, taxis, and emergency vehicles. All but one of the Indianapolis Transit System's seventeen basic bus routes radiate out from Monument Circle or very close to it. (The one exception spans the north side.) Ten routes terminate on the circle itself, where there are no bus-stop shelters. Claffey doesn't believe Washington Street's six lanes can carry efficiently the number of buses it would be required to if all buses were routed to it downtown and then through a circulatory system of one-way street pairs, even though his retired operations manager has mapped a downtown bus routing plan that would measurably improve local passenger distribution.

When the Chicago-based holding company acquired Indianapolis Transit in the mid-1950's, its first major action was to drop its public relations department, considered to have been of high quality by the now-retired superintendent of operations, who then worked for the company. There has been no significant advertising effort by the system since then. In addition, no transfer agreements exist with any of the eight smaller companies that operate suburban routes in the area, and there have been no advances made to institute such agreements. Claffey himself doesn't know, and says it would take "a real fancy origin and destination study" to determine, how many of his passengers transfer to or from the suburban lines.

He did take one bold step in 1968, however, when he purchased a route from the suburban Sheridan Bus Line. The route runs from downtown Indianapolis northward to the county line, crossing both the residential neighborhoods of inner-city domestic workers and the outlying affluent families to which they hire out. He charges a special 60-cent fare on the route, however, and doesn't even allow transfer privileges with his own company's other routes, even though he laments that his own household maid has to travel four hours a day to and from his home and that he has to pay $1.25 a day for her bus transportation. His maid lives west of the downtown, he in the far northeast section of the county, where his own buses don't go.

According to Claffey, most of the suburban companies, experiencing the same ridership declines and cost increases, are anxious to sell their operations to him, but "I can't afford to buy them. I'd just be buying a losing deal. I'd be buying a pig in a poke." Yet, he concedes that crosstown service, the bus routes most demanded by his captive riders, the inner-city poor, probably could only be effectively instituted if all of the local bus companies were combined into one system. At present, more than one-fifth of all the Indianapolis Transit System's riders must pay a nickel and transfer downtown to get to their destinations.

Indianapolis Transit had an ulterior motive in acquiring its one suburban operation. St. Vincent's Hospital, operated not far from downtown by the Catholic Church, plans to move to the far north side and build what Claffey describes as "one hell of a big hospital"; it will employ a staff of approximately 3,500 persons, a population his suburban route will be ideally suited to serve. Yet a 125-acre site just west of downtown is now developed into a major medical center, including the state hospital, a women's hospital, a Rotary Club hospital, a psychiatric hospital, the Veterans' Hospital, Marion County General Hospital, and the state Board of Health headquarters; only two of the Indianapolis Transit System's routes serve the area, both originating a block south of Monument Circle, not where persons in ill health or their families and neighbors are likely to be.

Twice during the earlier 1960's the transit company attempted to serve apartment conglomerates developed at the far edges of Marion County's east side. The most recent attempt, some five years ago, lasted only three months; unpleased with the poor ridership the brief experiment generated, Claffey terminated it.

His company had had a similar experiment in the preceding decade that had turned out quite differently—although with the significant difference that it was not made at the expense of the company. In 1957 developers of a subdivision northwest of the city were refused federal financing unless they gave assurance that their large subdivision of middle-class homes would be provided with public transit. They approached the bus company and promised to pay all operating losses for a route through their project, Eagledale, under a contract renewable every thirty days. As the homes were built and occupied, Indianapolis Transit opened and expanded its route to serve them. The developers paid between $700 and $800 monthly for about nine months, by which time Eagledale's new residents had developed the bus-riding habit and the routes were self-supporting and profitable. Reminded of the Eagledale story, the major developer now says he would never willingly incur such cost again, and Claffey retorts that it was "too long ago" to be of any significance. Claffey says that in more recent years the route has experienced the same ridership declines and need for fare increases as his other routes: no wonder, with automobiles now critically essential for any kind of movement in the city's sprawling highways-only era; public transit has little chance to develop ridership habits to compete with society's automobile addiction.

Even when ridership is at a peak, with all buses in use, the company's president moans that he is only serving as a "clearinghouse for money" because the fares don't do more than meet the costs. This occasion arises at least once a year in Indianapolis at the Memorial Day weekend's classic "Indianapolis 500" race in Speedway. For longer than Claffey can remember his company has provided a special six-mile shuttle service between the race track and downtown. In 1968 heavy rain and mud brought an unusually large number of race fans to his buses, but he was unable to get expected special lane privileges from traffic polie, and the tie-ups kept his buses in service until more than four hours after the race was ended. In 1969 and 1970, with better weather and better police cooperation, the shuttle service worked more efficiently, but in 1971 police again let other traffic into a route mapped for buses and taxicabs only.

Claffey worries about the crowds he has to carry on the race days. "There's a tremendous potential for liability involved. We've almost always run accident-free"—he knocks on his wooden desk top—"but if we have a bad accident, we're in serious trouble."

While local government has concentrated its effort on accommodating the private automobile, some of that effort has inadvertently helped the Indianapolis Transit System as well. Such an isolated instance was the banning of parking along the entire length of Washington Street (excepting the six-laned downtown portion) from Marion County's east border to its west border—a distance of some sixteen miles. Before the ban, the four-lane, strip-developed thoroughfare had the city's—and the bus company's—highest crash rate. Despite fifteen years of east-side merchant opposition along the commercial strip, the ban was imposed at the start of 1969 and within six months the accident rate declined by one-third. Concurrent with the parking ban, traffic signals were synchronized for 30-mile-per-hour driving and bus stops were relocated to the far side of traffic-light intersections, helping both bus and auto efficiency. Cars did not have to sit frustrated behind buses at stops, and buses were able to make time by getting through traffic lights before loading and unloading passengers.

While hardly aggressive in promotion of its product, the Indianapolis Transit System has at least initiated several changes aimed at improving service and, hopefully, luring more riders to buses. The company has built eight bus-stop shelters in the city and four at the Indianapolis campus of Indiana University, the latter at the request of the university, which paid half the cost. It also secured permission from the city to use one lane of a one-way street for a buses-only route, in the opposite direction from automobile traffic—a consideration for public transit that the DOT's director now feels should never have been made: it causes too much trouble in engineering automobile traffic flows. The bus company also attempted a noon-time shuttle service between the north-side concentrations of insurance company home offices and the downtown but discontinued it for lack of patronage after two years. On special "Hoosier Bargain Days" it provided free bus rides into downtown, subsidized by downtown merchants, but felt that the subsidy didn't cover the full expenses, since it believed regular riders probably changed travel schedules to take advantage of the free rides.

Since ridership began to fall rapidly again in 1968 and costs began outstripping fare-box revenues, the Indianapolis Transit System company has lost interest in such experiments. "We've been conducting a very conservative operation since that time," Claffey admits, "because we don't know where it's going to end. We've been ultra-conservative, I'd say."

Where it's likely to end, and sooner than Indianapolis would prefer, is in the throes of public acquisition that Dayton is already experiencing. The trends of automobile domination and far-flung dispersal of everything from housing and employment to movie-going and health care has progressed too far to be reversed in time to save even the modicum of public transit now provided by the Indianapolis Transit System. For the present, the system has to be salvaged if only to provide a skeleton on which to build a future urban transportation system that provides an adequate alternative to continued urban evacuation.

For the future of public transit, Indianapolis has a bonus: its railroads still exist in the radial pattern they first established more than a century ago. Most of the railroad-street crossings are at grade, causing severe automobile traffic problems that the Department of Transportation would dearly love to resolve. The railroad companies, caught in their own economic collapse as part of the cost of highways, automobiles, and trucks, are unwilling to share in the cost of constructing bridges to separate grade crossings and make things easier for car traffic. The railroads, out of their own selfishness, have successfully fought every attempt by the city to get their cooperation—with the single exception that one train was rescheduled to avoid conflict with shift-changing traffic near GM's Detroit Diesel plant in Speedway.

In 1969 the chairman of the Mass Transportation Authority said that grade separation of streets and rails was the second highest transportation priority in the city—behind highway and street improvements, naturally. At the time William Byrum recognized that this would also provide rights-of-way for future rapid transit should the city decide to want such. Two years later Byrum, now on the City-County Council, felt that the grade-crossing problem should be solved in quite a different manner: rerouting all rails *around* the city to yards on the far outskirts. "We don't need any trains in the city," he said in 1971. "I think trains inside the city are inimical to development. I'm not talking about aesthetics, I'm talking about efficiency."

In the name of efficiency, then, the rails may someday be removed from Indianapolis, and with them the corridors that afford a significant chance to develop efficient mass rapid transit alternatives to highways. There is a parallel in Indianapolis history: early in the twentieth century interurban rail lines existed in Indianapolis, but after they were abandoned some four decades ago they passed into private hands; most of the rights-of-way disappeared and now exist only in the basements of new plants, office buildings, and homes that have been built on them. Should existing rail lines be removed from Indianapolis, their rights-of-way may disappear in the same way. Their property is as valuable to developers as it is crucial to good public transit development.

Some few steps are being taken for public transit's future, but they appear too mild to effect the scope of change required. One is within the Department of Metropolitan Development, which has a $75,000 federal grant to study alternative courses for saving the existing bus service and adapting it to the needs of present-day Indianapolis—part of the region's continuing "comprehensive" transportation study hardly likely to produce challenging and innovative actions. Another is in an ad hoc group organized by Mayor Lugar.

The mayor himself speaks knowledgeably about transit and cities and about the need to limit the use of automobiles in the city. And well he might: Lugar once lived in the crowded Northern Virginia suburbs of Washington, D.C., and saw at first hand the terrible wastes involved in turning city environments over to automobiles. He foresees the day when Indianapolis may have to tax land for its "highest and best use," as is done so successfully in Toronto, Canada. Under such a system it would no longer be profitable for developers to leave acres of land barren as low-tax-yield parking lots waiting for a major development opportunity to arise; they would be taxed instead as though the parking lot contained the major office tower the site was fitted for. As a result, downtown parking would become considerably more expensive. Also, cars could be assessed tolls for entering the downtown area; downtown parking spaces could be taxed as a luxury; automobiles could be required to pay premium license fees to use city streets. Lugar sees the possibility of such measures for the future, but it is not politically expedient for him to discuss them publicly in the Indianapolis of the early 70's. Instead, in the summer of 1970, he created a Transit Task Force to discuss this and similar questions.

Young Doctor E. H. (Ned) Lamkin, Jr., who is serving his third term in the state legislature, is chairman of the task force. He is a lean and active man whose wife confirms what one lengthy conversation leads an observer to believe: the young businessman-doctor-legislator would like very much to be a "Renaissance Man." He enjoys exercising his mind on new thoughts, and that is what cities and city transportation need today. His thoughts led him to believe that the downtown, to be saved, should be considered primarily as an office-headquarters concentration and a "regional" shopping center for those who live closer to it than to other shopping areas—just as a suburban shopping center serves its neighbors. As such, he believes, it could be linked by fast rail service to major suburban concentrations, but any such rapid transit line should also be mapped to someday reach to the other metropolitan centers that ring Indianapolis—Chicago, 189 miles northwest; St. Louis, 262 miles southwest; Cincinnati, 111 miles southeast; and Detroit, 273 miles northeast. An "idea" by Indianapolis standards, but it is unlikely that a rebuilding of the interurban rail system of an earlier part of this century would satisfy the overriding need for an alternative to highways in the metropolitan area itself. Where DOT Director Wetzel wants to build a toll Northeast Expressway, Dr. Lamkin proposes a rail rapid transit system, but he is unlikely to get a receptive hearing from most of his constituents, one of whom is Wetzel himself. Lamkin's task force was an outgrowth of an attempt he made to create a state mass transportation commission that would have included large-city mayors, legislators from urban areas, and a non-voting advisory commission for the vested-interest groups such as highway lobbyists and engineers, transit operators, and suppliers. The state's highway interests successfully talked other legislators into watering Lamkin's proposal down to a powerless interim legislative study committee weighted in favor of non-urban areas and including a senator well known for his pro-highway stance. When Mayor Lugar named his task force for transit, he also named an advisory commission similar to the one envisioned in Lamkin's state-level proposal. Among its members are Wetzel, Claffey, and several railroad officials. Lamkin brought two proposals to the advisory committee—one to reserve some minor streets for buses only, another to attempt a rail transit operation from the downtown area northward, essentially along the same corridor that the regional transportation study in 1968 recommended using for a busway. The task-force chairman recalls that when he entered the meeting room he found "all the highway people on one side of the table and all the railroad people on the other side of the table." They listened to the doctor present his case, but the advisory commission chairman, a public relations director for GM's Detroit Diesel–Allison Division, took a great deal of time before calling a second meeting.

Lamkin also seemed to be having difficulty in getting enough interest among his regular task-force members to call meetings of their various committees, so low a priority do civic-minded business leaders put on public transit. Lamkin and four others, including Dr. George Smerk, a professor of transportation at Indiana University's Graduate School of Business in Bloomington, determined to "put together a proposal" themselves. Dr. Lamkin is interested in the northeast rail transit idea. Dr. Smerk recalls that another "idea that keeps coming up is turning Union Station [in downtown Indianapolis] into a transportation center" and running a high-speed rail line out to the airport west of the city. Dr. Lamkin says they also are looking into more futuristic urban transit schemes that would operate small personal-sized vehicles, either publicly or privately owned, along special guideways.

Whatever the task force comes up with, it will at least be the beginning of serious thinking about the future of the city. Indianapolis has aggressive, active leadership in government, a structure of government that meets its task well for the present, and a private business leadership that seems interested in the health and vitality of the city —assets not easily come by. However, unless the public transportation issue—and its corollary issue of future land-use patterns—is seriously addressed as a matter of significant priority at least as high as highway building, Unified Government will soon enough find itself in the same inadequate state that Indianapolis city government found itself in during the 1960's. Uni-Gov will not stop dispersal, and Uni-Gov most definitely will not stop freeway construction and all its attendant waste. The tunnel vision that has resulted in all of Uni-Gov's transportation resources being tossed into highways will only accelerate the coming of the day when Uni-Gov will find itself inadequate.

The city does have an active private industry leadership—within its financial and insurance institutions, within its professional class, and within such industrial giants as the home-based Eli Lilly and Company. The latter, admittedly, has grown so large that its topmost executives are more often away from the city than at home and are more interested in national and international economic and political developments than in the affairs of Indianapolis, but the corporation's second tier of leadership is deeply involved in the programs and government of Richard Lugar. That leadership must soon be turned to address the question of public transportation. The urban area cannot much longer afford to have its future guided by the concepts prevailing within its Department of Transportation. If it is, then it is a safe wager that Mayor Lugar's campaign slogan will have been proved wrong, at least insofar as highway transportation and the troubles it brings are concerned: Indianapolis may not be a city whose highway-dilemma time has come. Not yet.

4
Atlanta: A City Too Busy

Recurrently during the 1960's, full-page advertisements in national magazines and newspapers boasted of a new Atlanta in the South. The Chamber of Commerce, armed with a slick house magazine and a 1.5-million-dollar promotion budget, cranked up a propaganda machine designed to awaken the nation to its pocket of prosperity in Dixie: a city "too busy to hate," an island of reason in a sea of bigotry, a city of luxurious magnolia-shaded homes and glinting new skyscrapers. Interminable welcoming speeches were made telling the story of the rebuilding of Atlanta and the "New South." Because the nation had not earlier paid any unusual attention to Atlanta, it had little by which to judge the new propaganda. It believed, and the new money flowed in to build yet more. It was good psychology for investment, but there was one flaw, one that continues to afflict the city: its successful white leaders, and their juniors who wanted to be just as successful and affluent, came to believe their own propaganda. "Atlanta is a giant that sleeps with one eye open," a newsman once wrote to open a feature story about the city at night. He was correct, but more importantly—and usually left unsaid during the 1960's—Atlanta was a giant also *awake* with but one eye open.

The story Atlanta told and retold of itself was accurate enough as far as it went: it *was* the rebuildingest city around. It was born as a railroad settlement of saloons at the end of the line from Chattanooga, Tennessee. When it was incorporated it changed its name from Terminus to Marthasville and eventually to Atlanta but remained a dusty, noisy, and dirty out-of-the-way railroading spot located somewhere, it was agreed, between the more respectable towns of Decatur in DeKalb County and Marietta in Cobb County. In 1845, a South Carolina politician named John C. Calhoun passed through on his way to a convention in Memphis, Tennessee. When he arrived in Memphis he told his audience that if the Southeast were to prosper at all, it would have to do it with a system of railroads that "must necessarily unite at a point . . . called Atlanta, not far from Decatur." Because the railroads did finally come together there, the city grew into the major distribution center for the Confederate Army during the Civil War—a fact that attracted the attention of Yankee General William Tecumseh Sherman. Where Atlanta picks up the story for modern telling is at the "Gone With the Wind" rebuilding of the Reconstruction era (it skips over the dominant, terrorizing role of the Ku Klux Klan well into the twentieth century).

As if the railroads had not built and shaped, brought on the destruction of, and then rebuilt and reshaped the city enough, the turn of the century brought another form of transportation for the city to cope with—the automobile. Massive traffic jams of horses, buggies, fancy carriages, farm wagons, and primitive cars trying to mix with the railroad trains that poured through the downtown from every compass point forced the city to build viaducts across the tracks for the cars and carriages; it built so many of these overpasses that downtown Atlanta was turned into a two-story center. Buildings raised their main entrances to the new second story and most people eventually forgot the ground floor was there until a group of architects in the 1960's rediscovered the old architecture and turned a major part of the original downtown into "Underground Atlanta," a gaslit tourist mecca of ethnic and turn-of-the-century restaurants, clubs, taverns, and curiosity shops of almost every variety.

There had been a lesser rebuilding of Atlanta during the 1920's also, but the one the city itself told of most proudly was that of the 1960's, marking successive records in new construction, new jobs, retail sales, telephone listings, and every other economic barometer the city's promoters could conjure up.

One of the latest tellings of modern Atlanta's story is by Ivan Allen, Jr., its mayor for the decade, in his book, *Mayor: Notes on the Sixties* (Simon and Schuster, New York, 1971), a rather self-serving testimonial to himself and his circle of friends who ruled the city—the "power structure." (It is former Mayor Allen who consistently places the term in quotation marks, as though in a self-conscious denial of the fact and a vain attempt to hide his pride in his own membership in it—and, as a result, he draws the reader's attention to the phrase.) His apologia runs the entire litany of Atlanta's claims for itself—from racial harmony born of the power structure's benevolent, if "pragmatic" and "paternalistic" (his words), liberalism to the unparalleled economic boom born of the business craftsmanship that permeated both City Hall and the upper floors of the new downtown skyscrapers. Indeed, during the 1960's there was almost no way to separate an action of the private sector from an action of the political sector; they were identical.

There is another Atlanta, however, one closer to where its residents live and work, and one that has only recently come to center-stage, pushed there by the city's swelling black population. It is an Atlanta that demonstrates the mistakes that were made amid all the hustling for new business, new buildings, and major-league everything. Atlanta's white leadership concentrated so mightily on turning its home city into a major-league center—for sports, culture, conventions, business, air travel, you name it—that it tended to forget its own humanity. It went after quantity, and quality suffered.

Most cities are governed by not-too-clearly defined groups of leaders assembled into what most recognize as the local power structures. Flint, Dayton, and Indianapolis each has its own particular brand of power structure. Atlanta's, however, is a classic case of rule by elitists, and as such affords a clear study of how such rule is organized, perpetuated, and made manifest.

To one degree or another, what is true of power-structure rule in Atlanta is also true in the other cities. Atlanta merely provides the place where the system came into clearest focus. More than in most cities, the power structure of Atlanta was a readily definable clique of men from one generation, most of whom grew up as boyhood friends, went to the "right" schools, and inherited their leadership of the city from their fathers—a system not unlike the ancient dynastic orders and scented rather heavily with the divine right of kings. Ivan Allen, with his trim white hair, squared jaw, and manicured southern drawl, may have personified that power elite, but he was by no means its presiding officer. That title would have had to be assigned to the now retired president of the Citizens & Southern National Bank, Mills B. Lane, Jr., usually acknowledged as the man behind the throne in state and city politics. Bespectacled and circle-faced, Lane had good reason to proclaim on his office door and on each of his gift neckties that he decorated with a smiling sun and a bale of cotton, "It's a wonderful world!" His bank was the largest in the Southeast, it had quadrupled deposits in twenty years and, as Lane tellingly remarked to *Fortune* magazine in 1969, he had a good head start in life: "Hell! My old man owned the joint."

Lane was not the only one whose father "owned the joint." With him at the top of the Atlanta power structure were many other sons of the heads of its business community. They were the heads of the three or four other largest banks, the owners of its largest department and furniture stores, the president of its two jointly owned major daily newspapers, the heads of its major utilities companies, and, most importantly, Robert Woodruff, patriarch from the earlier generation who had developed the Atlanta-born Coca-Cola Company and owned the largest personal fortune in the South. Woodruff was the C. S. Mott of Atlanta, anonymously donating large sums to its United Fund drives and to City Hall for its more ambitious projects, even though during the 1950's he retired from active service and passed on to the younger generation his role of business and civic leader.

Just below this peak of control was the pyramid of the city's business leadership: the presidents of the larger local businesses, retail outlets, managers of national branch offices, realtors and attorneys from a select group of firms. Their home base rested in the Commerce Club upstairs from the Chamber of Commerce offices atop the Commerce Building just a block from the city's epicenter, "Five Points," where most of the banks built their skyscrapers. No one has better described this power structure in Atlanta than the former mayor himself in his post-mortem book on the 1960's:

> Almost all of us had been born and raised within a mile or two of each other in Atlanta. We had gone to the same schools, to the same churches, to the same golf courses, to the same summer camps. We had dated the same girls. We had played within our group, married within our group, partied within our group, and worked within our group. . . . [W]e had been fortunate enough to have certain benefits passed on to us from our fathers so that our devotion to hard work—once the low spot of the Depression passed around 1933—made it possible for us to enjoy spiraling success in business for all of our years. . . . We were white, Anglo-Saxon

Protestant, Atlantan, business-oriented, nonpolitical, moderate, well-bred, well-educated, pragmatic, and dedicated to the betterment of Atlanta. . . . When you talked about the "power structure" or the "establishment" in Atlanta, you really were talking about the leaders of the top fifty or so businesses in the city. We had, for a dozen or so years, warmed up to our task by working on projects like the Boy Scouts Council and the Community Chest fund drive and various other good works, and now (1958–1960) our time had come to replace our elders at the helm of the city. Nearly ninety percent of us lived inside a half-mile radius of (one) intersection . . . ten miles from downtown Atlanta, and we had shared the same problems, interests, and ambitions our entire lives. We were concerned with executive problems. . . . This gave us a further common large bond, and it should not be surprising that we also constituted a separate social set. . . .

This, then was Atlanta's closed circle of white elitists. Not invited into membership but vital to its success in the political realm was a similar but much smaller circle in the other Atlanta—its black society. Atlanta's black community had long had an upper class comparable in most respects to the upper middle class in the white society. It was composed of ministers, educators from Atlanta University (the blacks' "Harvard") and established black businessmen: a black banker, an attorney, an insurance company vice-president. But for their darker skin these men could have been cut from the same cloth as the white rulers. Because they were cautious professional men, mild-spoken, well dressed and well educated, they were picked to serve as communicators between the masses of black poor in the slums and the white men who lunched at the Commerce Club. They delivered most of the black vote in return for promises of what, during the 1940's and 1950's, passed for moderation—not integration, to be sure, but at least a small allotment of public services, a street light here and there, perhaps, and assurance that they would be protected from such extremes as Ku Klux Klan–inspired genocide.

In 1961 Allen inherited the presidency of the Atlanta Chamber of Commerce and later that year, when the late Mayor William B. Hartsfield, a flamboyant politician with a penchant for the grand public relations gesture, announced retirement from twenty-three years in office (he, too, had been the beneficiary of the salt-and-pepper coalition of the elite), also inherited the mantle of the power structure's candidate for mayor.

Allen's tenure as mayor lasted two terms, from January 1962 to January 1970. They were the years of flourishing power-structure rule, when City Hall and the Chamber of Commerce were in daily contact and decisions were made with equal force in either place. Allen entered office with the same six-point program of growth he had carried with him into the chamber presidency a year earlier, including keeping public schools open and obeying court-ordered desegregation ("integration" was a forbidden term around Atlanta and the South in those years) and construction of both expressways and rapid transit. While not successful on all counts, Allen and his coterie of friends did succeed where most immediately visible and where success earned quick praise from national city-watchers: a stadium, an auditorium, expressways, and a wave of skyscraper construction. The first nation-alerting success, however, came even before Allen's election, when, at the end of August 1961, the city peacefully entered nine black children into four of its previously all-white schools.

For a good part of the decade to follow Atlanta lived and grew off the national good will engendered in that September school integration. What was most obvious and most touted about the growth of the 60's was the construction that boomed through the city, partially as a result of that good will and partially as a result of the business community's eagerness to invest in the city once it had full control of its public conduct, as shown by both the school integration and Allen's election. Buttermilk Bottoms, a slum of rotting, leaning, and crowded apartments and trash-filled alleys just east of downtown, was bulldozed away and replaced with a $10-million-dollar auditorium–civic center complex. Another overcrowded slum, just south of the state capitol, was razed and replaced with an $18-million-dollar stadium (by closed-door decision of a selected band of power-structure men who chose to spend an extra $600,000 to build it in one year, though the Braves didn't arrive from Milwaukee until the following year) that resembles a gargantuan space cruiser adrift on a sea of asphalt parking. At the north end of downtown architect John Portman tore out shabby rows of buildings and constructed Peachtree Center, a $100-million-dollar complex of office buildings, restaurants, and the twenty-two-story, eight-hundred-room space-age Regency Hyatt House, topped with a blue revolving restaurant that looks like a flying saucer, the entire complex stitched together by pedestrian "skyways." A total of seventeen skyscrapers of at least fifteen stories each were built, including the First National Bank's forty-one-story tower at Five Points and three others each of more than thirty stories. Each successive building reached farther into the imagination for architectural distinctiveness, some reaching to absurd lengths to be noticed: towers of black, bronze, glass; a skyscraper flanged at each floor like a Japanese high-rise pagoda; a brazen glass silo. Atlanta could build a temple, it had proved, but it could not fill it with quality. It was still very

much a provincial town, with provincial tastes and provincial attitudes.

On a less visible scale the same was true in the lives of the city's
black population—that is, less visible perhaps to all but black people
themselves. It was a failure that led inexorably to the collapse of the
power structure's control over the city. Throughout the decade the
city continued to promote itself as "too busy to hate." The unspoken
corollary was that it was also too busy to love. It was building buildings instead of enriching people. The economic benefits that came with
the new skyscrapers and temples to big business, big arts, and big
sports failed to seep far enough down to the masses crowded into
slums of crumbling frame houses and shacks that looked as if they
had been transplanted from the dusty tenant farms of the South, slums
with such picturesque names as Vine City, Rock City, Summerhill,
Mechanicsville, Peoplestown, and My Blue Heaven. The speech-
makers could claim before the nation that their city was progressive
and racially harmonious, but beyond the tokenism of a few appointments for the "acceptable" upper black crust, the city was failing its
blacks. It desegregated public facilities, but only after demonstrations,
street confrontations, jailings, and threats of increasing militancy by
the new breed of black neighborhood leaders—leaders the city's
power structure was in no way prepared to accept. To the city's white
business elite, "leaders" were "reasonable" men of at least thirty or
thirty-five who dressed in suits, never raised their voices, spoke like
white businessmen, dined with the manners of white businessmen, and
said "sir." The Atlanta of the 1960's did not want to face the full realities of a black presence that did not conform to such norms. It was and
remains true, nevertheless, that the black presence in Atlanta, of whatever norms, was growing too large to be ignored. That presence sim-
mered beneath every question, every decision, every action to which
the city and its metropolitan area addressed itself.

The image of Atlanta on race, however, remained benign, and the
city's black population swelled during the 1960's as it had never
done before. During the decade the black population of the five-county
metropolitan area increased by some 82,000, considerably more than
the increase in black population during the entire first forty years of
the century. It was also the first time in the century that the black increase had kept pace with the total population increase—35 percent
for blacks, compared to 37 percent for the total population.

The white population was growing also, of course, and with
bounding strides since the opening of the suburbs during the 1940's.
The metropolitan area began the century with about 214,000 persons

and took forty years to top the half-million mark, but from 1940 to 1950 it added another quarter-million, and by 1960 it had reached one million; the 1970 census counted a total five-county population of almost 1.4 million.

With the growth the city also experienced the same sort of peculiar American malaise of urban-suburban racial isolationism that has plagued the rest of the nation. From 1960 to 1970 the City of Atlanta lost a net of 60,000 white residents and gained almost 70,000 blacks. While the census figures showed that the black population of the metropolitan area was holding to between 22 and 23 percent of its total (the Atlanta Urban League, which monitored the census, insists it is considerably higher), the city itself became one of the sixteen in the nation with predominantly black populations; in 1970, 52 percent of Atlanta's population was "nonwhite"—virtually all of it black.

As the black population swelled, it sought more room to relieve the agonizing pressures of overcrowding; it looked first to the edges of its already established ghettos of slums in the bottomlands that ringed the downtown, and then beyond. Unscrupulous real estate salesmen were quick to exploit white racial fears, and the whites fled. Most of the black expansion occurred in a wide swatch extending east and west from downtown: the north side was the Peachtree Street corridor—the avenue to the "liberal" white establishment and the city's most costly real estate, beyond the pocketbooks of most blacks—and southward was "redneck" country. East of the city, where its boundaries dip into the primary "bedroom" county of DeKalb, whites fled the expanding black population into southern DeKalb and beyond into Rockdale County; westward, where Atlanta University's large spread of black campuses gave the black community a cultural anchor, the black expansion came even more swiftly and whites fled their long-held neighborhoods to settle in southern Cobb County. In many instances, what had once been single-family homes for whites were carved into small apartments or rooming houses and rented to the blacks by absentee white landlords and exploiting real estate agencies. Meanwhile, as they fled to the surrounding counties, the whites, usually laborers and lower-middle-class families, carried with them a bitterness toward the black people and, by easy transference, a distrust for Atlanta. De-Kalb County, once headed by a progressive wing of politicians, turned conservative. The once rural lower reaches of Cobb County, which offered asylum to the white expatriates of western Atlanta, became a bastion of racially motivated white conservatism characterized by hate for Atlanta and any program of advance that Atlanta espoused. Southern Cobb County's abiding political theme became its recurrent "Stop Atlanta" drives. It was this new anti-Atlanta population which, in the mid-1960's, was largely instrumental in voting to exclude Cobb County from the regional pact that formed the Metropolitan Atlanta Rapid Transit Authority to be discussed later in detail.

The masses of blacks left in the city, meanwhile, found themselves repeatedly shunted about as the government needed room to build its expressways, its stadium, its civic center. Others were dislocated by other forms of urban renewal and, if they were lucky, found themselves in dreary public housing projects that bore no resemblance to the imaginative new skyscraper architecture they could see rising as the new downtown skyline, or the great rambling office and industrial parks locating in the distant suburbs. In the housing projects they begged for a voice in the city's public housing authority, and while their tenant associations were recognized after a time, their voices went unheard, their needs mostly unheeded.

In every aspect of city life the blacks found themselves receiving at best the crumbs of the new progress. Mayor Allen could boast that more than 22,000 jobs were being added to the area each year during his decade and that unemployment had slipped to a remarkable 1.9 percent at one point, but the fact remained that, according to the United States Department of Labor, the predominantly black inner-city areas represented 42 percent of all the unemployed male heads of households in the city, even though they represented less than 20 percent of the city's male household heads. The Atlanta Urban League estimated that blacks received only between 3 and 4 percent of Atlanta's white-collar jobs and represented four out of every five welfare cases. Blacks were the last hired, the first fired; they were virtually excluded from the highest-skilled and highest-paying construction-trades unions; "their" superhighway, the west expressway, was the last of the basic radial pattern built and served more to whisk Atlanta's white expatriates to town and back than to provide mobility for the inner-city captives. As in other cities, most of the new and better jobs were at the sprawled-out suburban plants—car assembly plants, Lockheed-Georgia's sprawling aircraft plant in Cobb County—where you couldn't go easily by bus.

Not only did Atlanta's blacks suffer at the economic table, they also continued to endure indignities at the hands of the "progressive" white leadership. In his first year in office, Mayor Allen erected a barrier across Peyton Road on Atlanta's west side to serve as a little "Berlin Wall" separating a white residential neighborhood from an expanding black neighborhood; only humiliation at the hands of the national press caused the wall to be quietly dismantled and removed.

A week before Christmas 1964, when the Reverend Dr. Martin Luther King, Jr., returned to the United States after receiving his

Nobel Peace Prize in Oslo, Norway, he was given a tumultuous welcome in New York City, was presented with that city's highest award, the Gold Medal of Honor, and was welcomed by Vice-President Hubert Humphrey, and in Washington, D.C., he met for about an hour with President Lyndon Johnson; but when he arrived at his home town airport aboard New York Governor Nelson Rockefeller's private twin-engine airplane, "Wayfarer," he was greeted by only a handful of friends from the black community and a few members of the press; welcoming him on behalf of Georgia's "moderate" governor, Carl Sanders, was a black state senator from Atlanta, and the highest-ranking Atlanta city official present was a black police lieutenant. Only after several weeks of private debate about likely repercussions was a biracial banquet held in his honor, largely at the initiative of the publisher of the *Atlanta Constitution,* the late Ralph McGill, and a rabbi, Jacob Rothschild.

Crowded along the spectrum between the internationally famous Dr. King and the unknown black people who lived behind the barricade erected on Peyton Road were the thousands of black families who suffered the daily indignities of second-class citizenship: street lights broken and not repaired; streets of gravel or chuckholes never resurfaced; garbage left uncollected in alleys; schools ill-equipped and overcrowded; police who did not protect but who harassed and talked rudely to blacks who stood around on sidewalks to escape the summer heat of the ghettos; police detectives who "raided" homes, broke down doors and intimidated the blacks for "information"; aides at the Grady Memorial Hospital emergency clinic who hurried to help white patients and left wounded and bleeding black men, women, and children waiting; landlords who evicted them without notice and without benefit of a hearing; a police court that disregarded the niceties of justice whenever a defendant was too poor to bring in an attorney, and judges that joked from the bench about the defeated men who came before them.

All of that led, inexorably, to the watershed year of 1966 in Atlanta. In 1965 Allen was reelected easily by the same white-and-black leadership coalition that had first installed him in office, but it was the last time that coalition would function successfully. It was the year in which Allen promised Atlantans that the racial explosion that had swept the Watts section of Los Angeles that summer could not happen in Atlanta, that racial harmony was too much a part of Atlanta's temperament to permit it. A year later few doubted that it most definitely could—and probably *would*—happen here. What was not so obvious was that once the thread of racial harmony in Atlanta snapped there would be long-lasting repercussions throughout the city. They would affect its politics, its government, its possibilities for regional cooperation and regional governance, the priorities the city leaders set, and the design of the city's public works programs, most notably its transportation network.

During the "long hot summer" of 1966, as cities went up in flames across much of the nation, Atlanta officials went about privately questioning each other on the state of affairs in Vine City. Police had their contingency plans, and special task forces were sent into Vine City to try to cool the summer with hastily devised programs of corner tot-lots, showers, street clean-ups, and garbage pick-ups. Everyone was certain that that small, crammed community of shanties on the hill across the railroad gulch from downtown's new skyscrapers would be the most likely to "blow." On September 6, 1966, rioting erupted, not in Vine City but in Summerhill, little more than a block from the new Atlanta Stadium grounds.

Mayor Allen came to the scene and walked with a grim face back and forth with the milling mob, appealing for reason, knowing too well that to the crowd he walked, talked, dressed, and looked like "The Man." When he tried to address the crowd from the roof of a police car he was shouted down with black power slogans, and a few blacks rocked the patrol car until the mayor fell off, rumpled but un-injured. The several hours of rioting that ensued left the area littered with glass, empty tear-gas canisters, and sore memories, and left the city with a soiled image.

On a rainy night a half-year later, at a meeting in a church surrounded by Summerhill's shabby houses, a black woman told the city's powerless Community Relations Commission, "We've been the step-child out here for so long. Why can't they just tell us we're illegitimate and stop asking us for taxes?" A commissioner asked what was most important to the people of Summerhill. Parks? Street repairs? Lighting? "We can't say that," the woman said. "No more than we can say meat is more important. Or water. Or bread. We've gone without for so long." And a man said, "When they first cleared the land up there they told us they'd put up housing, and then they put up the stadium."

Summerhill was not an exception. The same night that it exploded in rioting, another melee broke out in nearby Mechanicsville. Five days later three nights of mob violence began on the east side of the city. Homemade firebombs burned out stores and exploded under police cars. Atlanta's summertimes had exploded in flames and an-guish. In a sporadic, unpredictable pattern, racial uprisings occurred in succeeding summers, hardly ever twice at the same location—now at the heart of Vine City, now farther out in a cluster of apartments in a west-side community almost inaccessible on regular city streets.

Atlanta's blacks were attempting to tell the city's white leadership that they no longer *believed,* that they were fed up. They were declaring also that the polite black leadership that had for so long claimed to represent them to the power structure had done a far better job of representing the white ruling class to them. For years black students had marched in Atlanta's streets peacefully chanting their "Freedom, Now!" slogans, and the white leadership had failed to understand that "freedom" was not simply another sandlot park or a water faucet for cooling off in the summertime and "now" did not mean in a little while, that "freedom" did not mean another government study commission or program to provide jobs for more administrators and that "now" did not mean when white southerners could be educated to accept black southerners.

In April 1968 it was a tribute, not to the white leadership, but to the black community's deep love for its greatest citizen, the Reverend Dr. Martin Luther King, Jr., that there were no major outbursts of violence when 200,000 mourners, including the most respected political leaders of the nation, came to march side by side through Atlanta's streets behind the mule-drawn wagon that was taking him to his burial. It was Atlanta's saddest and finest hour.

None of this is meant to imply that racism and fear of blacks do not also pervade other American cities, regardless of where they are. It is because of the large numbers of blacks in Atlanta, and Atlanta's place in the South and its history, that no understanding of the course of events in Atlanta can be reached without a thorough consideration of the role played by the urban black community. The South *is* different. It has a history permeated by the black experience and built upon the subjugation of blacks. In the South, as much as whites fear blacks and flee from them to the suburbs, blacks also feared whites and had lulled themselves into hopelessness. If you travel through the South and stop in its dusty towns and speak to the black people, they will tell you they do not demand full voting rights and do not seek full integration of schools and better school facilities because "we have to go on living here," and they know that there will be retaliation by local whites if they demand full citizenship. It did not matter whether or not white retaliation *would* occur—and Atlanta's blacks knew too well the past conduct of police in the slums—the blacks of Atlanta and the South *believed* it would. They could see that, despite all its fine pronouncements of its status as a regional center and a progressive national city, Atlanta was not so much different from the rest of the South's towns. Deep within the core of its attitudes and responses, it remained a dusty, if overgrown, southern community. During its years of growth it had still found time to revel in a four-year centennial celebration of the war it lost, restaging the bloody battles, flying Confederate flags, and championing the right of white high schools to sing "Dixie." The blacks of the South know this, and only when it came time for Atlanta's blacks to outnumber its whites, only when Atlanta's blacks saw a *real* chance to control the conditions of their existence, did a growing number of them fling off the reticence and fear.

For those who cared to notice, the change first became apparent —irrevocably—in November 1968 referenda on the financing and construction of a modern, high-speed rapid transit alternative to the destruction and wastefulness of urban freeways. The history of the development of rapid transit before and since those referenda provides one of the best examples of how the city was governed, how it made its decisions, how it made its mistakes, and how it came to a changing of the guard.

The Atlanta Region Metropolitan Planning Commission, created by the state legislature in 1947 without federal incentives or assistance and the oldest publicly supported regional planning agency in the country, first warned its member local governments in 1954 that they would have to address themselves soon to the need for a high-speed public transportation system that could operate on its own right-of-way—rapid transit—"within a few years." In 1959 the commission, which had also had a heavy hand in plotting the city's exorbitant freeway network, again warned, "An auto-dominant system will never be able to carry radial loads adequately during rush hours, even with maximum possible use of expressway buses. Transit innovations, such as exclusive right-of-way rapid transit, will be absolutely essential and should be investigated as an immediate follow-up to this expressway study." Strangely enough, that expressway study was also recommending the addition of crosstown and by-pass superhighways to the already monumental program to carve up the city with concrete.

A year later the privately owned city bus company, Atlanta Transit System, Inc., advanced the city's first rapid transit plan—for a 16-mile, 59-million-dollar network of rails using high-speed, electrically powered trains. The following year the regional planning agency unveiled its own plan for rapid transit, a radial network of 60 miles of rail reaching into all five counties of the area and estimated to cost between $200 and $215 million dollars. The agency said that if preparations began immediately, the first parts of the basic system could go into service by 1967 and the entire 60 miles could be operational in 1969, "by which time the need for rapid transit will be keenly felt."

The Metropolitan Planning Commission's proposed radial system became the foundation for almost all future plans: one route northwest into the heart of Cobb County; a northeast line through DeKalb County's northern communities and a short distance into the more rural Gwinett County; an eastern spur through a more affluent section of DeKalb County around Emory University, and a major eastern route through East Atlanta, an area about to enter the throes of racial transition from white to black, and more urbanized central parts of DeKalb; a southern route along a commercial corridor extending to the mostly white suburban communities, past the Atlanta Municipal Airport and into the northern tip of more rural Clayton County. Only future lines for a "long-range system" were mapped for the city's most concentrated areas of black population, west and southeast of downtown. All of the lines would connect at a "transit center" downtown, three blocks from the city's largest department store, Rich's, owned by Richard H. Rich, a prominent member of the Atlanta power structure and named by Ivan Allen as chairman of the Chamber of Commerce's Rapid Transit Committee.

In 1962 the state legislature created a special Metropolitan Atlanta Transit Study Commission, a hand-picked group of eleven white men assigned the task of refining the Metropolitan Planning Commission's plan and producing a "master plan" by the end of the year. The study commission worked in secrecy, refusing to discuss publicly the system it was conceiving until it was prepared to publish its final report. It unveiled its proposal in December 1962—a more ambitious plan than the Metropolitan Planning Commission's, but not dramatically different. The study group suggested a 66-mile system to cost about $292 million dollars (not allowing for inflation—which became a key factor in public works ventures later in the decade) and to be built in three phases: initial operations were to begin in 1971 on 21.5 miles of track on the northeast and south routes; in 1975 operations were to begin on lines through black communities—the east line and, added to the Planning Commission's proposal, a short west-side line; by 1980, the full system was to go into operation. "Transit Center" was moved two blocks westward, diagonally across an intersection from Rich's downtown store.

That same year the state legislature also adopted an amendment to the state constitution authorizing the creation of regional transit agencies, and it was included on the general election ballot in November. It passed by easy margins in the Atlanta area, but it required a statewide vote; concern in other cities over local racial demands and threatened public control of "private-enterprise" public transit defeated the amendment. Meanwhile, an overwhelming majority of voters in the San Francisco, California, area were approving a property tax to build a 75-mile rapid transit system for that city's region. The import of the San Francisco vote was not lost on Atlanta. Spirits were up, it was the age of construction success in Atlanta, and local legislators tried again, this time drafting the amendment to apply only to the Atlanta region and, thus, requiring only a local vote. It was accepted by voters in each of the five counties in 1964. Atlanta's black voters gave their support, as requested; their alliance with the white power structure was not yet fraying.

In 1965, interjurisdictional discord raised its head when local legislators met to draft an act to create the Metropolitan Atlanta Rapid Transit Authority (MARTA), the agency that was to build and operate a modern, high-speed, automated rail transit system. For weeks a committee of legislators met at the state capitol at night and worked at compromises until the early morning hours. The key issues involved the apportioning of voting power on the board of the new agency. As drafted, the board would have had eleven seats—six for Atlanta (one each named by the Fulton and DeKalb County governments from their populations within the city limits) and one for each of the five counties. Atlanta insisted on its majority control; Cobb County insisted on two seats; a legislator from DeKalb threatened to scuttle the entire measure through local legislative courtesy rules unless the county received more voting power on the board; Fletcher Thompson, Republican state senator from Fulton County south of Atlanta (Fulton includes most of the city) astounded everyone by appearing early with a five-page list of changes he wanted in the proposed bill, most of them tracking mimeographed handouts being distributed by the John Birch Society, and demanded that at least one seat on the board be guaranteed to his geographical area of the county. (A year later the south Fulton Republican was elected to represent Atlanta in Congress, succeeding the city's sometimes-liberal Democratic congressman, Charles Weltner, who had resigned from his race for reelection rather than obey a party loyalty oath that required him to support the gubernatorial candidacy of racist Lester Maddox.)

A compromise agreement was reached with all legislators except Thompson after an impassioned appeal by the chief architect of the transit agency legislation, DeKalb County Senator Ben Johnson, the dean of Emory University's Law School. "Nobody wants to go it alone," he told his legislative colleagues from the metropolitan area. "We've just got to have something to go with. If we can't walk, we'll crawl, and if we can't crawl—we'll just sit and think about crawling. There are problems in the metropolitan area that have got to be

solved. I had hoped that the composition of this board for rapid
transit would serve as a prototype for solving other problems that are
metropolitan-wide."

The compromise agreed upon remained as constituted in Senator
Johnson's proposed eleven-seat board, except that Atlanta retained
only four seats and Fulton and DeKalb counties were increased to
two each with no requirement that one of each pair be named from
within the Atlanta city limits. More than one public official from
more than one local jurisdiction remarked that he had had to "swal-
low hard." With the help of rural legislators newly interested in state
office and city votes, Senator Thompson's obstructionist objections
were overridden on the Senate floor.

A provision written in at the insistence of suburban legislators
required a referendum in each area to determine whether that county
or city wished to become a member of the new Metropolitan Atlanta
Rapid Transit Authority (MARTA). Those referenda were held in
June 1965. Again the John Birch Society attacked, this time with an
essentially ineffective dial-a-message "Let Freedom Ring" campaign
that branded MARTA a plot to create a "private Gestapo" because
the legislation authorized the creation of a transit security force.
More effective, however, was the "Stop Atlanta" opposition from
Cobb County's south-side areas, the new conservative Young Republican stronghold of embittered white former Atlantans who, according to one legislator, "feel they were evicted from their homes,
so to speak, by the politics [blacks] of Atlanta." Cobb County was
the only jurisdiction to decline membership in MARTA, despite the
fact that it housed the largest single employer in the state—Lockheed-
Georgia, then a highly reputed aircraft builder with the United States
government's contract to build the behemoth C-5A cargo plane.
The company's employment at its Cobb County plant had fallen from
a high of 32,000 to about 17,000 by the end of 1971, but at its height
in the mid-1960's its suburban traffic jams were as bad as, or worse
than, downtown Atlanta's.

In January 1966, only a year before the original target date for
the start of rapid transit operations, MARTA became an officially
constituted agency. Its initial board, reduced to ten seats by Cobb
County's self-imposed exclusion, included as Atlanta's four appointees
Richard Rich, also elected MARTA chairman; L. D. Milton, a bank
president and the only black man on the board; Rawson Haverty,
owner of the leading downtown furniture retailing firm and a member
in good standing of the white power structure, and banker Mills B.
Lane. Roy A. Blount, president of a major DeKalb County bank,
and Dr. Sanford Atwood, president of DeKalb County's Emory Uni-

versity, were DeKalb County's appointees. MARTA's work was to be the work of the power structure.

Despite MARTA, the real work and the real transportation hopes of Atlanta were concentrated in the expressway program. The Chamber of Commerce had a rapid transit committee, but its highways committee was by far the stronger, even going so far as to publish its own monthly reports. Superhighways were given credit for inspiring the new downtown growth, but only in the small establishment of metropolitan land use and rapid transit planners were they also given sufficient credit for the increasing levels of pollution (it is estimated that automobiles account for more than 80 percent of the city's air pollution), for an approaching crisis in property taxes (50 percent of the downtown land space is turned over to expressways, streets, and parking), and for the accelerating suburbanization of retailing and employment. Massive shopping centers opened in the suburbs in every direction from downtown Atlanta, and downtown retailers were quick to suburbanize to the new centers: Lenox Square, Greenbriar, North DeKalb, Columbia Mall, South Cobb Center, to name but a few of the earlier ones. Nineteen suburban office parks opened during the decade of the 60's, and one of them became the nation's second largest. Expansive, land-gobbling industrial parks also spread out over the suburban landscape wherever the Interstates—and particularly the beltway I-285—went: in Cobb County, in Gwinnett, in the outer reaches of DeKalb, in Clayton. Despite the new skyscrapers changing the city's downtown skyline, most of the real growth in buildings and jobs was occurring in the suburbs.

The Atlanta expressway program had its genesis in a 1946 study that urged a simple north-south and east-west radial network of about 33 miles that it estimated would cost around 48 million dollars. Subsequent studies by the Atlanta Region Metropolitan Planning Commission and the State Highway Department kept adding to that, and by 1956, when the nation's Interstate Highway program was launched, Atlanta was ready with expressways programmed or in place southward, northeastward, and northwestward from downtown, and was continuing to map still more freeways in what would eventually become an even more ambitious superhighway program than that of Indianapolis—with a final price tag not yet calculated but likely to multiply the 1946 estimate by more than ten. Some 380 million dollars' worth of super-roads were programmed for the first half of the 1970's alone. Interstate 85 came southwestward from South Carolina, I-75 southeastward from Tennessee, and I-20 westward from the Atlantic coast. They all tied together in a massive downtown "connector" and an interchange that consumed some one hundred acres of top-value land just behind the state capitol on the edge of downtown. The "connector" was the last piece of the basic radial system built and opened, and it was not long before that mid-1960's opening that the downtown realized what expressway-sized traffic jams the new highways could bring, a traffic congestion that other cities banking on expressways, like Indianapolis, were yet to face.

In October 1969 Governor Lester Maddox, always ready to enjoy performing the antics of a court jester, rode on the hood of a convertible through a paper barricade to officially open the perimeter I-285, which formed a concrete noose around the city and tied together its suburbs. Well before then, however, highway planners had known that their superhighways were getting more traffic than they could bear, so they had several more in planning: an "outer" perimeter highway to relieve congestion on the new beltway Interstate; a major new north-south freeway to slash across east-side neighborhoods from beltway to beltway, made up of strange bits and pieces—from north to south, a North Fulton Expressway on a state-financed program to extend a superhighway out of Appalachia from the north end of Fulton County to the beltway, a Peachtree Connector to extend this to a crossing of the Northeast Expressway (I-85), an I-485 Interstate-funded bypass to the East Expressway (I-20), and another state-funded expressway to continue on to the south-side span of the beltway and, eventually, beyond to connect with I-75 in Clayton County; another north-south route for a west-side bypass, again mincing up long-established close-in neighborhoods; a special freeway east out of downtown Atlanta's "connector" to reach out to Stone Mountain at the far side of DeKalb County, a magnificent mound of granite where the Ku Klux Klan used to rally and where the state has now carved on the mountain's face the images of the Confederacy's heroes and built at its base a luxurious antebellum park; and various other connectors and bypasses to form an "inner" loop and neighborhood-slicing spurs. A master map of these grandiose highways built, programmed, and planned looks like a patchwork hodgepodge of tangled ribbons and swatches, looping here, crisscrossing in a grid there, and everywhere decimating the city topography with concrete rivers.

Some of the proposed superhighways are not included in the Interstate program, which receives 90 percent federal funding, so the state of Georgia has agreed to build them as toll roads—some 34 miles long, expected to cost about 190 million dollars; they include the state portions of the east-side expressway bypass, the Stone Mountain expressway, and an extension of an existing south-side freeway. If the routes should be added to the Interstate program, of course, the state may drop its toll-road plans, but highway builders are so anxious to get the superhighways built that their primary interest is to escape the long delays involved in federal financing and its prerequisites of hearings and other "controls."

In his book on the 60's, former Mayor Ivan Allen related a conversation that exemplified the highway-building pride of Atlanta and its suburb-dwelling leadership's failure to recognize the full implications of in-town super-roads. In early 1963 Allen was standing on a hilltop near downtown overlooking the urban renewal area that was to become the site of the Atlanta Stadium and trying to sell Atlanta to Charles O. Finley, the owner of the Kansas City Athletics.

> "What are those buildings down there?" he [Finley] said.
> "That's Five Points, Downtown Atlanta."
> "What's all that construction over there?"
> "Where four Interstate highways come together."
> "How big is the interchange?"
> "Thirty-two lanes," I said. "Biggest interchange in the South."

Though impressed, Finley never did bring the Athletics to Atlanta. The site became the home of the former Milwaukee Braves instead.

With such a promiscuous superhighway program in the works, it was no surprise that anti-highway sentiment surfaced. It happened in Morningside, one of the city's oldest and most stable neighborhoods of quiet, curving, tree-shaded streets and many exceptionally nice homes, a neighborhood of middle-class white families and retired and semiretired elderly persons who had lived in the community for much of their lives. The eight-lane I-485 is to slice through the neighborhood on its way toward the proposed tollways northward and southward to form the city's east-side expressway bypass. The Morningside–Lenox Park Association has been fighting the superhighway since 1965. At first residents only wanted it moved to one side or the other; the state highway department came up with four alternate routes, but each one promised to bring disruption and eventual blight to the neighborhood. Relentlessly the highway engineers moved on, despite mounting citizen opposition that boiled into stormy public meetings. Even the offices of a former state legislator and city alderman whose ward encompassed the area failed to win significant concessions from the state. In 1971 the citizens went to court, charging the state with failing to abide by federal laws covering environmental impact. They won a temporary halt to the condemnation of homes along a wide swath being bought by the highway builders, but their attorney warned them during the summer of 1971 that they would need more than court action to stop the highway: "I can only get you time," Michael Padnos told the citizens. He advised them to get the public support of the mayor, the governor, and other public officials. They were not likely to have too much success in getting high-level support. Only a few weeks later the power structure, under the standards of its Chamber of Commerce and its downtown component, Central Atlanta Progress, Inc., adopted resolutions calling for construction of the freeway at the "earliest possible" time.

A resident of the neighborhood told the attorney that Atlanta's mayor had told her he was "with us" but that "he isn't ready to say so publicly." Padnos retorted, "That's worth one lukewarm bucket of nothing." And a few months later the mayor himself proved Padnos accurate in his assessment. That came after another court decision and a resolution by the city's board of aldermen had gone in favor of the anti-freeway citizens: Mayor Sam Massell summoned the aldermen back into special session to hear pro-highway arguments and succeeded in getting them to rescind their earlier anti-highway stand.

Padnos also urged the Morningside citizens to recruit support from other neighborhoods in the paths of freeways. Their chances for recruiting support were considerably better in neighborhoods than in either the public or the private power structure. They could find enough likely allies on the west side, where black residential areas are to be chopped up by proposed freeways and toll highways, and even on the same north-south route as Morningside's I-485: a mile or so south of Morningside, residents had been trying to work with the state to alter exit and entrance ramp locations, but in 1971 had yet to recognize the full destructive effects the highway itself would have on their concerted efforts to revitalize what once was a declining neighborhood. They did join in a loose "coalition" with the Morningside group, however. Just south of those residents, another neighborhood being gulped up by the highway builders to construct a massive interchange for I-485 and the proposed Stone Mountain tollway presents further opportunity for building a broader urban opposition to expressways. Eastward, the Stone Mountain route is mapped to slash through the small city of Decatur on Atlanta's eastern boundary, where residents have insisted that none of the three alternate routes the state highway department is proposing are acceptable. The Decatur City Commission itself opposes the highway and allowed citizens to air their views at a town meeting. A young black man summed up the citizens' response to highway builders: "Let them take their asphalt and jam it on I-85 or I-75, but not on us in Decatur."

Allies in the anti-highway effort could also be recruited in the northern suburbs of Atlanta, because there, too, residents are getting vivid lessons about the community destruction that comes with highways. On Atlanta's affluent north side, where many from the city's professional class reside, many of the city's finer homes are in the path of the tollway that the state plans to pave as a link between I-485's eight lanes and the northern arc of the beltway. Already developers have come into the area hungrily seeking major commercial development opportunities, even though the North Fulton Expressway is presently stopped at the beltway without even an exit ramp to surface streets. Fulton County's government is more than willing to give the zoning and building permissions they need; its county commissioners feel that too much development has gone to other counties in the metropolitan area and that Fulton County's unincorporated areas have not cashed in enough on the flight from the city. (Fulton County Commission Chairman Charlie Brown, an old-time politician in the area who holds this view most adamantly since his west-side neighborhood became populated by blacks, might be surprised to learn the results of a Cobb County cost-benefit study which showed that every hundred acres of its bedroom community land developed in apartments has brought an average of $226,000 annually in increased taxes—but has cost the county an additional $351,000 in government services.)

As a result of these attitudes in the county's governing body and the eagerness of developers to reap profits from the coming of the highways, the wives of the north side's affluent professional men have been storming the county courthouse in Atlanta repeatedly to beat off rezoning that they feel will destroy the peacefulness of their neighborhood of large homes, spacious lawns, and wooded lots. In 1971 they were only beginning to address their attentions seriously to the tollway that will slice across those acres of rolling woodland and lawns and bring on more waves of developers. Just north of them, across the beltway in the unincorporated community of Sandy Springs, they have a lesson in point. There the white middle-class citizens of suburbia have been engaged in community planning and have repeatedly faced the same frustrating fights with public officials over the haphazard, sprawling development brought in by the North Fulton Expressway. "We've had nothing but trouble since the North Fulton Expressway was opened," a writer was once told by Dr. Eva Galambos, an economist who has been a leading figure in Sandy Springs local affairs. "We've had nothing but speculators and developers." As a result, Sandy Springs has become an ugly area of strips and clusters of commercial development, side-by-side small shopping plazas, large apartment conglomerates, service stations, and a swarm of parking lots. Residents who now fight the haphazard development that the superhighway has brought in its wake would have been better served had they focused on the highway itself in the first place; those residents living within the beltway could profit by the mistakes of Sandy Springs.

Other suburban allies for Morningside's highway fight are available on the northwestern edge of the city, where the perimeter superhighway flows not far from the Chattahoochee, once a lovely river extolled by poet Sidney Lanier in his "Song of The Chattahoochee" but now blighted by pollution, industry, and uncontrolled apartment and commercial development. In 1971 the state had contracted for construction of a new superbridge over the river, and developers won a zoning battle over planners' and residents' opposition to build a large apartment and commercial complex on the river's bank. Governor Jimmy Carter, sensitive to environmental issues, retaliated by canceling the bridge contract and calling for a moratorium on all development along the river until a land-use study could produce a development plan that would preserve as parkland what was left of the river's natural beauty, but residents of the area still had to go to court to get an order to stop the developers' bulldozers. Angry objections by Fulton County Commission Chairman Charlie Brown prompted one woman, Mary Day, to rewrite Sidney Lanier's poem in a letter to the editor of the *Atlanta Constitution,* lamenting the fate of the river once it left "the hills of Habersham . . . the valleys of Hall," two picturesque, rural counties in northern Georgia:

> In vain the pleas of the conservationists,
> In vain the friends of the river call;
> I've a date with a man who develops land—
> The hills are ripped open, the tall trees fall;
> Far from the hills of Habersham,
> Far from the valleys of Hall.
>
> A message floats in my polluted flood
> To the county commissioners, Brown et all.
> The mills of the voters grind slowly,
> But they grind exceeding small.
> We shall retire you to Habersham—
> Or why not go straight to Hall?

The battle was fought in the courts and newspapers until a compromise was struck that allowed development with some consideration for riverside beauty. Regardless of the ultimate fate of that particular site on the river, however, the exurban surroundings of Atlanta are hardly likely to escape more than a symbolic few of the developments urged on by growth zealots "Brown et all."

The highway fighters have still another, though obscure and unused, ally in a 1970 housing study by the Atlanta Region Metropolitan Planning Commission. Once the commission learned that a part of the area's critical housing shortage was due to the demolition during the 1960's of an estimated 34,000 homes, two-thirds of them inside the city limits, it adopted a set of policies that, though not mentioning highways, included this language: "Promote all appropriate actions to conserve existing housing resources and protect existing neighborhoods."

MARTA, too, could have profited by the disenchantment being bred by the urban superhighway program had it been ready to identify itself with the frustrated citizens—the urban "consumers"—who felt that their voices too often went unheard. Instead, MARTA chose the path of its pro-highway power structure creators, and left the citizens out of its deliberations. MARTA's staff was white; its board, led by retailer Richard Rich, acquired the habit of meeting privately at the Commerce Club to debate any questions and make its decisions before holding its required public meeting to rubber-stamp the decisions without discussion. The public was left unaware of the issues, if any, being grappled with by MARTA's directors.

Through 1966 and 1967, MARTA's primary task was the refining and updating of the 1962 master rapid transit plan to reflect the phenomenal growth and shifts in population taking place during the decade. Also, MARTA needed funds. Local governments were appropriating operating expenses and federal grants were paying for large shares of the planning programs, but construction money was another matter. MARTA sought—and in a state-wide vote in November 1966 received approval for—a constitutional amendment authorizing the state to finance up to 10 percent of the rapid transit system's construction costs.

While MARTA's consulting engineers were preparing their 1967 plan for rapid transit the privately owned Atlantic Transit System—like other citizens, unconsulted by MARTA in its rapid transit planning—unveiled yet another plan: "Rapid Busways." The company's president, the late Robert L. Sommerville, pointed out that his first plan had been presented seven years before and still "no trains are running, no final routes have been selected, no right-of-way has been bought; worse, in fact, is that no capital funds are in sight. Massive federal participation is so far a mirage. No methods of raising local shares have even been presented to the community. In a word, it is going to be a long time before any new system is in operation."

Sommerville's plan was to pave "throats" from suburbs to downtown for the exclusive use of buses as an interim measure. Eventually tracks could be laid along the busways for a rail system. In outlying areas buses would collect and distribute riders on regular surface streets, then use the special buses-only corridors for the high-speed trip to downtown. Sommerville said his proposed system of 32 miles of buses-only trunk lines would cost about 52 million dollars; he asked that a special test route be attempted linking Atlanta's east- and west-side concentrations of the black population's unemployed, underemployed, and domestic workers with the north side's white affluent employers of domestics and the outlying north-side industrial employment centers. Less than a month after MARTA's staff and consultants were asked to evaluate Sommerville's plan they returned with a recommendation that it not be implemented; they said the bus company had seriously underestimated costs and time requirements for land acquisition and such things as utilities and tenant relocations. Another major MARTA objection was that the bus company's proposal did not serve the 5.5-mile Peachtree Street corridor of offices and retailing—the white power structure's economic and investment base. MARTA's rapid transit plans were particularly designed around service to that corridor, the staff and its consulting engineers pointed out.

Later in 1967, MARTA's consulting engineers emerged from their private offices with their own plan. Again it resembled the basic radial system first proposed in 1961 by the Atlanta Region Metropolitan Planning Commission, to be developed this time in four stages, but with the noteworthy change that the black communities' east-west route would be started at the same time as the north-south routes. For the first time the inner city dwellers' need for better transportation was being given the same priority as the downtown investors' desires for development opportunities.

In 1968 MARTA targeted itself for a referendum on a bond issue in November, but not until early September did it reach its decision on how large a system to take to voters: a 40-mile route pattern that followed the same corridors as those recommended earlier by its consultants—east, west, south, and northeast from downtown—but limited only to Fulton and DeKalb counties. The routes would be built for 750 million dollars—a broad leap from the estimated 292 million dollars for a 66-mile system in 1962; inflation had taken its toll. According to the 1961 and 1962 plans, rapid trains were to be running by the end of the 60's; since that time some 2 million dollars had been spent in planning, Atlanta area voters had endorsed the idea of rapid transit in referenda in 1962, 1964, 1965, and 1966—and still no rapid transit construction was under way.

Of the 750 million dollars, it was estimated that 378 million dollars in local bonds would be needed, the remainder to come from federal and state aid. Deciding how to apportion that 378-million-dollar share among the local governments consumed another month of private debate and, at the end of September, the deadline for deciding whether or not the rapid transit bond issue would be placed on the November ballot, representatives of the governments of Atlanta and Fulton and DeKalb counties met behind closed doors in a conference room at the downtown Marriott Motor Hotel and at last reached agreement on a formula of cost distribution. This allowed but one month for a campaign to win voter support for the tax increases that would be necessary.

Nothing seemed to be done properly. When a black community delegation asked if there were to be any guarantees that blacks would have equal employment opportunities on the rapid transit construction projects, a MARTA official told them no. When they asked if a rapid transit spur line could be built to a public housing project, Perry Homes, in the northwest section of the city, they were told it was "under study" and that no decision would be made until after the voting. When a coalition of local black community leaders—those non-businessman black leaders who had arisen through the civil rights struggles of the 1960's—publicly announced opposition to MARTA's bonds, the manager of the Chamber-of-Commerce-financed "citizens' committee" directing the MARTA campaign dismissed them with the remark, "They don't represent anybody; we got our Negroes, too." (MARTA lost most of "our Negroes" to the coalition shortly before the referenda were held.) When union employees of the private bus company asked for agreements for MARTA's future employees, they were refused and as a result labor groups announced their opposition.

The citizens' "Committee for Rapid Transit—Now!" was a thinly veiled program of the Atlanta Chamber of Commerce, headed by the former governor, Carl Sanders, a businessmen's attorney from Augusta. The committee had no strategy for campaigning in areas where support would be hardest to get, in south Fulton and south DeKalb counties, where voters were conservative tax rebels and supporters of Lester Maddox and Alabama's George Wallace.

When Lester Maddox, then governor, went to Los Angeles and returned to announce that that city of 7 million seemed to get along fine without rapid transit, Sanders, his predecessor in the governor's mansion, declined to take issue with him publicly to point out his error. Los Angeles was to vote on a tax increase for rapid transit the same day that Atlanta was, and the city was always the first one cited by urban designers as the prime example of why cities should *not* be turned over to automobiles and superhighways. Helen Bullard, mastermind of Ivan Allen's mayoralty campaigns and now manager of the citizens' committee's effort, was bent on soft-selling the rapid transit graduated property tax increase. The Chamber's "citizens' committee" wanted no public confrontations with its opposition—but the tax-rebellious opposition was vocal and effective.

As though to inflict a final insult on the black community, MARTA saw fit to hire its first black employees only one week before the voting: a secretary and a black man who was to serve as community relations director. It was the community relations director's job to win back support from the black residential areas. One week was hardly enough time to reverse the antagonisms built up over a history of white power structure high-handedness. Intent on demonstrating that they would no longer follow meekly behind white leadership, black organizations refused to waver on the MARTA bonds. Ironically, this placed them squarely in the camp of their historical enemies—the south side's conservative, lower-class whites, who formed the bedrock of anti–power structure, pro–Lester Maddox support.

When the votes were counted, MARTA had lost in almost all areas. Inflation-squeezed middle-class whites had rebelled against tax increases; blacks had rebelled against white rule; Wallace-ite and Maddox-ite voters had rebelled out of anti-government instincts (MARTA was still a communist-inspired plot to create a "super-government," which by definition was evil). Only the power structure's small minority of voters in pockets of north and northwest Atlanta—those who had, in effect, created and governed the rapid transit authority—supported the bond issue. Inside the Atlanta city limits the vote was 58 percent against; in DeKalb County outside the Atlanta borders, 52 percent against; in Fulton County outside Atlanta, 64 percent against.

The significance of the vote count was not that black people had opposed rapid transit; they were aware that better public transportation was vital if the slum-imprisoned black people of Atlanta were to have a chance at the prosperity and growth occurring all around them —parks, schools, health care, jobs, suburban shopping. Much more to the point was that the blacks for the first time resisted the "way things have always been done" in Atlanta. No longer would they accept without question the plans privately drawn up by the white elite of the city; they had learned to say no—out of frustration, to be sure, but a unified *no* nevertheless.

Understandably, MARTA was upset. Richard Rich privately threatened to resign from its board until Mayor Allen and others of the power structure insisted that he stay on. (He resigned soon afterward, anyway.) Fulton County's delegates to the MARTA board insisted that it cut in half its appropriations requests for the following year's operating expenses, and MARTA complied. Mayor Allen suggested the creation of a broadly based citizens' "advisory" committee, but MARTA's board said that should be the responsibility of local governments. To trim expenses MARTA fired three staff members—including the two blacks hired the week before the voting—and when a group of black businessmen came to a board meeting to protest, Roy Blount, the DeKalb banker then presiding in Rich's temporary absence, brushed aside their remarks with a curt response picked up on radio and television: "If you had supported us, maybe we could keep them on the job."

To top off the board meeting—the first such MARTA meeting that actually included a public debate of the issues—several board members said the authority should go into "hibernation." Wounded, miffed at what it felt was lack of local government support, confused by the astounding defeat, and too tired to pick up its assigned duties of preparing a new rapid transit plan and carrying it through, MARTA tucked its tail between its legs and did just that, to await a new day.

The MARTA defeat also signaled disarray in the city's power elite. It had been starting earlier that year, in the liberal voice of the city, its morning newspaper. Eugene Patterson and Ralph McGill, the Pulitzer Prize–winning editor and publisher of the *Atlanta Constitution,* were having increasing difficulties with the ownership of their paper—Atlanta Newspapers, Inc., a subsidiary of the conservative Cox Enterprises based in Dayton, Ohio. Jack Tarver, president of the Atlanta Newspapers (the *Constitution* and the afternoon daily, the *Atlanta Journal*) and a key occupant of the inner sanctum of power in the city, was increasingly angered by the liberal bent of the newspapers' editorial pages, particularly the *Constitution*'s. In September 1968 the anger came to a head over a brief editorial column written by a young woman, B. J. Phillips, whom Tarver had repeatedly insisted that Patterson fire. The editor had just as repeatedly refused; he felt that her youthful and incisive voice on the editorial page gave it a broader base than otherwise prevailed. In September, when she wrote a column advising the public to attend a hearing to learn how the Georgia Power Company would seek to pass its war-financing income surtax on to its customers in the form of a rate increase, Tarver attempted to have the column removed from the paper. (He reportedly had warned earlier that Phillips's column should steer clear of the power structure's "big boys.") Patterson refused to remove the column and resigned to go job hunting. He stuck to his decision despite a hurried visit to the newspapers' executive offices by Mayor

Allen and Mills B. Lane, both interested in preserving for Atlanta's image Patterson's liberal voice. B. J. Phillips resigned that same day. A group of news reporters, the backbone of the newspaper's staff, also threatened to resign en masse until urged by Ralph McGill to continue on. In February 1969 Ralph McGill died at a private birthday dinner given in his honor. Within a few months, several of the newspaper's reporters had left, including its political editor, its investigative reporter, and its Washington correspondent.

By the turn of the decade there was also a massive turnover in the leadership of *Atlanta Magazine,* the slick publication that had trumpeted the Atlanta Chamber of Commerce's "Forward Atlanta" program to the nation's business community; aggressive, innovative, and liberal editors and writers were replaced by a team whose single common attribute seemed to be acquiescence in the ways and wishes of the power structure. As Opie Shelton, an abrasive and conservative man recruited from New Orleans to direct the Chamber's efforts of the 1960's, told the *Wall Street Journal,* the shake-up was due to "basic differences in philosophy." Earlier Shelton had pointedly told the award-winning magazine's editorial staff that its assignment was to "enhance the image and pride in which Atlanta is held by its own people and by the world at large." During the same period the Chamber's leadership was quoted as believing the magazine had become an island of liberalism feeding at the bosom of the establishment.

By 1971 Shelton had retired and Patterson's replacement as editor of the *Constitution,* a compliantly conservative southerner and former political editor named Reg Murphy, was lamenting in print that the Chamber had created a "mess" and that it was still trying to recruit a new executive director without a "clear indication of what the Atlanta Chamber wanted him to do." Murphy quoted a visiting city planning expert who had asked, "Is the rest of the city as confused about itself as this?"

The city wasn't, though the power structure of the 1960's most clearly was. Not only had it failed dismally on its rapid transit development dreams, it had lost control of its city. It proved itself unable to adjust to its city when it no longer managed the stage. The 1969 City Hall elections proved that strikingly. They signaled the completion of the changing of the guard in Atlanta.

In January 1969 Ivan Allen announced publicly what had been acknowledged privately for weeks: he would not seek reelection. While he did not say so publicly at the time (he didn't need to, it was known) he did confirm later in his book on his mayoralty that his "idea was to . . . pass the job on to some other younger member of the Atlanta business community"; clearly that was not to be his liberal, Jewish vice-mayor, Sam Massell, who had held the number two position at City Hall throughout the Ivan Allen years, who had won his elections with some of the city's largest vote margins ever—72 percent of the vote over five opponents in his reelection bid of 1965—and who had become popular in the black community for such actions as his public support for a young black attorney's race against United States Senator Herman Talmadge, a machine-politics relic from the rural, bigoted southern past. Allen, in his later book, said he opposed Massell because he had too little government experience, his vice-mayoral duties consisting of little more than presiding over the city's legislative body, the Board of Aldermen. Allen seemed to have forgotten that he himself had had *no* government experience before his election as mayor and that Massell had been credited with marshaling through the aldermanic board many of Allen's more important programs.

Maynard Jackson, the black attorney who had opposed Senator Talmadge, became the white power structure's choice for vice-mayor in 1969, but the white leaders had less success in selecting a candidate for mayor. Charlie Weltner, the former liberal congressman who had resigned rather than support Lester Maddox, had privately told Massell he would not run against him if Massell could put together a strong campaign. Others on the Chamber's list of "possibles" were relatively unknown business leaders—unknown, that is, outside the Commerce Club and its immediate environs—and their trial balloons drifted back to ground as soon as they were sent aloft. The chamber's choice fell to Rodney Cook, a young insurance man, an alderman and a state legislator whose political career had been characterized in large part by frequent leaps into public frays with loudly voiced, headline-making pronouncements that demonstrated his half-knowledge of the issues, a resident of the city's posh north side, and, strange for the Democratic power structure, a Republican. He was young, blond, and Anglo-Saxon. (Jews were also excluded from membership in the city's finest gentile private clubs.) Cook's selection came despite the privately conveyed warnings of the old-guard black leadership that they could under no circumstances accept him, largely because of his voting record on local zoning questions; the black leaders had come to Allen to help select a mayoralty candidate the black community could "live with" in order to try one final time to preserve the old coalition of establishment whites and assenting blacks. "This, of course, was perfectly satisfactory to me," Allen later wrote in his book. "That coalition had always been responsible for selecting and then electing candidates in the city, especially me, both in 1961 and 1965. . . . This was perfectly proper—the logical, traditional way to go about it. . . ." But when the white-anointed black leadership insisted that the choice not fall to Cook, the coalition fell apart. It was clear that in the white-black coalition, the white power structure insisted on calling the shots.

Massell and Cook were the front-runners in a field of four candidates and two weeks later faced each other in a runoff. Allen launched a telephone campaign to get out votes for Cook and, two days before the runoff, publicly called on Massell to withdraw from the race because of allegations of fund-raising among nightclub owners by his brother and a police captain. Allen states in his book that, without benefit of trial, "I found him guilty of mishandling the power he already had as vice mayor."

Massell won handily with almost 55 percent of the total vote. While Cook carried 73 percent of the vote in white precincts, Massell had 92 percent of the vote in black precincts. Once elected, he immediately became the butt of snide, anti-Semitic editorial cartoons in the once-liberal *Atlanta Constitution.*

Atlanta's governmental leadership had been overhauled by the elections. Massell, at forty-two, was the first Jewish incumbent and one of the youngest men the mayor's office had had, as well as its first self-described liberal; the vice-mayor was black; black representation on the Board of Aldermen increased from 1 to 5 of the 18 seats; Dr. Horace Tate, a black educator who had run for mayor and then endorsed Massell in the runoff election, was named chairman of the Board of Education. The new administration was to have a different style, one dedicated, as Massell put it, to the "quality of life." Blacks were named to the MARTA board, to other city boards, and to City Hall jobs. By mid-1971 the city's personnel director and its public works director were both black men.

Even the style of government was different. On a sunny summer morning Mayor Massell took an unannounced walking tour of Summerhill, chatting with residents on the streets, gathering large and small groups about him, and stepping in and out of the area's small shops. Later he disclosed that he was seriously considering establishing a special police precinct for the still tense area, as well as a community center and, possibly, a "little city hall."

Also typical of the new style was Mayor Massell's relations with garbage collectors, whose union had long been a thorn in City Hall's side. One morning Massell joined garbage-collection crews, donned their uniform, and worked beside them "because I wanted to find out what the union was bitching about." The primary complaint of the men was not dog bites or low pay but the rusted bottoms of garbage cans. "They couldn't go to the housewives who put the cans out," Massell said, "and they had to handle the mess that was created when the bottoms fell out, especially when it rained." To remedy the problem Massell had special fluorescent red stickers printed: "CONDEMNED—This Can Is Unfit for Storage of Garbage." After that, when garbage-collection crews found a rusted-out can on their rounds, they slapped a sticker on it and refused to pick it up again.

There were other changes, too. The starting salary for all city employees was raised to $100 a week; the police department was increased by one-third and its pay scale increased by 22 percent, with an additional 8 percent increase for college graduates; an archaic assumption that firemen and policemen should receive equal pay was finally broken to allow the police pay increase.

The skyscraping thrust of the city did not come to a halt, as some had feared. Massell proved that construction of buildings could continue alongside the "upbuilding of human dignity," as he termed it in his inaugural address. Indeed, the city continued to set new records of building construction permits issued each year. During Ivan Allen's last year in office the city issued building permits for $176,093,832 in construction—a record. In Massell's first year in office that record was broken by almost 3 million dollars.

The Woodruff Foundation donated (anonymously, as usual) 9.4 million dollars' worth of stocks for the city government to sell in order to purchase the city's choicest downtown block—1.7 acres at Five Points—and turn it into a park. A major developer of suburban office parks revealed that he was assembling some eight acres of shabbily developed land at the north end of downtown to build the city's largest single complex of office towers, a hotel, and retail stores, a complex to rival the 100-million-dollar Peachtree Center complex developed by John Portman during the 1960's and nationally heralded as the skyline symbol of the new Atlanta.

Also included in the downtown's continuing construction boom under the Massell administration was a 17-million-dollar sports coliseum for the Atlanta Hawks, the professional basketball team that had been playing at Georgia Tech's smaller facility. At the start of the 1960's such a project had been part of Ivan Allen's six-point program. (The coliseum, being built by Cousins Properties, owners of the Hawks, is to open in time for the 1973 basketball season.) Once the development package was put together and the coliseum planned for construction in the railroad gulch on the west side of downtown, Massell ran headlong into the power structure's style of doing business, a style that had left City Hall with the turning of the decade. The business leadership consulted the mayor's office about a ground-breaking ceremony and was told Massell wanted it informal, without speeches. Instead, the ceremony that was planned was to be attended "by invitation only," with specially engraved invitations, and was to include a luncheon at the Commerce Club and a round of speeches—including one by Mayor Massell—from an on-site portable stage. When Massell learned of the preparations he let it be known that he would probably have other plans that day. Instead, he planned his own ceremony for the day after the ground-breaking: an on-site "community party" without speeches, but with a basketball and backboard where throwing a basket would be worth a free ticket to the Hawks' opening game in the new facility, with gift bottles of dirt from the site, and with a general party atmosphere of peanuts, cokes, and fried chicken (Georgia's three main "crops")—all citizens invited. The business establishment decided to drop its ground-breaking plans and joined in Massell's.

It was in the field of rapid transit that the new administration most vividly shook the community out of its doldrums. Near the end of Massell's first year in office, MARTA had awakened enough to pose a list of alternative ways for financing rapid transit construction and asked local governments to choose. Local officials were unable to agree until Massell proposed that they seek a local-option sales tax from the state legislature—something often attempted but never received from the rurally controlled legislature during the 1960's—and use it to build rapid transit, buy the privately owned bus company and expand its service, and operate transit as a free-ride system. His no-fare proposal captured the imagination of the nation's press and public transit proponents, but it had to be diluted somewhat when attorneys pointed out that the legislation which created MARTA had specified that it build a system of transportation "for hire"—which didn't mean free rides. Local legislators prepared to take the sales-tax measure, now set at three-fourths of one cent on the dollar, to the state legislature, and in January 1971 Massell told Central Atlanta Progress, the power structure's contingent of downtown interests, "If you will but help us pass this tax program in the legislature in this session . . . I'll guarantee you the passage at the polls in a referendum of the general public . . . and I'll be back next year to call that last year's success."

A sales tax was regressive; it taxed the poor disproportionately, Mayor Massell agreed. But it would be the poor who would most ride public transit and, as he repeatedly pointed out, a reduction in fares to 15 cents from the 40 cents plus 5 cents for transfers charged by the Atlanta Transit System in 1971 would mean a weekly saving of $3 by each worker using public transit, more than enough to offset the sales tax. It won the support of most urban blacks and suburban whites alike.

In the Georgia House of Representatives the three-quarter-cent sales-tax measure was raised to a full cent at the initiative of the state's new governor, Jimmy Carter, a peanut farmer and student of urban affairs and planning from the unlikely town of Plains, Georgia (population about 500), who had been elected over former Governor Carl Sanders, the candidate of Atlanta's out-of-power white power structure. In exchange for the extra quarter-cent tax MARTA agreed to forfeit its 10 percent state aid. The measure passed and went to the state Senate where the presiding officer, the former governor and now Lieutenant Governor Lester Maddox, vowed his opposition. Governor Carter assigned his own floor manager to marshal the bill through and won passage by a mere two votes after conceding a ten-year limit on the tax to Lester Maddox. (After the ten years the sales tax is to drop to a half-cent.)

To secure adoption by the Senate, promises had been intimated—if not made outright—that the 15-cent fare would remain in effect for at least the ten-year duration. MARTA's staff, however, tried to steer away from such promises. With the annual 60 million dollars or more that the tax would bring, the staff saw an opportunity to finance an entire system on an almost pay-as-you-go basis, bypassing the need for costly long-term bonds. This, however, required that they not promise a ten-year 15-cent fare. The black community became enraged, and a coalition of its leadership presented a list of more than two dozen demands—including 35 percent representation in all MARTA operations (a Washington-imposed "Atlanta Plan" set quotas for black employment on federally financed construction jobs at 22 percent, based on the 1970 census, but the Atlanta Urban League still insisted that blacks in the suburban areas had been grossly undercounted, so it raised the level to 35 percent), a ten-year 15-cent fare, a rail rapid transit route to the still controversial Perry Homes project in northwest Atlanta instead of a MARTA-proposed "busway," other route alterations, and—a boon to the freeway fighters—"a moratorium on the planning and construction of all expressways and freeways through residential areas." The coalition now included both the old-guard black leaders, the new community leadership, and the city's vice-mayor, already bent on succeeding Massell as mayor.

As one MARTA staff member observed in mid-1971, "The politicians see only the politics, the transportation people see only the transportation." The two had to come to terms if MARTA was to mount a successful campaign that would correct the errors of 1968. Negotiations with the black leaders had to be undertaken and compromises had to be reached. MARTA had advantages now: increased black membership on its board, black participation on its new MARTA advisory committee, and a 32 percent black representation on its staff, including a new community relations director, Morris J. Dillard, who had led a school integration boycott during the 1960's.

MARTA promised a rail transit route to Perry Homes, equal employment for blacks in all its work and a 15-cent fare for seven years beginning with immediate purchase and improvement of the local bus system. While short of meeting all demands of the black leadership coalition, the concessions were impressive, and more than enough to save MARTA from a repetition of the 1968 debacle.

The system MARTA now offered to its voters in the full four-county area (Fulton, DeKalb, Clayton, and Gwinnett—Cobb still remained outside MARTA) was the outgrowth of a regional transportation study completed in 1969: 56 miles of high-speed rail transit extending east, west (including the spur to Perry Homes), south, and northeast, and 14 miles of busways reaching as branches from the rail lines northward along the median strip of the Peachtree Connector superhighway (should it be built), and north and south off the east line. The east-west line serving the "black corridor" would be the first ready, in five years; the north-south line would be ready a year later. The 1.4-billion-dollar package also included the immediate acquisition by MARTA of the private bus transit system, the addition of 430 buses to its fleet of 501, the establishment of eight new crosstown bus routes, eight new radial routes, and six new rush-hour express routes, and the construction of a hundred bus passenger shelters. MARTA estimated that 90 percent of all residents living inside the perimeter I-285 would be within walking distance of a bus route.

In contrast with the Chamber-directed 1968 attempt, the 1971 campaign was managed by politically sensitive elected officials and involved a wide range of citizens in an all-out speakers' bureau effort. Though well financed, the campaign seemed nonprofessional—just the tone rapid transit supporters had hoped to strike. Less than a month before the voting it seemed that MARTA would get an easy victory. Its own pollsters tabulated a 70–30 percent split among voters in rapid transit's favor. Then Atlanta's old nemesis raised its head again: race.

Bussing of children to achieve racial balance in schools was injected into headlines by outside court rulings. White Atlanta reacted with knee-jerk fear. Rapid transit's opponents were quick to strike the theme that rapid transit and public ownership of the city's bus system would hasten the bussing of school children. Racists even claimed that MARTA would be moving inner-city blacks into suburban public housing. MARTA's advocates protested against such tactics but by voting day they knew it would be close. Not until all results were in did they know how close. Had the important vote count been a single, four-county total, rapid transit would have lost again, this time by a dismal 99,158 to 110,182. Instead, an approval vote was required only in each of the two most urban counties—Fulton and DeKalb.

While the other two counties each voted almost 4 to 1 against the transit sales tax, DeKalb and Fulton voters saved it. In DeKalb County the margin was a narrow, but comfortable, 3,358 votes: 39,565 to 36,207. In Fulton County the final count was 53,793 to 53,322—a margin of only 471 votes! Beginning in 1972, the new sales tax for transit is being levied in the two counties; the remaining two will have to try again later. Bus fares are a record-low 15 cents, bus lines are expanded, but rapid transit has not yet gone under construction. Most important, Atlanta showed that it had yet to act as a region.

If anyone questioned that a modern, comfortable, high-speed public transportation network was needed for the Atlanta region, he need only look at what had occurred during the preceding decade. Highways had proliferated, carving up the city, alienating neighborhoods, creating artificial walls between peoples, and spreading the population and tax base of the city in ever-widening circles of suburban clutter, so much so that with the start of the 1970's, the Bureau of the Census decreed that two more counties be added to the Standard Metropolitan Statistical Area. While the five-county region's population had grown 37 percent during the 60's, its automobile population had soared 91 percent, mostly in the suburban counties—120 percent in DeKalb, 145 percent in Cobb, 155 percent in once-pastoral Gwinnett, and 194 percent in Clayton. The population was "moving out" on wheels.

As could be expected, the bus company, one of the country's most progressive and successful in earlier years, was suffering considerably at the hands of such an automobile explosion and was needing MARTA's rescue. The late Robert Sommerville had bought the company in 1950 from the Georgia Power Company, which had operated it mostly as a network of outmoded trackless trolleys. It was Sommerville who first planned a rapid transit system for Atlanta in 1960; who converted most of the bus company to "New Look" coaches and removed the unsightly overhead trolley lines during the early 1960's; who in 1966 was first in this country to propose, in a speech at an international meeting in Pittsburgh, that public transit be regarded as merely "sideways elevators" and offer free rides subsidized by the business community as a cost of doing business, just as are office tower elevators; who in 1967 proposed the busways plan that was scuttled in short order by MARTA, only to be revived in the regional transportation plan two years later—after Sommerville's death—and incorporated in MARTA's 1971 proposal to the electorate.

Sommerville, though the head of one of the city's most vital private enterprises, was never fully invited into its inner circle of business leadership. He was a public-minded businessman who recognized and tried to serve the needs of his major audience, the captive poor of the inner city and the domestic workers who lived east and west of downtown and worked north of the city. He was a rare figure in the bus transit industry's ranks of aging men no longer capable of innovation and ideas. He instituted express routes on the city's freeways, but the buses there also became mired in the same mounting traffic jams. He kept alive a special downtown "Shoppers' Special" shuttle along Peachtree Street at greatly reduced fares. He established a special, heavily used shuttle service for all stadium events.

Yet the bus company could not long survive under the rapid suburbanization and the overbearing dominance of the automobile and its inherent freedom of choice: freedom to ride in the type of automobile you choose, to travel at the time you choose, to listen to the radio program you choose, and to sit in the traffic jam you choose. In 1945 the company had carried 118 million revenue passengers; by 1964 it had fallen to less than half that. During the rest of the 1960's its progressive business practices enabled it to make small increases in its passenger counts, but by 1970 and 1971 it was falling again, by more than 5 percent a year. To meet rising labor costs it had been forced to follow the same practice that other bus companies used—fare increases. In 1963 basic fares increased to 25 cents, in 1968 to 30 cents, in 1969 to 35 cents, and in 1971 to 40 cents. Still, during its fiscal year that ended in April 1971, the company lost $185,700 on operations.

Special services were tried. With a federal grant it inaugurated a "Town Flyer" shuttle arcing through downtown between the large parking yards of the Atlanta Stadium at the southeast corner of downtown and the auditorium–civic center at the northeast corner. When the federal grant program expired, downtown businessmen agreed to pledge enough funds to keep the Town Flyers running.

Rich's department store, the only major commercial property south of what had come to be known as the "black wall" of Marietta Street (it bisects the prosperous north half of downtown from its more shoddy south half), entered into an unusual subsidy arrangement with the bus company in late 1970: the store pays a charter rate to double the number of buses on the low-fare Shoppers' Special route through the downtown area; additionally, patrons of these "Red Ball Express" buses are given special tickets which the store validates for free return trips. It was an attempt by Rich's to break through the new racial polarity of the downtown—blacks south of Marietta Street, whites north of it. In the past, large numbers of secretaries and other white-collar employees in the office buildings north of Marietta Street had come to Rich's for lunch and noon shopping; with the increase in the black population and the concentration of its activity in the south half of downtown, racial fears had been keeping the whites away from the store. To save white workers the fear of walking downtown's sidewalks at noontime, Rich's was willing to pay the bus company between $2,000 and $2,500 a month for the "Red Ball Express."

Meanwhile, the bus company was also being relieved—at least temporarily—of its city franchise taxes. Mayor Massell agreed to delay the bus company's payments on an interest-bearing promissory note. Unlike other cities, where public transit service has been severely curtailed to cut costs until public transit was limping to its death, the Atlanta Transit System had been able, with initiative, new ideas, and subsidy help from the federal and local governments and from the business community, to maintain its service routes. As a result, in 1972 MARTA was starting from a firmer foundation than its public agency counterparts in numerous other cities—Flint for example—were forced to start with.

With these developments, Atlanta is well on its way to providing, although belatedly, a modern alternative to in-city automobile travel, automobile headaches, and automobile pollution. Yet the city is still hamstrung by a failure to grapple with the need for a more logical government framework—something that should seem even more necessary and possible as a result of the region's long, arduous, and often frustrating rapid transit planning and implementing effort of the 1960's. Complicating any regional efforts in Atlanta, however, is the ever-abiding issue of race. With the black population now dominant in the city itself, whites can be expected to seek suburban retreats from the city in even greater numbers. Only a regional approach to government that realistically faces the fact that the region's population is really the city's population—white *and* black—can hope to bring the city together again.

Atlanta was first with regional urban planning, and at the start of the 1950's it became one of the first to take a small step toward regionalism under a Plan of Improvement which annexed large urbanized territories and entered into city-county contracts for the sharing of a few selected government services. But the creation of a Metropolitan Atlanta Council of Local Governments during the mid-1960's proved of little value: it served mostly in an advisory role, with the exception of regional police services of record-keeping and the setting up of a regional "Metropol" police communications network.

In 1966 the city tried a second major annexation—its largest and one of its fastest-growing suburban neighbors, the north-side unincorporated sprawl of Sandy Springs. A liberal-minded minority of the area's white population agreed that it should be annexed to Atlanta, but Sandy Springs's dominant population of conservative, middle-class, Republican whites refused to go along. They pointed out that Atlanta's black schoolchildren might come to their white schools, that their taxes might rise too drastically, that Atlanta in 1951 had annexed the area of Buckhead under the Plan of Improvement to help solve the city's problems but "the problems are still there" (caused largely by flight to such areas as Sandy Springs itself) and that they would incur "hidden obligations" if they "married" the city. Mayor Ivan Allen, out to debate the opposition at a Sandy Springs school one evening, was correct but scored few points when he remarked that Sandy Springs had "been sleeping in the same bed with [Atlanta] and they [*sic*] better go ahead and make provisions to marry it." Voters rejected the annexation in a special referendum.

By 1971, racism in the suburbs had grown even more acute. Court decisions required that school systems distribute black and white teachers among all schools equally, and massive transfers of white teachers to "black" schools and black teachers to "white" schools had followed in 1970 to achieve a balance. The same had been true in Fulton County outside Atlanta, but there whites accounted for some 90 percent of the population and most of the teacher population, so transfers had had minimal effect on school complexions. County residents were hardly inclined to annex themselves to the city's half-black population and become part of its school integration; additionally, though no court had even indicated that it might be necessary, even "liberal" suburbanites feared that the bussing of school children would soon be required to finally eradicate the city's dual school system, one kept in unofficial being by persistent segregated housing patterns.

"Bussing" became a red flag of racism and anti-Atlanta sentiments in the affluent northern suburbs. As a consequence, even some of the "liberal" pro-annexation voices of 1966 were by 1971 talking of suburban isolationism—despite their recurring skirmishes with a backward and unresponsive county government over zoning and related issues. "We're just tired of government," remarked Dr. Eva Galambos in 1971,"—at all levels." By then Sandy Springs had moved far away from any regionally logical approach to administration of the urban area's affairs. Its leaders were ready to incorporate it as a separate city or to annex it to some other municipality—perhaps Roswell, an old farming town farther north in Fulton County only recently approaching the age of urban living. Even Chattahoochee Plantation, a small community of some one hundred residents just across the Chattahoochee River in Cobb County, was mentioned not entirely in jest.

The concept of regional government should be nothing new to Atlanta. Consolidation of Atlanta and Fulton County governments was suggested as early as 1912, and more recently, the idea of metropolitan government was espoused both by the late Charles O. Emmerich, Commission Chairman of DeKalb County during an early 1960's era of progressivism, and by Glenn Bennett, now retired executive director of the then Atlanta Region Metropolitan Planning Commission.

A commission formed in the late 1960's studied the controversial possibility of merging Atlanta and Fulton County's school systems, but nothing came of it. Then, in the waning months of Ivan Allen's administration and the decade of the 1960's, the New York-based Institute of Public Administration did a $150,000 study that recommended a merger of Atlanta and Fulton County governments—an unrealistic plan that ignored the spreading master-bedroom communities in DeKalb, Clayton, Cobb, and southern Gwinnett counties but included within the proposed merged government the still mostly rural—and mostly white—areas in the far southern and far northern reaches of elongated Fulton County. The Institute's report received the endorsement of the lame-duck mayor, Ivan Allen, but not of mayor-elect Sam Massell, the black community, or most urban legislators. It was shelved without action.

The most significant new approach to metropolitan government for Atlanta came at the hands of a small band of young and innovative Atlanta-area legislators first elected in 1968. During the summer of 1969, three of them toured Toronto, Canada, Minneapolis–St. Paul, and San Francisco and returned to write legislation for an "umbrella" regional administrative and planning unit patterned after the one they had studied in the Twin Cities of Minnesota. They made one tactical error: they included the Twin Cities' provision that permitted the "umbrella" to levy a quarter-mill property tax—just enough for opponents to label it with that old bugaboo—"supergovernment." While it was reported favorably to the floor of the Georgia House of Representatives in 1970, it was subjected to a resounding defeat. The 1970 legislature did give the small band of legislators a few stepping stones, however: it adopted legislation that required the state government to set up regional planning and development councils throughout the state, not as the customary voluntary pacts between local governments, but as state-imposed and state-defined commissions responsible for reviewing development and approving plans for receipt of state aid—unheard of in Georgia before the planning-student governor, Jimmy Carter. It also created a new standing committee on State Planning and Community Affairs in the Georgia House, to include as chairman and members a significant number of the progressive Atlanta area legislators writing the regional "umbrella" legislation, and it set up a special study committee of those legislators to draft a new "umbrella" bill for the Atlanta region.

The study committee's chairman was Howard Atherton, mayor of and legislator for Marietta in suburban Cobb County and chairman of the Metropolitan Atlanta Council of Local Governments, and it included among its members the key legislators who had worked with him in drafting and engineering the first "umbrella" bill: Gerald T. Horton, an urban planning consultant, Mrs. Grace Hamilton, a black woman, and Sidney Marcus—all of Atlanta—and Larry W. Thomason of DeKalb County. They distributed copies of their legislation to other committees, the involved regional agencies, and local officials, redrafted repeatedly to meet objections, and carefully excluded such objectionable material as taxing powers and control over local zoning decisions; they also steered clear of describing their proposal as an "umbrella" or a metropolitan government prototype. Reminiscent of Dayton's alphabet soup merger attempt, their new agency was intended to merge the Council of Local Governments, the Metropolitan Planning Commission, and the Metropolitan Area Council on Health. It was primarily for planning, coordination, and review, they said. The Metropolitan Planning Commission was already serving these functions, but it did not qualify under the new 1970 law for state-imposed area planning and development commissions: half its board members were not elected officials (all were appointed) and consequently it was not authorized to review programs for state aid. The drafting legislators said the new commission simply would do for Atlanta what the state law had done in 1970 for the rest of the state. The legislation was adopted without difficulty. When Governor Carter signed it into law, Representative Sidney Marcus presented him with an umbrella, and soon umbrellas were appearing everywhere—on office doors and, auspiciously, hanging from the ceiling over the desk of Glenn Bennett, the retiring director of the Atlanta Region Metropolitan Planning Commission that was to pass out of existence, submerged within the new Metropolitan Area Planning and Development Commission.

It was with good reason that, at the closing of the 1971 session of the Georgia General Assembly, Atlanta's first self-styled liberal mayor, Sam Massell, erected a billboard on the front lawn of City Hall facing uphill to the gold-domed state capitol. With a batch of new legislation that included the local option 1-cent sales tax for transit, the umbrella bill and several other state assistance measures safely written into law, the billboard read simply: "Thank You, Georgia Lawmakers."

An "Abolish Atlanta" movement, the city-county consolidation attempt, the city-county school merger effort, and the Sandy Springs annexation referendum had given rise to considerable public furor and acrimony, even though each was at best a fractional step toward improvement in public administration of the Atlanta community's affairs and, as a result, each came to naught. Ironically, the seemingly innocuous "umbrella" bill, though it encountered some old-guard opposition, managed to gain the support of everyone from the whites of the state's farm communities to Atlanta's City Hall and almost all black leaders and black legislators (with the prominent exception of Vice-Mayor Maynard Jackson and his closest allies) and contained within its provisions the vehicle for true regional government built on a logical framework that meets metropolitan-wide needs. While it remains too weak to involve itself in zoning or taxing and cannot directly control member government actions, it does have increasingly important review powers that can determine whether or not crucially needed state and federal aid will be forthcoming for any project.

The breakthrough that represents its primary and future strengths, however, lies in the form and makeup of its board. By law, the commission consists of the County Commission chairman from each member county, the mayor of Atlanta, one mayor from each county chosen by a caucus of the mayors within that county, a member of the Atlanta Board of Aldermen, and appointed non-officeholding citizens named from special districts equal to one less than the total number of elected officials on the board. Thus, with a five-county area, twelve board members are County Commission chairmen, mayors, and an alderman, and eleven are selected from special districts. The citizen districts were carved by a caucus of legislators from the affected counties, and the citizen appointees were elected by the elected-official members of the new umbrella agency—a division of powers agreed upon to remove the final opposition to the measure by a reviewing committee that had insisted that the new agency was to be "umbrella government—pure and simple."

Most significant, however, was that the law provides that, as the Census Bureau increases the size of Atlanta's Standard Metropolitan Statistical Area (as other counties become increasingly dependent on Atlanta economically and culturally by virtue of spreading bedroom communities), so also is the new Metropolitan Area Planning and Development Commission required to grow. Thus, no sooner had the new commission entered into its first year of official existence than it was required by the results of the 1970 census to expand from five to seven counties to keep up with the Atlanta urban community's expansion along the freeway corridors.

Even the carving of the citizen districts is a notable departure from the history of petty local jealousies that once led the then local senator, Fletcher Thompson, to insist that one MARTA board member be appointed from his south end of Fulton County. The legislators who carved the districts made sure that as many of them as possible crossed a major jurisdictional boundary—either a county line or from the City of Atlanta into a county area, and in many cases both. Thus it was possible to name four citizen members to the initial board from predominantly black areas of Atlanta, their districts to cross over into white suburban areas, including the south-Cobb County area of embittered Atlanta expatriates. (Three black citizens and one black Atlanta alderman were named to the initial board, giving blacks but one seat less than what they would require to match their 22 percent share of the region's population.) The rationale for cross-jurisdictional gerrymandering was simple: it was an attempt to require that citizen members speak for more than their own home communities, that they represent areas with a wide range of regional problems. Time would tell whether the drafters of the legislation had succeeded.

The new commission has also an additional virtue: given a situation that needs dealing with—drugs, water and sewerage, airport development, even rapid transit—the commission provides a place to assign it, and the commission is required *by law* to deal with it; it cannot spin away its duties to some other agency, as was done with the rapid transit program of the 1960's by the Metropolitan Planning Commission; given a crisis, the commission can quickly become the vehicle for regionalization of government. Sadly true is the fact that in all but rare cases regional government has been a reaction to crisis and not a well-thought-out program to meet needs. Atlanta now has a vehicle that can, if it will, meet the crises and grow eventually into a viable regional government.

Atlanta during the 1960's was too busy growing to pay adequate attention to its social needs. True, the economy needed strengthening with major investment and construction of new facilities to provide the taxes and employment an expanding city needs, but it left a legacy born of the undemocratic manner in which the power structure's high-speed growth program was carried out, and a legacy of the failure to recognize the human needs of the larger and growing population that was more impressed by street lighting than stadium lighting, more interested in a voice in its government than in playing sidewalk superintendent to a new skyscraper, and more excited about preserving home and neighborhood than about another superhighway interchange or a cavernous auditorium complex. Atlanta during the 1970's is trying a different tactic—growth with attention to little-league people instead of temples and monuments to the major leagues of business, sports, and "culture." Success will require a new spirit of cooperation between city and suburbs, a cooperation not yet evident under the heat of racial polarization. It is to be hoped that the newly developing regional rapid transit alternative to city- and neighborhood-destroying automobile travel and the "umbrella" planning and development agency can serve as vehicles to finally eradicate the racism that threatens Atlanta's future and to build instead a true urban community out of the estranged fragments that now exist.

5
Washington: Our National Urban Policy

The nation's capital has many cities in it. There is the Washington of the tourists: the Washington Monument, the White House, the Lincoln and Jefferson memorials, the Kennedy Center and the Kennedy brothers' graves, the Capitol, the Mall and Reflecting Pool, the Smithsonian, the long lines waiting in the summer humidity, the street-corner vendors of balloons, mementos, ice cream, soft drinks, and hot dogs, the eager expectations of meeting a TV news personality in a hotel elevator. There is also the Washington of the headlines: committees in debate, votes on "the floor," the press conferences and presidential proclamations, intrigues and rumors, the lavishly overladen and overrated soirees of the glamour set, the embassies, the demonstrations. There is the Washington of the thousands of civil "servants" who go to cocktail parties that are not written about in the society pages; the Washington of the many who strive for power, which everyone recognizes is the name of the game there, who trust no one, who do not smile an honestly friendly smile or say "hello" on the streets, who "deal" each in his own large or small way, each playing lobbyist for his own cause—a federal or foundation grant, a program, a promotion, a job, a consultantship (My God, how many consultants they have in Washington!), a fashionable wife, or an "up-and-coming" husband. There is the Washington described at the start of this book, the city of neighborhoods filled with people striving, working, and playing in a turmoil that might be the world's best polyethnic, social, and economic mix. And there is the black-and-poor Washington of frustrated hopes, dingy alley apartments, disease, poverty, rats, low wages, joblessness, poor schools, anger, bitterness—the Washington that exploded in rioting which frightened the nation the night the Reverend Dr. Martin Luther King was killed.

Washington is a blend of all these parts, and all are there because the city is the nation's capital. The single fact of the federal presence pervades every activity of the city—government, business, social life, social unrest, social action, finance. The federal presence accounts for the waves of black migration that made it the nation's first large city with a predominantly black population. The federal presence accounts for its chronic lack of funds. The federal presence accounts for the proliferation of tax-exempt organizations, the large assembly of national institutes of and for everything, the overwhelming domination of the region by the office-worker class. The federal presence brings to the city large demonstrator groups anxious for reform, be it prohibition, bonus payments for World War I veterans, jobs, women's suffrage, civil rights for blacks, or an end to a war, and the city is forced to make preparations for receiving them, housing them, policing them, providing health care and sanitation for them, and cleaning up behind them when they leave. Above all, the federal government rules the city and makes of it, in the phrase of the home-rule bumper stickers, the nation's "last colony."

The Congress and the President have ruled the city directly and totally since 1874, but even before then the federal government made the major decisions affecting the city. Its location on the marshy bottomlands beside the Potomac River was a compromise reached over a dinner table by, among others, Thomas Jefferson, the secretary of state, and Alexander Hamilton, the secretary of the treasury, in 1790. Its original design as a city of wide boulevards, public circles, and "magnificent distances" was the work of Pierre L'Enfant, a French planner hired by the new federal government and then fired by President George Washington because he thought the planner too meticulous in drawing his maps and charts. The President was impatient to get on with building the new city to keep at bay the speculators he feared would buy up the most valuable land in the mapped Ten Mile Square. (The speculators, however, were less than interested, and even a syndicate of buyers who came to the rescue to buy land unneeded by the federal government went bankrupt a short while later.) The first of many major alterations in L'Enfant's basic plans came at the hands of another impetuous president, Andrew Jackson, who in 1833 decided to settle a long dispute about the location of the Treasury Building: he stormed from the White House, planted his cane nearby, and declared, "Right here is where I want the cornerstone." It was built there, and it has ever since blocked the White House's view of the Capitol—some may argue in more ways than the physical. L'Enfant's plan had called for a long, boulevard-like Pennsylvania Avenue stretching open from the White House to the Capitol; the Treasury forced Pennsylvania Avenue to make two right-angle turns before continuing on its way to the Capitol grounds.

Since 1874, federal dominion of District affairs has been even more heavy-handed, reaching into every aspect of local life. Congressional committees have spent hours closely examining such "issues" as the hiring of a city clerk and the cost of building toolhouses for street cleaners. Dominated by rural politicians and, most remarkably in the last several decades, *southern* rural politicians, the congressional committeemen who most control local affairs have demonstrated a consistent lack of knowledge and understanding of urban affairs, a cavalier attitude of unconcern for such understanding, and a zeal for exploiting the District of Columbia for their own political, financial, and ideological ends.

The nation's government was never designed to be a local government. Quite the reverse—it was designed as a federation representative of the broad spectrum of communities in the country. That such a government took on the assignment of administering local affairs for the District of Columbia is a historical anomaly that affords a concrete lesson in how the nation looks upon its cities—and why, at base, its cities are failures. As both the home and child of the national government, Washington is the storm center of the nation's domestic issues and a crucible in which the ingredients are melted together into a compound that is, if anything is, a reflection of our true national "urban policy."

In May of 1800, when the first sloops carrying the government's records from Philadelphia docked between Georgetown and what was to be the nation's capital city, Washington was a village of 372 buildings, 3,210 residents, and muddy roads built on the Potomac River's marshy tidelands. Within the first few years the infant city faced the problems it was to endure for the rest of its life: the federal government brought laborers in to build the new government buildings—the Capitol, the executive "palace"—but had to lay off men when it ran out of funds; in 1802 more than 40 percent of the new city's revenue was used for relief from poverty among these transients, a responsibility usually assumed by the states (Elizabethan English law had shielded cities from responsibility for the "transient poor") but not assumed by the Congress despite the fact that it had brought the men to Washington in the first place and was, in fact, the "state" government for the District of Columbia. Additionally, so much of the most valuable land was being held in reserve by the federal government, and as such was exempt from taxation, that by 1804 the city was unable to raise enough money to provide necessary services and had to borrow funds. It was hardly the last such occasion, and only as the city government repeatedly tailspun into debt during the succeeding decades was the Congress prevailed upon to bail it out with emergency grants or loans.

The same month that the federal government arrived with its documents to set up shop in Washington, the city's first reported public transportation system began operations. Horse-drawn coaches began twice-daily runs from what is now the heart of Georgetown—a much older and at that time more stable town and, because of its higher and drier terrain, the residential choice of most of the first congressmen and executive officials—past what is now the White House and down Pennsylvania Avenue (at that time an open bog) to a tavern on the site of what is now the Supreme Court on Capitol Hill. That Georgetown-to-Capitol-Hill corridor became the first area of urban development, a fact that was to beleaguer the east side of the District with neglect for the next 170 years.

Not having a direct effect on land development, but having perhaps the most significant effect on the city's future economy, was another transportation decision. City leaders determined early that they could best build a strong economic base free from the vagaries of federal government by carving a barge canal beside the Potomac over the mountain ridges to the fertile Ohio River basin. They reasoned that this could turn the city into a major port for transoceanic commerce in the nation's produce. During the entire first half of the nineteenth century they repeatedly tried to dredge the canal, but silt and mud just as doggedly clogged it. Still they persisted, in a race with Baltimore for seaport leadership. While Baltimore, thirty-five miles northeastward, banked its hopes on the railroads, Washington futilely poured its limited funds into canal development and, in a final crippling blow to its chances in the race, even refused to permit locomotives to operate within the city limits until 1852; up to that year trains had to be drawn by horse from the city limits to the terminal near the Capitol. Baltimore became the major seaport, and Washington's economy became ever more reliant on the federal establishment.

The first great wave of change to strike at Washington came during and immediately after the Civil War. Once attacked and burned by the British with little resistance, the city was now ringed by a system of forts. Bread was baked in the basement of the Capitol to feed the Army of the Potomac. Thousands of soldiers came through on their way to war, then returned wounded and bloodied. A triangular area between the White House and the Capitol became a red-light district for "Joe Hooker's Division." During the six decades before the war the city's population had grown steadily from 3,200 to 61,000, and while its black population had steadily increased from about 750 to almost 11,000, fed largely by freed slaves who were forbidden to remain in Virginia more than six months, the black share of the population had slipped from 28 percent in 1810 to 18 percent in 1860; in 1870, after a decade of war and "reconstruction," the city's population had swollen to almost double—to 109,000—and almost one-third of its population was black. The blacks had come out of the South to reap the fulfillment of the promises embodied in the Emancipation Proclamation.

Washington's older families and small merchants feared the economic strain placed on the city by the new residents, mostly poor and uneducated in the ways of the city. Their city had been turned overnight from a quiet town of a few scientists, government aristocrats, high-ranking military officials, artisans, tradesmen, and clerks to a city of racial fears, squalid shacks, control of financial institutions by new and ambitious businessmen from New York and Philadelphia, and Reconstruction Republicans bent on making the District of Columbia a proving ground for racial equality. In December 1865 the whites of Washington and Georgetown voted 7,056 to 35 against black suffrage; if they were not able to control their own society and economy, they were not going to let the newly freed slaves control it either. Still, the Reconstruction Congress forced integration of public facilities, including a brief experiment in integrated schooling, and gave the vote to blacks in the District.

Dismayed and appalled by the change that had swept their once-peaceful settlement, the city's long-term residents willingly acquiesced in 1871 when Congress decided to assume control of local affairs. An 1869 newspaper editorial, cited by Washington's Pulitzer Prize-winning historian, Constance McLaughlin Green (*Washington, Village and Capital, 1800–1878,* Princeton University Press, 1962), portrayed the eagerness of the capital city for a return to stability, in any form: "If it works badly it would be easy to return to a charter government. . . . The citizens of Washington would like a change." Washington's citizens have never since been able to make that "easy" return to home rule.

In 1871 the city charters of Washington and Georgetown were abolished by Congress, and in their stead was created a "Territorial Government" to rule the entire District of Columbia. Its governor and upper legislative chamber were appointed by the President, and only the lower house and a non-voting member of Congress were popularly elected; Congress retained the right to annul any act of the territorial legislature. Before the creation of the new government, blacks, elected by the new Reconstructionist population of the city, had held six of the seven seats on the City Council; after the new government was installed they were elected to only two of the twenty-two seats in the district-wide elected chamber.

Both elective and appointive posts in the new government were filled by Republicans who immediately unbridled the spoils system, expanded the local civil service from 160 positions to about 400, and used the new jobs as political plunder to distribute to their friends. It took only three and a half years for the Territorial Government, led by its overzealous public works director and second governor, "Boss" Alexander Shepherd, to bankrupt the District. Squandered public funds, massive but hastily and poorly planned public works projects, spoils system contracts, high taxes, incredible fiscal irresponsibility, and a rigged bond-issue referendum combined to bring on an economic crash in 1873. Jay Cooke's bank closed, and his brother resigned as territorial governor; the local treasury was bare, and civil servants went upaid. In the face of such collapse President Ulysses Grant named "Boss" Shepherd the new governor. When a congressional investigation the next year discovered that Shepherd's irresponsibility had sunk the District almost 19 million dollars into debt (almost twice the congressionally permitted debt ceiling for the District), the Territorial Government was abolished and the federal government assumed complete control. In despondency, the District's residents again tacitly submitted as Congress took away their right to any voice in government. Once again the city's landholders were prepared to give up what little vote they had retained rather than give the franchise to the propertyless, the poor, the black, and the transient who filled the city.

Under the new governmental form, the President appointed three commissioners, and Congress acted as the local legislature, busying itself with the mundane matters of local governance—budgets, personnel, ordinance-writing. In addition, the federal government assumed half of the debt incurred by the Territorial Government and promised to pay half the costs of running the District's new government, since the federal government owned half of the District's assessed property value. (The latter was a promise not kept by the Congress.)

What had emerged from the turmoil of Civil War, Reconstruction, and Territorial Government was the city that was to remain to the present. "Boss" Shepherd had cleaned up the front yard of the city, had paved and lit its front streets, and had installed sewer lines, but his work on the marble front of the city, at which tourists still marvel, concealed the rot that was creeping across the city's back yard: alley shanties, disease, squalor, poverty, unemployment. To complete the preparations for modern Washington it remained only to open the suburbs.

Once Congress took control away from the public, the process began in earnest; conditions were at last right for the exploitation of the land. The city, once confined to a small geographical area on the flatlands beside the Potomac, now officially included the entire Ten Mile Square mapped by L' Enfant (except for a one-third trans-Potomac portion ceded back to Virginia in 1846), and most of it was open land on higher—and drier—terrain. After the Congress had organized its new committees to oversee public affairs throughout the area, seats on those committees became eagerly sought plums: a congressman on such a committee would have valuable foreknowledge of public works ventures that could bring handsome rewards to those interested in land speculation and development.

Additionally, the city had its new financiers who had come from the North after the war, and they, in league with realtors and developers, were bent on reaping the profits of development. Together in 1889 they organized the Board of Trade. Initially the board turned its attentions to basic community research, but it never succeeded in developing any understanding of the working classes or of the teeming black slums behind Washington's marble face. Within but a few years the Board of Trade was confining itself primarily, and then exclusively, to the interests of developers and their financiers and to the preservation of a stable, healthy governmental environment in which the wealthiest could go about business as usual. This was best accomplished by establishing a close working relationship with the new congressional committees, to their mutual benefit, and within two years of the Board of Trade's formation it became generally acknowledged that its advice was sought privately on most District matters and that even the District's commissioners owed their appointments to the Board of Trade. The board itself, meanwhile, was ruled by a small number of the business leadership's top strata, not unlike Atlanta's power structure. They were the directors of the seventy-seven major development companies, banks, and utilities, many of them often holding key positions in the directorates of several of the companies. In the second volume of her history (*Washington, Capital City, 1879–1950,* Princeton University Press, 1963), Constance McLaughlin Green described the Board of Trade as an organization "ruled by a handful of men for the sole benefit of real estate speculators and the bankers who financed them." During that turn-of-the-century era the same could also have been said of the congressional committees to which the government of the District of Columbia was entrusted. With such control vested exclusively in the hands of a few financiers and their willing colleagues on a few congressional committees, Washington experienced an unprecedented real estate boom that continued almost unabated to World War I.

At first the new suburbs were developed haphazardly. They were not coordinated with the District or with each other. If street patterns in the new developments happened to tie in with the older city street grid first plotted by L' Enfant, it was mere accident—that is, until the Congress, belatedly in the 1890's, ordered that all further streets in new developments be patterned after those in the city proper. Thus, it is not unusual in the Washington of the 1970's to find upon reaching the old city limits that numbered streets often crook and twist from their paths, sometimes dead-ending altogether only to begin anew several blocks away but probably not in direct alignment with the streets closer in.

Anxious to harvest the largest possible profits from the lowest possible investments, the developers of the late nineteenth and early twentieth centuries were also crowding the highlands of the District with the narrow brick row houses that now give Washington its distinctive residential style and appearance. But in 1909 the *Washington Post* was still lamenting "the lack of foresight, in some quarters, that is permitting the erection of so many unbroken rows of houses in localities that ought to be filled with detached residences surrounded by green lawns." That same issue of the *Post* (December 5, 1909) gave a detailed description of the suburbanization that was spreading over the District:

> Where yesterday were vacant lots and virgin groves, today stand substantial homes and around them what were by-paths and rough roads are now paved streets and avenues. The surface (rail) car lines have crept farther toward the ever-receding city's edge until

at the present time full loads of passengers are drawn in both directions past points which only a very short time ago cars passed practically empty . . . . Every day the city is reaching out, reaching out, not in one direction only, but in several. As above stated, what are now thickly populated resident districts, built up solid with handsome dwellings, were a very few years ago vacant tracts entirely outside of the city proper. Gradually the Capital is creeping up to and over the Maryland line, into Montgomery County, into Fairfax County [Virginia] and out farther and farther to the North.

During that same era Congress issued two orders that were to have long-term influence on the design of the urban community. In 1899 it restricted all buildings in the District to a height of approximately twelve stories, based on the limitations of fire hoses and ladders in that day, but in subsequent years, as fire-fighting equipment improved, the Congress refused to modify the building-height rule, now insisting that it was in the interest of preserving visibility of the Capitol's dome from every direction in the city. As a result, developers later built their skyscrapers in the suburbs, where land was both cheaper and easier to aggregate into large plots, and where a building could be built high enough to provide considerably more usable—and rentable—floor space per square foot of land purchased than the archaic, congressionally imposed zoning restrictions permitted inside the District.

The other major city-shaping decision concerned public transportation. During the Civil War years of chaos, public transportation had begun a transition from horse-drawn omnibuses operating on bumpy, mud-holed streets to horse-drawn cars operating on rails imbedded in the streets being newly paved by "Boss" Shepherd. So many of the rails eventually crisscrossed the city and were snarling private-vehicle traffic with their slow-paced movement that in 1890 Congress ordered that a different, swifter form of locomotion be installed on all routes. Some companies switched to cable-drawn cars, but most installed electric trolley systems. The electric rail lines that fanned out over the city, carrying residential development to the "ever-receding city's edge," as the *Post* termed it in 1909, can still be traced by the legacy of strip commercial development they brought after them. The corridors of small shops that collected along these fixed rail lines were especially suited to the frequent-stop system of public transportation, but today they cause a havoc of stop-and-go, park-and-shop, in-and-out local traffic.

Once most of the choicest land within the District of Columbia was under development after World War I, the seats on the House and Senate District committees lost their appeal and were passed on to southern congressmen. By the 1930's the combination of seniority rule and the one-party South assured southern domination of District affairs, so much so that for four decades southern states have enjoyed more than twice their proper representation on the District Committee of the House of Representatives, which in recent decades has held District government in a dictatorial hammerlock. So heavy did southern domination of District affairs grow that for the past two decades 40 percent or more of the seats on the House District Committee have consistently been assigned to southerners. The sum of their contributions to the government of the District was probably best typified in a remark by a Mississippian, Representative Ross Collins. He was chairman of the District of Columbia subcommittee of the House Appropriations Committee when the District's welfare director, Elwood Street, appealed for funds to build more space and hire more supervisors for homeless teen-age black girls during the 1930's. "If I went along with your ideas, Mr. Street, I'd never keep my seat in Congress," Representative Collins told him. "My constituents wouldn't stand for spending all that money on niggers."

The 1930's were unusual years for Washington. Not only did they signal a conservative take-over of District government, but while the rest of the nation was in the throes of its worst depression, Washington enjoyed relative prosperity. Its population climbed from 487,000 in 1930 to 663,000 in 1940, a 36 percent increase while every other major city in the country, with the single exception of Los Angeles, was losing population. The New Deal brought to Washington a wave of eager civil servants—Franklin D. Roosevelt's brain trusters, who were going to set the nation on its feet again. Public works programs flourished. Massive, block-formation federal office buildings were built in the "triangle" between the Capitol and the White House grounds; galleries and museums were built alongside the Mall, and a new District government building was constructed.

Despite the handsome renewal of "official" Washington again, conditions in the inner city were worsening. The Board of Trade, careful not to upset the *status quo,* opposed all citizen efforts to regain home rule and sought only to hold an unwilling Congress to its promise of 1874 that it would pay half the costs of running the District, a promise which was whittled back annually until, by 1940, only 11 percent of District revenues were coming from federal sources. Local tax revenues, meanwhile, had to be deposited with the United States Treasury and left there until Congress determined the local budget and made appropriations for it, leading the rest of the nation to believe that it was actually federal taxes and not local revenues that were paying the District's bills. Even President Franklin D. Roosevelt became confused, and when he was shown that the Treasury had accumulated a large surplus of unspent District revenues, it was assumed that the funds belonged to the nation's taxpayers; the President and the Congress refused to release the surplus to the financially exhausted local government. Because the Congress and the Board of Trade, which had so eagerly assumed command of the District, had failed to treat it responsibly; had let its schools deteriorate from among the nation's best (the all-black "M" Street High School in 1916 had set a national record for sending its graduates on to college); had refused to provide decent health care, penal institutions, courts, or welfare programs; and had declined to reverse the blight that was crawling across the city—because of all these failures, those citizens who could afford it were fleeing farther into suburbia, blaming the growing black population instead of themselves and the leadership they had allowed to take command. While the city's population grew by 36 percent during the decade, the entire region's grew by 46 percent.

It was estimated that the New Deal brought some 120,000 whites and 55,000 blacks to Washington. Many of the whites were well-educated upper-class families whose men were qualifying for new government positions; most of the blacks were from the bottom of the socioeconomic ladder, without a share in the white man's local boom: if they were fortunate enough to find work, it was custodial. The "decoloration" of Georgetown, the old city of urban charm, offers the best evidence of what was occurring in Washington during the New Deal. In 1930 one-third of the area was inhabited by blacks living in deteriorating homes; during the 1930's the young "New Dealers" moved in, offered prices the blacks could ill afford to pass by, bought up the old homes, renovated them, and established the area as one of the most prized residential addresses in the city. The whitening of Georgetown continued until well into the 1950's, while blacks were forced to crowd ever more thickly into the slum ghettos of alley shanties.

Suburbia was similarly posted "for whites only." The policies of developers, realtors, and their banker-financiers saw to it. So did the new Federal Housing Authority's loan policies. Its "Underwriting Manual" recommended a model racial covenant and advised appraisers against racially mixed neighborhood developments even "to the point of rejection." As the new suburbs opened in the former farmlands of Montgomery and Prince Georges counties in Maryland and in the farther reaches of northern Virginia's Potomac River border, new roads were built to bring the suburbanites to the city. The city bustled with traffic jams. Washington came to outrank other major cities 2 to 1 in the number of cars being daily driven into its central business district during the 1930's.

Only World War II's gas rationing and halt to auto and auto-parts production temporarily braked the trend of travel domination by automobiles and the sprawling consumption of suburban acreage. Public transportation had its field day. The District's rail-free buses, first introduced during the 1920's, and the still-thriving electrically powered street railways carried more than 536 million riders in 1943, but with the end of the war, the suburbanization of white Washington and its concomitant reassumption of the automobile craze renewed themselves at a runaway pace. An eminent national commission, including such personalities as Mrs. Eleanor Roosevelt, Walter Reuther, Marshall Field, and Hubert Humphrey, published a report in 1948 that launched the beginning of integration in Washington—and sped fearful whites even more quickly on their way to suburbia. The whites fled poor schools, black migration, and inner-city blight, but mostly they fled simply to enjoy their postwar prosperity with new homes, automobiles, and spacious yards—as elsewhere, caring little about the problems they left behind them in the city.

In 1954, the Supreme Court handed down its decision in the case of *Brown vs. the Board of Education of Topeka, Kansas,* ordering complete school desegregation. By the end of that year the dual school system of Washington, which had persisted since a brief integration attempt of Reconstruction, was abolished, schools were integrated, and, by the end of the 1950's, all public facilities in the District were racially opened. Racism spurred on the development of suburban retreats for whites as the city opened its facilities to blacks. In 1957, the District of Columbia became the first major American city to be more than 50 percent black.

It was not only the white exodus that caused the quick change of complexion, however. As word spread farther and farther through the die-hard South, where most blacks still lived, that the nation's capital was becoming an "open" city where blacks could find the fulfillment of the Supreme Court's promise, black migration swelled the nonwhite population inside the District—from 281,000 in 1950 to 412,000 in 1960, a 47 percent increase, while white flight had reduced the total population of the District by almost 5 percent during the same decade.

There was another migratory pattern that was helping to push the black proportion of population in Washington over the halfway mark. Much of the rural land in Maryland had been deeded to freed slaves after the Emancipation Proclamation, and the descendants of the freedmen had stayed on the land, living in shacks and hovels hidden in the woods of Maryland until the developers came to claim the lands for the newly suburbanizing whites. As in Georgetown earlier, the blacks found it difficult to resist the seemingly high prices being offered. They little understood that the money being paid for their land was but a pittance compared with the profits the speculators and developers would harvest from the property. They sold and found themselves homeless; the new homes being built on their ancestral land were far too expensive—precious few of them priced under $40,000. They had no place to go but into the District of Columbia or other surrounding cities such as Baltimore, or smaller Rockville closer to the District.

It was against that background that one small island of resistance called Scotland came to be called a "miracle."

In 1965 Scotland was but a scattering of shacks hidden along a heavily wooded hillside in Montgomery County, the seat of such suburban communities as Chevy Chase and Bethesda, which recorded among the nation's highest average income levels in 1960. The shanty dwellers of Scotland had resisted the developers' bulldozers for more than a decade and had been persistently refused such vital public services as water and sewerage lines, garbage pickup and street lighting. The community's elders could remember trying to "save" Scotland and improve its services as far back as World War I, their efforts always in vain. Still they wanted to remain in the rural peace, beauty, and spaciousness they had come to appreciate during their century of occupancy. Yet, by 1964, the sixty-five remaining descendants of the freed slaves were giving up hope in the face of repeated rezoning efforts by white developers when Mrs. Joyce Siegel, a housewife from Bethesda, "discovered" them and assembled other whites to help the community save itself. The black families found new hope, cleaned up some six decades' accumulation of trash, hired the first garbage collectors that had ever visited the area, persuaded the local transit company to institute a bus route to the nearby shopping mall, established a wide variety of community programs of education and recreation, traced the deeds to their properties, pooled their holdings, and, with the ultimate help of a federal grant, created a distinctive community of a hundred town houses complete with playgrounds, commons, and—a luxury—an automatic garbage-disposal unit in each kitchen.

That the small community of pastel town houses called Scotland should be labeled a miracle is an indicator of the degree of whitening the suburbs of Washington endured at the hands of overeager developers who understood too well the drive that was moving white government workers and their institutional cohorts out of the city. Remarks by residents of Scotland who made the "miracle" work stand in vivid contrast to the human destruction wrought by other suburban developments:

A father of nine whose family had lived in a tar-paper shack that had repeatedly lost its roof in driving rainstorms—"I don't have the slightest idea where I would have moved if it hadn't been for Scotland. If Scotland hadn't come along, I would think the best outlet

would have been the District, which—that would have been terrible."

A man whose new town house overlooks the ancestral shack he
and his family had lived in for decades without electricity, running
water, or any appliance more modern than a coal-burning stove—"All
the people have the same feeling, that they want to live better, that
they don't want to live like they used to live."

And his wife—"You know, you live among the people so long
you don't want to move away, and we didn't want to destroy this
community. That's why we fought so hard to save it. . . . And there's
nothing better than to walk in to look at all your kids in their
beautiful beds and their nice, pretty rooms and lovely sheets and
just—just look at the kids."

This, then, was the picture of the Washington region that faced
the leaders of the city during the middle 1950's: a black population
about to claim dominance; polarization along racial and urban-
suburban lines; a white flight to suburbia that was causing uncontrolled sprawl and land consumption and freeing taxpayers from the
District while driving rural blacks into the city's slums; rising crime,
poverty, disease, and general squalor inside the city; F Street, in 1909
called by the *Washington Post* "a favorite promenade of a host of
girls and ladies every afternoon," becoming shabby and abandoned
by merchants for less centrally located sites; the arrival of a new
superhighway era with the adoption in 1956 of the Interstate Highway program, a long-debated idea rising out of the new suburban
movements and the eagerness of highway builders; and the total lack
of local control by citizens of the District.

To confront what was apparently going to be the ultimate destruction of the city—not by design, but by selfishness and fear and a
consequent failure of understanding—a few leaders emerged, scattered over the city and suburban areas, to urge on a rebirth of
interest. The counter-strategy was simple enough: (1) regional coordination, because the automobile had now permitted the city to
splay itself over the terrain of the entire District and large sections
of the two adjoining states; (2) improved planning, because so much
planning had been so ineffectual for so long; and (3) creation of a
more sensible, regional pattern of transportation to channel future
growth and to try to tie the disparate pieces of the region together. All
three efforts began at about the same time, when the economy was
still enjoying its postwar health.

The movement toward regionalism began in the private sector,
as an effort to realize economies. Strangely, the first step taken came

from that bastion of no-change leadership, the Board of Trade, which in the mid-1950's helped assemble the United Givers Fund out of the myriad of private fund-raising appeals in the area. Once that effort was seen as a likely success, the Boy Scout councils and Leagues of Women Voters in the major jurisdictions of the region banded together to effect similar economies, and at last government officials began stepping gingerly toward the same end.

In the spring of 1957, with a few regional cooperative ventures launched into such things as transportation planning and traffic safety and a Metropolitan Regional Conference established as a model prototype in New York, the local government officials and state legislators responded to an invitation by the president of the District's Board of Commissioners and formed the Washington Metropolitan Regional Conference, a voluntary association of local officials pledged to metropolitan cooperation. While it eventually evolved into the Metropolitan Washington Council of Governments and assumed the important review powers for the region's planning and federal grant applications, it steered clear of anything remotely resembling metropolitan government. Indeed, it proclaimed loudly and often that its reason for being was to see to it that regional government did *not* become reality. It was essentially a cautious federation that repeatedly stressed its role as one of "a vehicle for the exchange of information of mutual interest," lest it offend its weakest links and cause them to snap.

The council's first activity of any significance was the establishment of a committee to deal with water pollution problems and adoption of a "no effluent" policy for the Potomac River. That took it into its first show of weakness, over the Civil Aeronautics Administration's announced plans to build a new international airport—now Dulles International—more than twenty miles into the outskirts of Washington's Virginia suburbs and to dump its sewage into the Potomac above the District's drinking water intake. A Congressional Joint Committee on Washington Metropolitan Problems called the action a "flagrant disregard of community interests" and recommended that a Regional Sanitary Board be established to review all projects involving federal funding (except direct District appropriations). The Council of Governments formed the sanitation board, but under its own "cooperation" umbrella instead of as the autonomous board recommended by the joint committee. Public furor over the airport-sewer plans caused repeated delays in the project until a program to build an interceptor sewer line was adopted, with little active participation by the council or its sanitary board. The best that could be said for the COG in the sewer dispute was said in 1964 by Royce Hanson, then associate professor of government and public administration at the American University, in a report, *The Politics of Metropolitan Cooperation: Metropolitan Washington Council of Governments,* published by the Washington Center for Metropolitan Studies, a nonprofit research and educational institution of which Hanson is now president. In his 1964 study, Hanson gave this analysis of the COG's function in the controversy:

> Its role, specifically, was to create a situation which demanded a solution. The council was able, through its voluntary procedures, to agree on the existence of a problem, and to reach a consensus that something had to be done . . . . No member during the long debate over the location of the sewer could extricate himself from his own jurisdictional interests and assert a position which contained a regional interest in the sewer . . . .

The same was to be proved true repeatedly in subsequent years—for example, when Maryland's Montgomery County temporarily dropped its membership in the COG and branded the council's interest in assuming regional planning activities as an attempt to establish "supergovernment" (despite the COG's repeated professions of the opposite), when the council decided against becoming involved in a regional study of public housing because there were controversial implications that this would involve public housing in the suburbs, and when the council decided against taking any position on a controversial highway through Washington and other regional transportation issues.

Two of the Council of Government's major non-roles emerged in the evolution of planning and transportation for the Washington metropolitan region. In planning the council took a forward step for itself that is proving a step in quite the reverse direction for the region.

A measure of the effect that external political considerations—national as well as local—have had on Washington is in the struggle it has had to plan its own environment. Politicians have meddled in planning everywhere and at all times, perhaps, and in this respect Washington is little different from such cities as Flint, Michigan. What is significant in the national capital's planning efforts is that there the national attitude toward rational urban growth—as reflected in the Congress, the presidency, and the suburban governments—has been made manifest with little camouflage. That attitude, prevalent in Washington as elsewhere, has insisted (in practice) that buildings be *built,* not planned; that investors and speculators be given free rein; that cities are haphazard affairs anyway and only a laissez-faire policy befits them. Despite the renaissance of urban and regional planning in the past decade, the attitude still persists in the national character: planners are paid to draw pictures and paint maps and are tolerated but kept aside when a developer has a major new project in mind. Nowhere has the cost inflicted by such an attitude been more dear than in the capital, a city that was to have been "planned" from the start. As Charles Dickens once disdainfully observed, what was to have been built as a "city of magnificent distances" has become a "city of magnificent intentions."

George Washington's peremptory dismissal of L'Enfant, Andrew Jackson's temper tantrum over the location of the Treasury Building, private construction's filling in of sites that had been set aside for public buildings, small parks, and boulevards, and, ultimately, "Boss" Shepherd's bankrupting public works escapade of the 1870's, when even sewer lines were laid with ends that failed to meet properly, were but advance warnings of what was to come. In 1893 Congress created a Highway Commission which planned an area-wide roadway system extending the major avenues out to open up the suburbs (now parts of Washington) with little or no regard for the often steeply sloping terrain, so that the plans frequently had to be changed. Also in 1893, architect Daniel Burnham unveiled his "White City" at Chicago's Columbian Exposition and gave birth to the "City Beautiful" movement that spread across the country. In 1901, Congress created a Parks Commission and named Burnham as one of its members. The commission made ambitious proposals in keeping with Burnham's advice to planners, "Make no little plans"— grouping of government buildings around the Capitol, development of museums and galleries on the Mall, sunken gardens and the Reflecting Pool at the foot of the Washington Monument, a Lincoln Memorial and Arlington Memorial Bridge, parks development including the setting aside of the entire Rock Creek gorge as a natural preserve spanning all of northwest Washington—but a year later the commission was disbanded, ignored by a House of Representatives that was piqued because it had not been consulted in the planning. Eight years after that, in 1910, Congress created the commission's successor, the National Commission of Fine Arts, and gave it the less ambitious assignment of "advising" on the location and design of public buildings, fountains, and memorials; that commission soon became the arbiter of taste in federal architecture (now regarded as uniformly dull), landscaping, and the placement and design of statuary in the capital. In 1924, with a new revival of prosperity, "normalcy," and interest in the city environment, Congress again stepped in to create the National Capital Park Commission to plan and acquire parklands, and two years later broadened its name to the National Capital Park and Planning Commission and its assignment to include development of a comprehensive plan for the city. For the first time this established a regular and continuous planning program for the federal and District governments, to be done, of course, by federal appointees. The commission, however, was given few funds with which to work and was unable even to save many of the park sites it planned. Though a 50-million-dollar federal building program was launched to create the monotony of federal office structures in the "Federal Triangle" along the Mall, the commission was unable to stop developers from acquiring other sites it wanted to set aside and from building on them without regard for the planners' plans.

The same had been true of earlier planning: though L'Enfant had envisioned a Supreme Court at a distance east of the Capitol to attract development eastward as well as westward, it was built adjacent to the Capitol instead, and while the west entrance to the Capitol fronts on gardens and the expansive Mall to the Washington Monument, the east fronts on an expanse of parking lot and, beyond it, a dense residential neighborhood chronically troubled with crime and blight that reaches to the far eastern edges of the District.

One recurring failure in all of the planning commissions and planning programs of Washington was their uniform blindness to the needs of the total city. They planned monuments and marble faces, statues and parks and gardens for official Washington, and ignored the poverty, the alley communities and the blight that was spreading over the rest of the landscape. After World War II the National Capital Park and Planning Commission did recognize the city's mounting black population in the slums and advanced a city-wide redevelopment plan that will stand as a monument to Washington's planning: it would have segregated the city's blacks into "the rear of Anacostia," land within the Ten Mile Square beyond the Anacostia River where it flows into the Potomac south and east of the Capitol. A large segment of the area had been bought and set aside by the Reconstructionists in 1868 for development as a new community for freed slaves. According to a later report by the District's housing office of the 1868 development:

> The land was subdivided, and most of the lots were sold to "freemen." Land owners, with the help of government supplies and government technical assistance, built their own houses. Certain military barracks were renovated and rented as low-cost apartments in which the housing code was strictly enforced. The government paid the costs of moving persons. The residents set priorities for two churches and a school, then built them.

Despite that impressive, modern-seeming start, during the ensuing century the east side was abandoned by the planners and de-

velopers of the prosperous years and became one of those corners of
the District where the rug was lifted and the problems of poverty and
blight were swept safely out of view from the annual migrations of
politicians and tourists alike. The post–World War II planners were
prepared to put an official stamp on such a policy by segregating the
city into two societies, one master and one servant, the one white and
the other black, the one residing in the Washington that had received
the best development and public concern, the other banished, like
Cain, to the east side.

Blacks, now organized into the Urban League and the National
Association for the Advancement of Colored People, protested ve-
hemently, and, with the backing of the voluminous 1948 report by
the prestigious National Committee on Segregation, managed to win
the beginnings of public facility integration that culminated about a
decade later and put away forever the segregated-city plans of the
National Capital Park and Planning Commission.

In 1952, with the approaching "regionalism" efforts already in
the embryonic, conversational stage, Congress shortened the Park
and Planning Commission's name to the National Capital Planning
Commission and created a new National Capital Regional Planning
Council. The commission was assigned to provide "comprehensive
planning" for the city and the regional council was assigned to adopt
a general plan for the entire metropolitan area, which already included two counties in Maryland and four in northern Virginia.

Neither agency turned out to have much strength. The National
Capital Planning Commission, assigned to rule on the wisdom, location, and design of federal building projects in the region, timidly
chose instead to negotiate with the federal agencies doing the building. As its director, Charles Conrad, stated, "We don't ramrod things
through," a tacit recognition that real control rests not with the
planners but with the Congress and the Office of Management and
Budget. The net result has been federal building programs in careless
disregard of the maps and plans adopted by the Planning Commission.
On local matters the Planning Commission constructed a map of
colors and special circles marking off where "uptown centers" should
be developed, but gave too little detail for the District's zoning office
to base decisions on the plan if it wanted to. Net result: zoning with
little planning. The commission did produce an ambitious redevelopment plan for Pennsylvania Avenue, the decaying heart of the government district between the White House and the Capitol, but in
the mid-1960's that plan fell on its face; it had failed to take into
account that private developers were not interested since their potential profits would be too severely limited by the archaic building-

height regulations of the District. Similarly, the commission developed
a plan for an International Center of chanceries and embassies in a
close-in neighborhood of Washington's northwest side, an area of
old row houses and small neighborhood shops that remains well
tended and racially mixed. Citizen opposition stopped the plan, and
the International Center is to be built around a new office structure
for the Organization of American States on large acreage being
abandoned by the Bureau of Standards farther out from the downtown area.

As for the Regional Planning Council, it fared little better. Its
one major legacy to the archives of planning was a planners' day-
dream called "A Policies Plan for the Year 2000," published in 1961,
widely discussed in the region for three years and finally adopted as
official regional policy (if any *regional* policy could be *official* in
Washington) by the Washington Council of Governments in January
1964. That plan stated that the region would continue to grow and
spread over the outer landscape, to more than five million by the end
of the century, and that the growth should be channeled into a system of "wedges and corridors." The "wedges" would be preserved as
parklands and natural preserves that local governments would acquire
and otherwise retain from development; the "corridors" would be
swaths of developed urban land coursing outward between the
"wedges" and alongside major transportation throats of superhighways and a regional rail rapid transit system.

There were a few flaws: by the end of the 1960's, with regional
population standing at 2.86 million, it was obvious that in the year
2000 the region would be approaching 8 million, not 5 million, and
that at the present rate it would spread itself over the land in a great
scattered blotch that bore little resemblance to "wedges and corridors." The plan had failed to recognize the suburban governments'
avarice, which would not permit such a sacrifice of large land areas
to "open space" when developers were so eager to build and provide
the government with an expanded tax base, and, less often acknowledged, a demand for more public services for more residents spread
over a greater geographical area. No sooner was the "Year 2000"
plan published than suburban planners in Maryland prepared their
own subregional plan with major diversions from the metropolitan-
wide concept—in the interest of more intensive—and widespread—
development for its area. President John F. Kennedy issued an order
that all federal agencies abide by the "Year 2000" plan also, but
federal administrators didn't bother to obey. Additionally, the "Year
2000" plan failed to take into account the nature of the development
magnets that the highways the planners had been mapping were to

become. A map of the region's actual, programmed, and planned network of highways showed, not a radial corridor system, but a spiderweb of freeways, parkways, and other divided, major thoroughfares crisscrossing throughout the region. True, the nine freeways themselves were radial, but by the late 1960's they were linked by a full beltway super-road and an "outer beltway" was programmed, and the crosshatching of other major routes between these radials was sure to continue spreading development into the proposed open "wedges." In fact, forty intersections of present or future superhighways with each other or with the radial rapid transit system proposed for the area were generously scattered over the map of the metropolitan area. In 1971 a Council of Governments planner conceded that, owing largely to indiscriminate highway building, the "Year 2000" plan was "crumbling at the edges." In his words, "The beltway cut off the wedges."

The Council of Governments assumed the plan in 1966 when it stepped into the planning arena after years of mounting pressure by staff members had driven Montgomery County, Maryland, into its temporary exile from the COG. With the Marylanders not present to register protest, the COG officially took over the planning functions of the Regional Planning Commission and even became the regional agency responsible for reviewing local projects before they could be qualified for federal funding. Such a review, mandated by the Congress, represented a major strength to those agencies willing to exercise it to control and guide regional growth. It was a positive step for the Council of Governments in Washington, but it is clear that the council, with its self-imposed limitations as a "voluntary" federation of local officials, still declines to use its now six-year-old powers. A council researcher, Stuart Bendelow, even believes that regional planning is "putting together composites of local plans and saying, 'There's the plan of the region.'" Instead of actually planning for the metropolis, the COG is "coordinating" local planning among the member jurisdictions—through "meetings, committee structures and . . . writing a hell of a lot of reports." Once again the Council of Governments is serving, as Royce Hanson said in 1964, as merely "a collection of local interests." Conditions have not changed materially since 1964, when Hanson had these additional comments to make about the Council of Governments and the planning process it was shortly to assume:

> When in harmony, a concert of local interests may look like a regional interest but may not necessarily be one . . . . For six years [1958–1964] the council has gone through the agony of becoming without ever arriving. Thus, it might be characterized as having

been in a position of perpetual contemplation of its navel . . . . The local members, in the absence of region-oriented leadership or a regional executive staff, have been products of their own local political and administrative conditioning. Their metropolitan perspectives have been from the jurisdictions looking up, not from the metropolis looking down . . . . Without speedier procedures and stronger leadership on critical issues, regional planning could remain a process of *post hoc* ratification of operating agency decisions.

The effort to design and build a transportation system capable of service to both the sprawled-out region and its decaying core was the third major component of the urban strategy that came into being during the 1950's. Its course ran concurrently with the courses of regional approaches to government and planning, but it represented a considerably greater willingness to confront issues. As in Dayton, Indianapolis, Atlanta, and a host of other cities, transportation issues also provided the vehicle whereby the urban region developed its first and, thus far, only significant metropolitan-wide implementation program: transportation "forced" the issue of regionalism. In Washington the often stalled, always obstacle-strewn course toward a logical transportation skeleton has also made manifest the weaknesses in the Council of Governments, the failure to develop an actively regional approach to urban government, and the overriding injustices and lack of logic in congressional dominion over the city's affairs.

In contrast with other cities, Washington did not stand idly by and watch its public transportation system die after its major bus and streetcar company suffered the same fate as those in other cities during the first ten years after World War II. From a peak ridership of 536 million in 1943 it plunged 42 percent to 312 million in 1950 and then to 129 million in 1955. That year a crippling fifty-two-day strike against the Capital Transit Company resulted in a congressional order to terminate the company's franchise. (Control of the company had been acquired in 1949 by the later-to-be-legally-troubled financier, Louis Wolfson, whom Congress accused of "milking" the system.) The Senate passed a bill for public acquisition of the company, but the House refused to accept it; the next year both agreed to pass the franchise on to a new company, D.C. Transit System, Inc., with a congressional expression that the company deserved at least a net annual profit of 6.5 percent and that, "if the corporation does provide the Washington Metropolitan Area with a good public transportation system, with reasonable fares, the Congress will maintain a continuing interest in the welfare of the corporation and its investors."

The principle "investor" was O. Roy Chalk, a New York lawyer and real estate entrepreneur who, through stock splitting and what a senator was later to call "some kind of financial legerdemain," was able to acquire the company, then estimated to be worth about 23 million dollars, for only 13.5 million dollars, but to "invest" no more than an initial $500,000 down payment from his Trans-Caribbean Airways. The down payment was soon paid back from the bus company's cash on hand, property sales, and fare collections. When he acquired the Capital Transit Company, it was relatively debt-free and had large property holdings in the city. By the end of 1969 Chalk was reporting about 28 million dollars in liabilities (about $24 for every $1 in equity), including some 2.3 million dollars owed to his own employees' pension fund, and had sold off or heavily mortgaged most of the properties. It was Chalk who was now being accused by congressmen of "milking" the company, and once again the bus operation is heading toward public acquisition.

In the process, however, Chalk had managed to hold at bay the trend being followed by urban public transit in almost every other city in the country. In 1956 ridership climbed back to about 135 million and held there until 1967, despite the rising American dependence on private automobiles. Then its ridership began to slip; the rioting of April 1968 caused an epidemic of fear of the inner city and its downtown, where the buses went; fares rose to 32 cents in 1969, and to 40 cents the following year, and ridership continued to plunge downward, to 116 million in 1969. By 1971 the company was even blaming renewed public interest in urban bicycling for the slippage of its patronage.

The company was not entirely at fault for the falling ridership and actually had logged an impressively better record than most privately owned transit companies. Under congressional orders Chalk had converted the entire system to buses by 1962 and had torn up most of the street rails (but in 1971 still owed a regional transit authority $160,000 for some of the work); he had built up a fleet of 1,185 buses, three-fourths of them air-conditioned, and had instituted a free "Gold Bus" shuttle service for downtown shoppers during 1960's Christmas season, put it to full-time use (with a 10-cent fare) in 1962, and, with $240,000 in federal aid, converted the downtown service to minibuses in 1963. (It was recently abandoned.)

There were other success stories in the modern history of public transit in the Washington area. Though the stories were of small successes in the face of massive public transportation needs, they proved that affluent suburbanites would, in fact, leave their cars at home and take the bus to work when provided with a proper level of service. The most notable of the stories happened in Reston, Virginia.

Reston is a "new town" located on 7,400 acres about twenty miles west of Washington, not far from Dulles International Airport, and bisected by the Department of Transportation's access super-highway built for airport trips only. The new town, one of the most successful preplanned communities in the nation, has apartment towers, town houses, and beautifully landscaped and designed split-level homes, a community center, a shopping district, and the nucleus of an employment center around the United States Geological Survey offices. Most remarkable in the light of its isolation from the densely urbanized areas of Washington proper, Reston has developed into an "urban" community. While its residents are racially mixed, they are still homogeneous—the young families of professional men, execu-tives in federal service, and the white collar-and-attaché-case men who run the many private institutes and associations located in Wash-ington because of the federal government. They make Reston's popu-lation sophisticated, interested in civic activities, and well stocked with intelligence, education, and management abilities. Henry Bain, a senior associate of the Washington Center for Metropolitan Studies, has compiled a detailed history of the community's transit experience, *The Reston Express Bus—A Case History of Citizen Action to Improve Urban Transportation* (Washington Center for Metropolitan Studies, 1969). In it he points out, "While some (residents) were busy forming the Reston Chorale, the Reston Players and the Reston chapter of the Virginia Museum of Fine Arts, others were at work on the express bus service."

Most of Reston's work force was employed in and near the federal center of Washington. Commuting to work by car was arduous, since Reston was denied use of the Dulles Airport access highway. The only bus service was infrequent, did not come close to most residential areas in Reston, did not have a morning "rush-hour" schedule, involved a seventy-minute wandering ride that made numer-ous local stops, and cost $1 a trip. It was provided by the Washington, Virginia and Maryland Coach Company (WV&M), a subsidiary of Chalk's D.C. Transit System, Inc. The president of the WV&M in-sisted that there wouldn't be enough riders to warrant establishing rush-hour express service between Reston and Washington but said he would be glad to provide a bus on a charter basis if he were guar-anteed against losses. In November 1966, Reston's management agreed to try an express service to Washington and underwrite the costs, but the service was dropped two weeks later when it drew only about seven commuters a day. In 1968, the Reston Community

Association and its small band of interested Washington office workers decided to try a two-week experiment again, this time with a $150 maximum subsidy from the new town's new management, Gulf Reston, Inc. (Gulf Oil had acquired the property.) The citizens' association sold advance tickets to make up the rest of the charter fee of $270 a week for one daily round-trip bus route and promoted its service widely through the community; on March 4, twenty-nine pioneering passengers boarded the first express bus for Washington. The wife of the service's chief organizer, the administrator of a major federal agency, Karl Ingebritsen, provided thermos bottles of coffee. The second day a local drugstore added doughnuts. A Reston realtor provided twenty free copies of the *Washington Post,* and within a short period riders had organized a Friday afternoon "happy hour" on the ride home. Sometimes riders would provide hors d'oeuvres, and drinks were on a "bring your own" basis; eventually they involved a weekly raffling of a bottle that pooled resources to provide drinks. Most important to the project was its personal touch, described by Bain:

> It was impossible for a new rider to remain a stranger to the "club" of regular riders. When a newcomer boarded the bus in the morning, Ingebritsen would welcome him, inquire as to his destination and introduce him to some of the others. This attention gave the rider a chance to ask any questions he might have about the service and alerted the other riders to expect him on the return trip. . . . More than once the watchful eye of an experienced rider saved a newcomer from missing the evening bus homeward. The riders likewise looked out for one another in the mornings, even to the extent of asking the driver to wait a moment when a regular rider was not present at his usual stop.

The routing of the bus was as flexible as the imaginations and personal driving experiences of the passengers, who kibitzed friendlily whenever it seemed that a traffic jam ahead would slow the progress of the bus. Still, despite the "club" atmosphere and the personal touch, ridership during the first two weeks fell short of the number needed to sustain the costs of operating it. The bus company was skeptical that the project would succeed over the long run, and Gulf Reston declined to underwrite any part of the experiment further. Only the cash collected from advance ticket subscriptions provided a financial base from which the community association could meet its bills and continue the service, convinced that its approximately 125 riders a week would increase to the break-even point in time. The citizens also developed the conviction, contrary to all the transit "wisdom" of older city system operators, that only expansion of the service would make it succeed. Still not at the break-even point but holding remarkably close to it, a second route was instituted in May 1968, and the organizers were proved correct: they passed the break-even point in August and immediately expanded to still a third route, and then a fourth in January 1969 and a fifth in June 1969. The network of routes served different sectors of the office-building heart of the metropolitan area: federal office buildings near the Mall, the K Street cluster of institutes and trade associations and smaller federal agencies, the burgeoning new office buildings of Rosslyn in Arlington just across the Potomac River from Georgetown, and the Pentagon and National Airport across the Potomac from Washington's federal establishment. One Friday afternoon trip was even reserved for tee-totalers and nappers. The bus service, now counting 550 riders and 17 buses daily, not only in paying for itself but has become a full-time management enterprise by the Reston Community Association and is reaping substantial rewards: reduced auto insurance rates for its riders, new mobility for housewives left at home, removal of the one obstacle to new home sales in Reston—its poor accessibility to Washington—and thus an increase in sales and rentals, and, not least in significance, provision of a vehicle for community spirit.

There were slips, of course. The bus company from which the coaches were chartered did not always provide the best and most modern buses; coffee and doughnut service was discontinued after the first few days, and the free newspapers were stopped after the *Washington Post* forbade free distribution of papers bought at wholesale price. Even the Virginia Alcoholic Beverage Control Board got into the act, putting a halt to the traditional happy hour and the work of volunteer "boosemeisters" under legal interpretations that denied the buses official charter status. Repeatedly the Reston Community Association asked for federal and other government assistance for expanding the service and for other aid, but was uniformly turned down, with the exception that it was eventually permitted to use the Dulles access highway. Yet, that the express, rush-hour commuter service is a success is beyond question. Each new route introduced has brought a sharp increase in ridership. Most importantly, it is a bus system planned and executed by the community itself, and thus tailored to meet the needs of the community. The developers of Reston, the local government, the state government, and the federal government has done precious little to assist. Yet, as the result of the community spirit that bred the project and the community spirit that has grown out of it, "The trip to and from the city became a positively valued social experience," according to Bain. No one could imagine a motorist saying that about his traffic-jammed drive to and from work each day.

Two service expansions for which the Reston group sought federal aid were an express route to Tyson's Corner, a regional shopping complex eight miles away, and a "reverse commuter" route to carry Washington workers to Reston's growing industrial and commercial employment and to carry inner-city domestics to Reston's homes. The federal government rejected both. Instead it gave $671,000 to the ineffectual Washington Council of Governments for a two-year demonstration project to provide express bus service for suburbanites into the city and reverse rides at 25-cent fares for inner-city workers needing transportation to suburban job sites. That two-year experiment ended in June 1971, and the routes it had inaugurated reverted to the D.C. Transit System, Inc. As suburb-to-city express runs the three "Capital Flyer" routes from Virginia and Maryland suburbs proved successful enough, averaging between 30 and 34 passengers per trip by the time the lines reverted to D.C. Transit. The lowest ridership of the three was on the route from Tyson's Corner, which Reston had wanted to serve by bus, to downtown Washington. Some of the "reverse commuter" routes were hardly so successful: one from the inner city to a shopping center in Montgomery County, Maryland, was averaging 30 riders per trip, but others ranged downward from 23 per trip to 8 per trip. When the private bus company took over the service, it raised the fares on the reverse-commuter trips to its regular suburban-route pricing structure—65 cents for the route to Arlington and 90 cents for the trip out to Montgomery County north of Washington; two of the reverse routes were abandoned by the bus company.

If the Reston and COG projects were not proof enough that suburbanites could be lured from their cars by good, rapid public transit service, the Shirley Highway "busway" program was enough to convince any lingering skeptics. Shirley Highway is part of Interstate 95 southward out of Washington and through one of the area's most densely populated suburban corridors. By 1969 it had long been notorious for its enormous traffic jams during rush hours, and President Richard Nixon, taking a helicopter tour to view it and other superhighways that converged their traffic streams into what localites picturesquely call their highway "mixing bowl," was moved to remark that he was "glad I don't have to drive to work." The Reston and Capital Flyer buses have to fight the same traffic jams as automobiles, but on Shirley Highway buses now have exclusive rush-hour use of reversible lanes along a major section of the traffic-clogged through-way, "for-buses-only" median lanes have been built in the highway to the river, and the last stretch of "busway" is under construction for its river crossing into the heart of Washington itself. About two hundred buses of the suburban transit operator—the Alexandria, Barcroft and Washington Company—make use of the automobile-free route, and a special ninety-bus fleet of carpeted, air-conditioned coaches is being acquired for special express service along the corridor. Within the first twenty months of the four-year demonstration project's operation, ridership on buses using the reserved lanes climbed 80 percent, while the rate of automobile traffic growth has declined to about a thousand less than the average annual increase.

The significance of the special bus program successes is not that they carry *large* numbers of riders that would otherwise commute by car (they don't) but that they prove that suburbanites will choose public transit over their automobiles if given a reasonably desirable option—a telling blow to the highway lobby's insistence on the national "love affair" with automobiles. The *real* hopes of developing a regional, mass-carrying option to the private car and the superhighway is not in buses, however, but in "Metro," a high-speed rail transportation network that promises to be the most modern in the world. It is currently under construction in the heart of Washington.

Such a system was not exactly a new idea for Washington, nor was recognition of the impact that good public transportation could have on land development. As far back as 1888 the Rock Creek Railway Company, an operator of electric trolleys, was organized with the expressed intent of opening up for development land in northwest sections of the District, on the west side of Rock Creek Park and north of the bluffs above the original city limits. High-speed rail transit itself was proposed as early as 1909, when the *Washington Post* proposed a core-area subway system that would have expanded upon the already operating underground rails connecting House and Senate office buildings with the Capitol by extending them into a triangular route serving the Union Station, a few blocks north of the Capitol, and federal and District office buildings to the White House, at the third point of the triangle a mile and a half west of the Capitol. The *Post,* detailing the then already tangled and congested traffic on the city's streets, called it "an assured fact that eventually Washington will find a subway indispensable." In 1931 a newspaper headline again asked, "Will Washington Need a Subway?" and five years later an editorial optimistically predicted that, "if talk can ever bring a subway, this is the winter when Washington's underground will finally get started toward some action. For talk certainly is increasing." By the end of that decade the Board of Trade completed a feasibility study for a subway, but the proposal never outlived congressional hearings when congressmen argued that such a system would be too costly.

By 1952 traffic generated in the new suburbs changed Congress's collective mind. In creating the National Capital Planning Commission and the Regional Planning Council it directed the two agencies to prepare a transportation plan for the metropolis. Already the region totaled about 1.5 million people with only slightly more than half of them living inside the District of Columbia. The states of Maryland and Virginia, where the "other half" lived, were also concerned, and two years later their legislatures created a joint study commission, the Tri-State Transportation Commission, to study public transportation facilities in the metropolitan area. It was this joint commission and not the local or regional planning agencies—and most definitely not local governments—which in 1959 presented President Dwight Eisenhower with a plan to build a 500-million-dollar rapid transit system.

At this stage at least, the region's governments should have assumed an active role in rapid transit planning, but their one vehicle for adopting such a role, the recently formed Council of Governments, found the transportation issue so "controversial," according to COG analyst Royce Hanson, that it declined to even organize a transportation committee during its first six months and took no hand in a mass-transportation survey conducted in 1959. Instead, it was eager to have a regional transit regulatory agency created separate from the rapid transit construction program, even though the Institute of Public Administration had told a joint congressional committee studying metropolitan Washington problems that a regulatory agency by itself would have little worth. The institute recommended instead "a federal corporation endowed with the powers to control, own, and if necessary, operate mass transportation facilities, and to institute a systematic control over arterial roadway traffic and parking, particularly parking in the District." The institute added, "Such a corporation could also undertake the construction and operation of a rail transit system, pending the establishment of an interstate compact agency." Maryland and Virginia opposed the creation of such a federal corporation, however, and still another controversy was being injected into the issue: the federal Bureau of Public Roads was demanding that an Interstate freeway that extended northward from the beltway in Maryland also be extended southward through some of the finest residential neighborhoods of northwest Washington, including historic Georgetown. (Congress eventually yielded to heated protest and froze all freeway construction in most of the west side of Washington but was to be considerably less responsive to public wishes on other superhighway programs.)

The Council of Governments remained true to its intention to follow the lead of its weakest elements: it did nothing. When the transportation issues came before the council in 1960, its chairman and the president of the District's Board of Commissioners, Robert E. McLaughlin, objected to a freeze on the northwest freeway project and told the COG steering committee, "My suggestion is that since we can't take the unanimous action [on the transportation legislation then pending in Congress] we take no action at all upon it." He reasoned that it had grown even "more controversial" since the full Council of Governments had earlier decided not to act on the creation of a rapid transit planning and building agency but instead to push for only a transit regulatory commission. The committee became tangled in conversation, not on the merits of the proposed legislation but on its own lack of unanimity.

"Do we always have a unanimous position?" one member asked.

"I think that is the concept under which this organization has worked in the past and I assume that we are going to work that way in the future," McLaughlin told her. Later he added, "We are still in the situation of having to wrap up the interstate [regulatory] compact on the Hill and it seems to me it would be very unwise tonight to take a divided action on it. . . . I knew this problem would come up sometime. . . . If we proceed on less than a unanimous vote tonight we are going to have an effect that I don't think was the purpose in organizing this organization. . . ."

In keeping with its nature, the regional "steering" committee settled the "problem" in its own best fashion: someone pointed out that there wasn't a quorum present and suggested, "Why don't we go home?" It did, without taking action. Its regulatory commission was created soon afterward by the Congress, and, true to predictions of the Institute of Public Administration, it had little impact on the shaping of the region's transportation network, except for the raising of bus fares. Also without input by the area's local governments sitting in regional confederation, Congress created in 1960 the National Capital Transportation Agency, which returned in 1962, again without benefit of local government participation, with a proposal that a regional authority build an 83-mile rail rapid transit system, another 15 miles of improved rail commuter lines, 52 miles of express bus operations, and *50 more miles of freeways.* Congress was not pleased, and it bottled in committee a plan for even a basic 23-mile rail system to await plan revisions by the National Capital Transportation Agency. In 1965 Congress approved a package requested by President Lyndon Johnson: a 25-mile "bobtail" system for the District itself, to cost 431 million dollars and eventually to be extended into a regional network. Both Maryland and Virginia, meanwhile, moved ahead with the creation of subregional transportation agencies empowered to enter into a compact with the District to build a system. In 1967 the federal agency was abolished and in its place was constituted the Washington Metropolitan Area Transit Authority (WMATA), charged with planning, developing, building, and financing a rail rapid transit system for the region. Each major jurisdiction was given two seats on the authority: two from Virginia's suburban counties and cities already banded into the subregional Northern Virginia Transportation Commission, two from Maryland's two suburban counties banded into another subregional agency, the Washington Suburban Transit Commission, and two from the District of Columbia, still essentially rudderless and plannerless. Each jurisdiction was given veto power by a provision that an action could be approved by WMATA only if at least one vote from each subregional jurisdiction was recorded in its favor.

In 1968 WMATA adopted what was to be its basic system: about 98 miles of rail rapid transit routes crisscrossing in the core area of Washington and then radiating suburbward with approximately one-third of the mileage in each state. Buses would be used for an extensive "feeder" network, and future rapid transit lines would extend the system farther out into the sprawling urbanized region, including a line to Dulles Airport which consultants found (probably to later cheers by Reston dwellers) "entirely feasible."

(In 1971, before the consultants' study was completed, Transportation Secretary John Volpe showed that high federal officials were still as eager as ever to tinker with local Washington affairs. He proposed to build a relatively useless but twenty-first-century-looking tracked air-cushion vehicle—TAC–V—line down the median strip of the Dulles access highway, but he was ridiculed to the point of dropping the proposal: the line would not have penetrated into Washington's most urbanized areas, would have been too costly a "toy," would not have phased in properly with the proposed Metro system, and would not have served a large enough passenger flow, since few people would be likely to drive to the Dulles highway's starting point at the beltway, park, and then take the "TAC–V" for the remaining, and easiest, leg of the trip.)

With the adoption of the basic system in 1968, everything seemed clear for a start-up in construction—some sixty years after the *Washington Post* had warned that rapid transit would be "indispensable." Maryland's Montgomery County Council authorized the issuance of bonds to finance its share of construction, and in November 1968, while Atlantans were turning down rapid transit by a wide margin, the remainder of Washington's suburbanites in each local government jurisdiction were approving their rapid transit bond issues by margins as high as 79 percent, with an average 71 percent in favor region-wide. Those votes, however, did not take care of the District of Columbia's local share for transit construction. Those funds had to come from Congress itself, still the rulers and purse-holders of the city.

During that same period, citizens of the District had succeeded in irritating powerful members of Congress by their unyielding op-position to a freeway-building program that threatened to crosshatch the city and its neighborhoods with concrete troughs. As Ben Kelley, at the time the public affairs director for the Federal Highway Ad-ministration, later observed in his book, *The Pavers and the Paved* (Donald W. Brown, Inc., New York, 1971):

> No catalogue of urban highway grief would be complete without recognition of the District of Columbia's years-long running war of resistance to freeways—a community-wide movement that has remained alive and vigorous despite heavy-handed maneuvers by road lobbyists and their congressional collaborators to put down more pavement in a city already crisscrossed with more freeway miles per capita and per square mile than any other in the United States, including symbolic Los Angeles.

The list of wastes that would be wrought by the District's planned and programmed highways was impressive: a cost of 65 million dollars a year for eight to ten years; dismemberment of several of the city's finest neighborhoods; destruction of 180 acres of residential property and displacement of 15,000 residents; destruction of 225 acres of commercial property, 245 of parks, monuments, and other government-owned land, 41 of schools, churches, cemeteries, and other charitable purposes, and removal of 6 million dollars a year in taxes from the District's already starved treasury.

Once built, the highways could play even greater havoc. Already the metropolitan area has some 800,000 cars, buses, and trucks reg-istered, and the District of Columbia has set the unenviable record of the nation's most densely auto-populated city. Washington has nearly 4,000 cars per square mile. More freeways can only cause this car population to grow—along with the inordinate problems that attend such growth.

The battle line between highway builders and the coalition of citizen groups was drawn at three small rock islands in the Potomac River near Georgetown, the "Three Sisters," where the highwaymen wanted to build a sixth river bridge, a superspan they say is vital to the success of the District's freeway plan. In December 1967, after extensive public hearings, a new City Council in the District (a mini-step toward home rule granted earlier that year) voted not to build the bridge and to restudy the rest of the highway system programmed for the District. The House Public Works Committee, responding with what Kelley called "a mixture of amazement and fury," succeeded in tacking on to the 1968 Federal Aid Highway Act an edict that the District build the bridge and freeways whether it wanted them or not. Each side had its studies. This time, even the National Capital Planning Commission sided against the Three Sisters Bridge. Not content with the City Council's ruling against the freeway program (no one believed the local "governing" body had the final say, anyway), the citizens' groups had also tangled the highways in court suits and won a favorable ruling in February 1968 from the United States Court of Appeals for the District of Columbia.

Congress retaliated again in August 1968. The House Appropriations subcommittee for the District of Columbia deleted the District's local share of subway-building funds from its fiscal-1969 budget, and the subcommittee's chairman, Congressman William H. Natcher of Bowling Green, Kentucky, remained true to the legacy of tyrannical congressional dominion over the District's local government. He stated: "As soon as the freeway system gets under way beyond recall, our committee will recommend the appropriation of funds for the rail transit system."

The freeway-subway impasse remained just that for a full year, as others attempted to mediate behind the scenes. Secretary of Transportation John A. Volpe, riding on a past reputation as an energetic highway builder while a governor of Massachusetts but also anxious to fashion for himself a new image as a friend to urban public transit, privately offered to release the federal matching funds even though the District did not yet have its local one-third share, a course clearly illegal. Then he tried to mediate, drawing President Richard Nixon himself into it after a helicopter tour of the morning rush hour. In August 1969, to a storm of angry shouting by citizens in the council chamber, the City Council reluctantly reversed its no-highways position: it agreed to build the bridge and freeways. As construction began on the bridge—with angry students and housewives lying in the paths of bulldozers—Natcher triumphantly released the first year of local funds for the Metro. Ironically, the strategy that jarred the impasse open was that a Virginia congressman, Republican Joel T. Broyhill of Arlington, threatened to hold as hostage for the freeway program not only the subway money but the District's entire budget.

To great fanfare in December 1969, the region's officials broke ground for the start of construction on the Metro. Almost symbolically it was a cold, gray, drizzling day that promised future troubles for the Metro. First, a halt to construction was ordered by the United States Department of Transportation after black groups protested that, despite promises, blacks were not getting anywhere near their share of jobs on subway contracts. The federal Labor Department stepped in, held hearings, and finally issued a "Washington Plan" for fair employment in federally aided construction, and WMATA reached agreements to help black contractors overcome hurdles to win construction contracts.

Congressman Natcher also reentered. The highway department had tried to start building the Three Sisters Bridge despite protests by citizens at "design" hearings ordered by the courts, so the anti-highway coalition had again tangled the bridge project in court appeals based on environmental-impact issues. Natcher, in renewed retaliation, used the weapon he had come to know best: he held hostage the District's 1971 appropriations earmarked for the District's local share of subway-building costs. (This was not "federal" money being held back, but District taxes still being deposited with the Treasury.) Metro construction was able to creep forward, however, as suburban government continued paying their local shares—albeit with increasing wariness that Congress would eventually fudge on its commitment—and their federal two-thirds matching grants continued in. Repeatedly, however, WMATA found itself with its bank account depleted of uncommitted funds.

In November 1970 Transportation Secretary Volpe gave WMATA a 57-million-dollar short-term rescue loan as an advance payment of the federal share, and it kept the awarding of construction contracts going to the end of that year, but then again WMATA ran dry. In February 1971 Volpe offered 68 million dollars more in federal funds, but the money never came; this time, again, it was unquestionably illegal. There were signs that the long series of impasses might be coming to an end, however: two of the Congress's most avid highway-building flag-wavers had been removed from their seats—Democratic Representative George Fallon by an irate, anti-freeway citizenry in Baltimore, and Republican William Cramer of Florida resigning his seat to run (unsuccessfully) for the United States Senate. Additionally, when Natcher's subcommittee voted to add fiscal 1972's 37 million dollars to the 34 million dollars already held back for fiscal 1971, four members of the subcommittee issued their own minority report calling for release of the funds. The effort, led by Representative Robert N. Giaimo, a Connecticut Democrat, forced a floor vote, and the House assumed the guilt that earlier had been heaped on Natcher and his committee alone; the vote was 219 to 170 for Natcher and against Metro.

A half-year lobbying effort ensued in an attempt to reverse that posture. In private communications Secretary Volpe tried to assure subway-kidnapping congressmen that the District would indeed proceed with freeway and bridge construction once legal technicalities (environmental impact hearings and considerations) thrown in the way by the United States Court of Appeals could be surmounted. Suburban governments, meanwhile, served notice that they would refuse to put another dollar into the subway program until Congress freed the District's share. Dire warnings that the subway was "as good as dead" came from every direction, and congressmen opposing release of the funds were subjected to a stream of public criticism. The region's local government and WMATA sent direct appeals to President Richard Nixon seeking his intercession. The President sent his own chief House lobbyist into the fray and himself issued three direct appeals—a personal public statement in mid-November, another through his press secretary at the end of the month, and a personal letter the following day to House Speaker Carl Albert when the speaker announced that he was siding with Natcher and the Appropriations Committee. He also ordered the Justice Department to ask the Court of Appeals to reconsider its ruling on the Three Sisters Bridge and, if that didn't work, to appeal directly to the Supreme Court.

The showdown vote came in December, with junior congressmen, led by Representative Giaimo and Representative Silvio Conte of Massachusetts, the second-ranking Democrat and top-ranking Republican on Natcher's subcommittee respectively, pitted against most of the leadership of both parties. After seven hours of sometimes angry debate over a federal judge's right to hold up freeway and bridge construction ordered by Congress, word came that the Court of Appeals had just refused President Nixon's request that it reconsider its position. When the vote was taken in Congress, the subway won continued life by a stunning upset victory of 195 to 174. The District's 72 million dollars in 1971 and 1972 subway appropriations was released, and with it federal matching funds that brought the total to 211.5 million dollars. WMATA announced that it would now be able to begin subway operations on 4.5 miles of line on July 4, 1974—"sort of a curtain raiser for the bicentennial celebrations," the community relations director for WMATA called it.

But despite the elation among urban anti-highway forces, it was hardly likely that pro-highway forces in Congress would thereafter decline to continue using strong-arm tactics when annual Metro appropriations came due again.

When the Metro was being planned, its designers promised heady things for the District. President Nixon had declared after Natcher's initial release of funds in 1969, "More than a subway will begin in December. A city will begin to renew itself, a metropolitan area to pull itself together." Secretary Volpe was equally ecstatic at the ground-breaking: "It will bring new life to Washington, new growth, new development, new improvement, and this progress will be far greater than most of us realize. The development of this rapid transit system will give us a tool for shaping a better quality of life for all people in the District and in nearby Maryland and Virginia. . . . This transit system offers a proud and significant hope for altering the course of the forces of urban decay. This transit system can and must help set in motion the force and momentum of urban revitalization." The District's appointed mayor, Walter Washington, cited the fifteen thousand jobs the system's construction would create, the new mobility it would afford, the "more intensive development" and increased employment and taxes it would bring, and added, "It will stimulate community development along the system and around each subway stop."

Throughout the 1960's, when few yet believed a subway system would actually be built, such promises had been made in abundance. Indeed, it was such promises and the development that had paced alongside rapid transit construction in such cities as San Francisco, Toronto, Montreal, and European centers during the past two decades that had caused the Regional Planning Commission to bank so much of its "wedges and corridors" scheme for the metropolis on its radial rapid transit network, then still only dotted lines on a map. Turning the promises into a reality was quite another matter.

In that regard the suburbs had far outdistanced the District of Columbia by the time construction began on the subway in December 1969. Arlington, across the Potomac from Georgetown, had put together a massive skyscraper community called Rosslyn on what had formerly been acres of junkyards, pawnshops, and shabby dwellings (the pawnshops came after suffragettes, early in the century, had staged a torchlight march across a bridge to Arlington and burned the area's houses of prostitution). Crystal City, another large cluster of glassy towers, had arisen near National Airport in Virginia. Other, even larger centers were being mapped by developers along the Jefferson Davis Highway corridor in northern Virginia. In Maryland, Friendship Heights was a skyscraper city of office, commercial, and apartment space just across the line from the District of Columbia,

Rockville had skyscrapers many larger cities would envy, and Silver Spring had Falkland being planned as a major center by another developer. In each case these places had been identified on the rapid transit maps as stops on the routes. They were not always planned with rapid transit's and the community's best interests at heart, but they were built large and quickly by avaricious developers and local governments just as eager to reap tax revenues from new rapid transit cluster growth.

The Maryland and Virginia suburban communities each had sub-regional planning commissions designing new zoning structures that would encourage the "planned unit developments" that took large acreages and fashioned them into mini-downtowns. The District had only its decaying core and its archaic zoning regulations inherited from the days when firehoses were not strong enough and fireladders not long enough to reach higher than a dozen stories.

At the groundbreaking in 1969 Mayor Washington proposed that the District government, "together with the [National Capital] Planning Commission, the Zoning Commission and the Redevelopment Land Agency [a federal agency responsible for urban renewal in Washington] develop specific programs designed to take advantage of this opportunity." All the National Capital Planning Commission had done thus far was identify certain proposed subway stations as ideal for major development as foggily defined "uptown centers."

In 1970 conditions were becoming right for change in the District. For years the Senate had passed home-rule legislation for the District only to watch it killed in the House of Representatives, usually without even committee hearings. In 1965 it happened again, and in 1967 President Lyndon Johnson devised a new strategy: he drafted a reorganization program for the District (not one to give its voters control over their own affairs, but one that at least placed its government a little closer to the non-voters). Because it was "reorganization" and not "home rule," it did not need active adoption by the Congress and was routed away from the death-mill of the southern-controlled House District Committee.

Under the new government, the city is administered by a mayor and deputy mayor appointed by the President, and a nine-member City Council, also appointed by the President, serves as a quasi-legislative body. President Johnson appointed as mayor Walter E. Washington, a black man who had once served as head of the National Capital Housing Authority and, briefly, of New York's public housing agency. (Johnson had earlier tried to name Washington one of the District's three commissioners, but Congress had balked; it didn't want a black man in charge of the District's police department!) Black majorities were named to the City Council and the initial school board, and future school board seats became elective positions. Congress, however, retained its proprietorship over the District's purse and its budget, including that of the school system—a fact that led quickly to the new government's first lesson in power when it tried, a month after taking office, to represent the District's residents in the highway controversy.

Mayor Washington, though given little but in-house powers, attempted to use them effectively. In reorganizing the administration of city government, he moved into new consolidated departments under his direct executive control several functions that had previously been performed by seemingly autonomous units which had had little responsiveness to any central urban command post. He placed trusted aides in charge of the new consolidated departments "by sidetracking administrators he feels are unresponsive," according to the *Washington Post*. Community improvement programs came under the umbrella of his special assistant for housing. Into a "human resources department" he consolidated health and welfare. Another consolidated office became an "environmental services department" that brought together trash disposal, air and water pollution, sewage, food inspection, and highway beautification. Mayor Washington was also able to satisfy one need that had been neglected by all the planning and "city beautiful" movements for a century— planning for the city's ignored east side, and most particularly, its farther reaches across the Anacostia River. From within his new housing office came a plan for renewal of one-half of the area, the "Far Southeast," where in 1868 a farm had been converted into a residential compound for freed slaves, complete with many programs of public assistance and community control thought radically liberal by conservatives even a century later.

At about this juncture, just a week before Metro's ground-breaking, a black city councilman named Joe Yeldell, then also serving as chairman of the Metro-building authority, called together the leading officials of the District and its still persisting proliferation of federal and quasi-federal planning agencies and told them:

> We are here to find ways to take advantage of—to use the energizing force of—a once-in-a-lifetime chance to improve our city and improve the national capital region for all the people who live and work here. I think this is the most important city and region in the world. So when we succeed in this difficult task, we can be very very proud.
>
> If we can't do it now, we can't do it ever.

If we *don't* do it now, we won't do it ever.

But I am certain we *can* do it. That is exactly why we are here this morning . . . . We have time, too, if we are creative, uninhibited, if we really use our imagination . . . .

Now we are here in this room to see to it that this million-volt energizer [Metro] does become the spur to a better environment as was intended all along. Specifically, we are in this room to see to it that the areas around Metro entrances, around Metro stations, are seed areas for a better city, that the improvements spread out from these centers. With the coordination of you in the public agencies in this room working with the creativity and imagination of the private sector, we can do things now that we have never been able to do before.

It will not be easy. We must overcome our own inertia, and, perhaps, some of our old ways of thinking . . . .

Out of that meeting and several more grew the October 1970 creation of the Transit Development Team. At first it was to be an assemblage of representatives from several sources, most of them contributing a staff member or two for full-time service: the National Capital Planning Commission, the Redevelopment Land Agency, the District Highway Department, the District Zoning office, the District Office of Community Services. Only the District seemed interested enough to do the work, however, and the "team" became a unit within the mayor's housing office, staffed by District personnel, receiving only funds from the Redevelopment Land Agency and holding some "coordination" meetings with the National Capital Planning Commission.

Though the "team" was initially established within the executive branch of the District government, the City Council expressed so much interest in its work that it soon was answering to both the mayor and the council. Even its function came to shift away from its initial assignment of planning development *around* transit stations. The first chores it undertook concerned transit routes and station designs themselves.

The readjustments of the roles and assignments of the Transit Development Team were clear indications of the shortcomings of Metro planning that had preceded it during the 1960's. Engineers, cost analysts, economists, traffic statisticians, and a host of other specialists had planned the system as a sound transportation network. But highway planners had done that with their highways also, and the highways were still destroying cities everywhere. What had not been done with highways, and what was only now beginning to be done with Metro, was the orchestration of the *impact* the technology, routes, station locations, and station designs would have on the community—not simply how well the transportation would work, but how it would alter the shape of the region. That a new transportation system will change the shape of the city and its environs is beyond question; that the change could be planned and made to benefit the community was the new challenge, ignored consistently through the decades of unplanned zoning and unbridled speculation and development attendant upon superhighway routing and Metro mapping. Only in 1971 was it confronted by the District of Columbia.

In its evolution the Transit Development Team could not avoid butting heads with the Washington Metropolitan Area Transit Authority, the agency of specialists that had adopted the transit plan and was immersed in trying to keep it financially afloat and under construction. It came with the "team's" release of its "Far Northeast" plan, which examined the impact of Metro's line across that long-neglected sector of the city. The prickliest thorn between WMATA and the District "team" was over parking lots. WMATA had designed its system with a considerable amount of parking spaces around Metro stations; the "team" urged sharp reductions in the amounts of parking to be provided, arguing that suburbanites' cars should be intercepted before entering the District and that auto usage in the District should be discouraged, not encouraged. In many ways it was a harkening back to the 1950's recommendation of the Institute of Public Administration to Congress that the regional transit agency yet to be born be "endowed with the powers to . . . institute a systematic control over . . . parking, particularly parking in the District."

About half of the 4,650 parking spaces planned for Metro stations by WMATA were to be located at four stations on the line through northeast Washington. As the transit team pointed out in a hearing before the D.C. City Council, "It would be ironic to wake up in a few years and find District residents using the transit system to commute to new transit-related employment centers in the suburbs, while our stations' areas remain undeveloped. Present plans call for thirty acres of prime land, adjacent to transit stations, to be used for parking." Most important to the "team" in its proposals was what the mayor's special assistant for housing programs, James G. Banks, called "a sense of place," something, he pointed out to the City Council, a Metro rider certainly would not feel upon leaving a subway station and finding himself on an asphalt desert of parking. Station by station the Transit Development Team's director, John Fondersmith, recommended reducing parking facilities by half or more, even eliminating parking at one station. WMATA and the National Capital Planning Commission protested that the parking facilities were needed to draw riders from those who might otherwise drive into the downtown, but

Fondersmith pointed out that even WMATA's estimates showed only between 2 and 5 percent of its riders would be lost if they had no parking facilities. The D.C. City Council accepted its "team's" recommendations and instructed its delegates to WMATA to vote against the parking: cities were for people, not cars. Then WMATA, too, changed its mind.

There were other issues as well—access points, the number and placement of entrances to stations—but it appeared in 1971 that WMATA, cost-conscious with a recalcitrant Congress still hanging on to the District's funds, and the transit "team" bent on reshaping the Metro plan for maximum community benefit, were negotiating their differences. In some cases the transit team's input was reaping major rewards. In others WMATA was able to show that the changes sought would cost more than the system could bear. Already, inflation during the lengthy, congressionally imposed delays had pushed Metro's estimated building costs from 2.5 billion to almost 3 billion dollars.

Understandably, WMATA was miffed that what it thought was a locked-in design for constructing the Metro system was now being reopened by the "team" in the District Building, but the city was in vital need of such a reopening, and Metro did present what seemed to be a last chance for the District to revitalize the urban core of the region. The Transit Development Team, "catching up" on its review of station designs within the District, is now reverting its attention back to its original assignment, planning development for the neighborhoods around the stations themselves, in effect attempting to turn each station into the "sense of place" nucleus for a revitalized community—parks, sky-rises, apartments, offices, shopping, or private homes, or perhaps a blend of several of these—and thereby renewing, little by little, the entire city area.

The city still has to confront the failures of its past, however, and even Metro cannot hope to blot all of them out.

Schools are in more disarray than ever, the quality of most of the city's public education is scandalous, and teachers, administrators, and parents are in an uproar over how best to make the schools serve the true needs of their almost all-black constituency.

During the 1960's blacks rapidly concentrated inside the city and whites continued their flight to suburbia: in 1960 blacks accounted for 54 percent of the District's population; by 1970 they had reached 72 percent, and total population had declined. An analysis by the Washington Center for Metropolitan Studies showed that housing for blacks and for large families was worse at the end of the 1960's than it had been at their start.

The city had been wracked by three days of rioting, looting, and burning during April 1968 and had been left scarred by deaths, injuries, boarded-over buildings, and vacant lots; the damage and the costs of quelling the eruption had totaled 27 million dollars. In the 1970's the suburbanites who use the city by day and flee it by night still think of Washington as crime-ridden, alien territory, yet in 1967, a year in which politicians heading into the 1968 elections were particularly fond of labeling Washington the crime capital of the nation, the Federal Bureau of Investigation's own count of violent crimes per unit of population showed Washington not first but sixth of the major cities—even behind such a choice and "charming" city as San Francisco, which ranked third. Still, it was not a crime rate to be proud of.

Washington's new city government responded to the image-wrecking political propaganda that gave its crime rate such high visibility by instituting major changes in its police force and increasing patrols and, as a result, effecting a reduced crime rate by the 1970's that still did not seem to mollify suburbia's fears. During 1970 Washington's metropolitan area ranked not first in the nation for crime but twentieth, behind such other well-known "crime capitals" as Albuquerque, Denver, Fort Lauderdale-Hollywood, New Orleans, Phoenix, Seattle-Everett and Stockton, California. And the crime rate of Washington proper is now dropping by an astounding 14 percent annually while in some of the city's suburbs it is climbing—by as much as 7 percent in Montgomery County, 14 percent in Alexandria, and 22 percent in Prince Georges County.

Several citizens' groups want the National Capital Planning Commission abolished and its planning of the District transferred to the one place where it belongs, within the District government itself: only then can planning have any significant effect on public policy. Earlier, a retiring board member proposed abolishing the planning commission, and President Lyndon Johnson's Bureau of the Budget even drafted an executive order to that effect, but it was never signed by the President. Under Mayor Washington's reorganization and the creation of the Transit Development Team it appears that the District government will accomplish by fiat what the federal government failed to do—turn control of planning of the District's environment over to the District itself.

In the face of blight, poverty, and tremendous community service needs, the city has only its meager powers, unresponsive federal agencies, and collapsing financial health. Its resources are extremely limited. The federal government still owns property equal at least to the value of its contribution in revenues to the city, and yet it imposes considerable demands on that city: playing host to everyone from ambassadors, presidents, and princes to the Poor Peoples Campaign, Honor America Day thousands, and anti-war demonstrators; maintaining a city of monuments, parks, and clean public grounds for the tourists, including the preservation of large open spaces and low building heights that not only save the view of the Capitol dome but also discourage private developers and cut deeply into the city's potential property tax income; preserving the image of a "model" to the nation and the world. For these services Washington receives little more from the nation it serves than disparaging remarks. The city serves suburbia, too, but, thanks to Congress, it cannot even collect income taxes from the scores of thousands of Virginians and Marylanders who work in the District, daily bringing their streams of cars to bang the District's pavements, demand more and more low-tax-yield parking lots downtown, and pollute its air. (It has been estimated that almost 85 percent of Washington's air pollution, now growing critical, is due to automobile traffic, and even Washington's many monuments are crumbling at the edges from the corrosive air pollutants.)

Many of the city's problems, of course, are the outgrowths of racial fear and the legacy left by a century of rule by federal "outsiders" whose hidden—and sometimes not so hidden—motives for refusing home rule to the District were similarly based on race. The Congress, and particularly the House, has consistently refused to admit that in a democratic nation the capital cannot claim to be a "model" for the country unless it, too, is given democracy. During the 1960's the District's residents were at last given the right to vote in presidential elections; their high proportion of voting astounds the politicians who long called them apathetic. Their government has been "reorganized," and their new appointed city officials are trying to represent them but are denied significant powers; true home rule still remains only a wishful dream for the thousands of residents who display bumper stickers protesting "D.C.: The Last Colony." In a fractional gesture of generosity in 1971 the District was finally permitted to elect a single delegate to the national legislature that rules it with such a heavy hand, but the delegate is not given full membership rights: he is denied a vote on the floor of the House; the non-voting delegate is simply the reinstitution of a provision made by the Reconstruction Congress when it first took home rule away from the city in the switch to three and a half years of Territorial Government a century ago.

The congressional grip on District affairs remains vise-like, as exemplified only too well by the strong-arm strategy of Kentucky's Representative Natcher in holding subway funds hostage for highways. Nor is Natcher alone. South Carolina's Representative John L. McMillan, chairman of the House District Committee, rivaled him in considering Washington a Southern plantation, with himself installed as plantation boss. In callous disregard for history, democratic traditions, and basic humanity, his committee had the temerity to state as official dogma in a 1971 report:

> Washington is a federal city, established exclusively for the benefit of, and as home for, the federal government and its agencies . . . .
> It is not the Congress, or the federal establishment, which is the interloper here . . . but rather the thousands of persons who have swarmed here, most of whom add little or nothing to the day-by-day operations of the federal government . . . who are the intruders and who are not vital to the federal government's operations
> . . . . Washington is a federal city, occupying its own land, and owes nothing to the District residents thereon.

Presumably the South Carolinian chairman would have had all non-federal employees expelled from the District of Columbia without so much as a relocation payment. His public posture, were it not so tragic for Washingtonians, would be ludicrous for its display of ignorance; even he must recognize that as much as any other city a "federal city" needs its store owners and clerks, its doctors and lawyers, its custodial workers and sanitation engineers, its druggists and barbers, its secretaries and typewriter repairmen. As a "city" it is even likely to have its poor, its jobless, its ill, its hopeless, and its criminals. Perhaps even a South Carolina congressman can recognize that these elements also "swarmed" to Washington at least in large part *because* it is a federal city. What the city's congressional overlords have been unwilling to admit is that they do, in fact, "owe" Washington and its residents—federal employees and non-employees alike —something: the right to self-government, for starters.

In 1972 the wall of congressional dominion was crumbling further, with liberal members of the House District Committee expanding ranks and gaining momentum in their push for home rule and Chairman McMillan on his way out of the Congress (defeated in his reelection bid in South Carolina) after 17 terms. Assuming no further upsets, the District chairmanship passes to a liberal, black Congressman Charles C. Diggs, Jr., of Detroit. Appointment of a liberal to take McMillan's committee seat would probably assure District residents of their long sought right to govern themselves.

It is to be hoped as well that a return to popular control will end such grandiose in-town highway schemes as one still being promoted by highway interests—a tunnel slice through the best of the city's monument and riverfront parklands.

Aside from the District's own problems, there is the legacy of regional failure. The "Year 2000" plan was a farce, ready for the dusty back shelves of planners' libraries the moment it received formal "adoption." There is no regional plan for the area, only a collection of local and subregional plans that the Council of Governments is prepared to call a plan for the metropolis. Highways and racism have scattered the city throughout the region and are rapidly expanding it further. By 1970, when the population of the region numbered 2.86 million, the metropolis had sprawled to two additional counties in Virginia and was threatening to reach even farther; in Maryland it is rapidly closing the gap of relatively vacant land between Washington and Baltimore and turning the capital into a contiguous part of the East Coast megalopolis. Thanks to congressional backwardness and tinkering, Metro is coming too late to stop the wild scattering of the city for some time to come. The region's land is being consumed at a pace that can be called nothing but an ecological disaster, while the District's tax base is shriveling. Not only has Washington lost a net of 1 percent of its population during the past decade, but employment and retail sales are also migrating to the suburbs. Possibly the height of irresponsibility, even the federal government is suburbanizing its jobs by moving several agencies to new, outlying facilities in Maryland and Virginia.

In the face of this, the Council of Governments is still a timid group of local politicians insisting that theirs is a voluntary venture which, far from bridging the region to a logical metropolitan form of government, is in fact an agency that will keep regional government away. This despite the recommendation of the joint congressional committee, which studied metropolitan affairs as far back as 1958 and even then recognized:

> It is the hard decisions that face the Washington metropolitan area with the greatest urgency today . . . . Confederations—particularly informal confederations—by their very nature have difficulty in making hard decisions. They are particularly ineffective in making decisions over an extended period of years.

To this, Royce Hanson added his own anaylsis:

> Unless the council, through the planning process, succeeded in asserting some policy guidance or even direction over regional programs, the initiative for a metropolitan program will come from the operating agencies, the highway departments, NCTA [National Capital Transportation Agency, forerunner of the Metro-building WMATA], the parks authorities, the sanitation agencies. The council, planning power or not, would still ratify decisions over which it had no control and little influence.

In the 1970's Hanson's warnings of the 1960's sound like prophecy. By its own choice, the Council of Governments performs little more than such a role. The nation's capital region deserves better.

6
Urban America Adrift

Viewed from one perspective, each of the five case cities seems uniquely the product of its own peculiar combination of personality traits that makes of it a gentleman financier or a tough factory foreman, a wealthy *belle dame* too conscious of her appearance or a highly placed government official also too conscious of his dress and not conscious enough of his "public trust." Viewed from the perspective of the specific, every city is unique. From the perspective of underlying generalities, however, urban communities have much in common. All of urban America shares the experiences that are common to the five case studies: Flint may be unusual as a General Motors town, but it is more typical than unique for its disdain of public transit. Washington, D.C., may be the federal city, the meeting place of the world's power, but in its rush to suburbia and its powerlessness in the face of urban needs, it is quite like every other large American city, from Kansas City to Portland, Oregon, to Miami,

Florida. Atlanta, Georgia, may be unusual for its power structure's rekindled interest in rebuilding the city during the 1960's, but that was typically American, short-lived profiteering, and through it all the city fitted the American urban pattern of sprawl, waste, and consequent erosion of environment and of the city's ability to salvage its own health. Indianapolis, unusual for its Uni-Gov, is typical for its highway mania. Dayton, a manufacturing center, mixes all of these into its own peculiar blend of progressivism (for instance, its leadership in regionalizing public housing) and backwardness (for instance, its knee-jerk fears of regional government), yet it is probably the most American of the five case studies—diverse economically yet broken financially, unable to serve its population and faced by growing population demands, forced by sharply cut revenue into a tax race that is sharpening a bitter crossfire between confined city and spreading suburb, trying to carry on its urban functions and improve urban living but doing so without planning, coordination, or systematic goal and strategy design: Dayton is a city adrift, as urban America is adrift.

As was stated at the outset, almost any five American cities could have been selected and the pattern of growth and decline would have been the same. City locations were often the choices of industry seeking trade and shipment routes. Their growth came at the hands of migrations to feed the hungry factories of the few industrial revolution decades that closed the nineteenth century and opened the twentieth. In city after city the dismemberment began only a short while later— with the paving of streets, the switching to automobile traffic, and the federal program of subsidizing suburban home-buying during the New Deal 1930's—too soon after the nation had started its move to the cities and much too soon to permit an urbanizing nation to develop also an urbanly cultured civilization. The war temporarily stopped auto production and the slippage to the suburbs, but once the war was over the nation turned back to rapid suburbanization, burgeoning auto production, massive highway-building projects, and rampant suburban bulldozing for new development. What has resulted is the familiar pattern: domestic isolationism in the suburbs; fear of the cities by their former inhabitants, whether grounded on race, crime, decay, slum ugliness, disease, poor schools, high taxes, or simply the urban density and diversity of peoples; the fragmentation of urban areas into self-protectionist fiefs; the decimation and strangulation of cities by super-roads and super-traffic in the service of suburbanites.

The costs imposed upon us by our enforced dependence on roadways and automobiles for ground transportation can be counted in many ways: the 16 billion dollars a year in so-called "highway user" taxes diverted annually from local, state, and federal treasuries and earmarked for use only in paving yet more square miles of the planet's surface; the domestic programs that wait in dire want as these billions are poured into concrete; the perilous concentrations of carbon monoxide and other pollutants in the air that are destroying vegetation, buildings, and lives; the exorbitant waste of natural space, energy, raw materials, and dollars, all blended into the most inefficient mode of transportation ever devised by man; the wasted thousands of acres annually paved for parking in downtowns, at suburban shopping centers, and along the ugly suburban strips of hamburger stands, gasoline stops, and drive-in everythings; the 4 million Americans injured and 52,000 killed each year by roadway crashes; the wanton destruction and resource waste of crumpled fenders and aluminum-foil bumpers in "fender-benders"; the ecological waste of raw materials represented by the acres of automobile graveyards reposing languorously across rural landscapes in most parts of the country.

Our utter dependence on an inefficient piece of steel machinery calculated to be the second largest investment most Americans ever make in their lives—the automobile and its appurtenances of pavement, petroleum, and space waste—is also bound to have a major impact on urban areas. The five urban case studies of this book have looked at the costs of superhighways and automobile mania in that other way—one which, far from reducing the significance of other criticisms of the unbridled highway-building programs, adds to them the cogent reality that highways *are* in large measure responsible for the destruction of the urban root of whatever America has that future historians might choose to regard as civilization.

While highways and automobiles may not be destroying the urban cores of the nation single-handedly, they most certainly are dealing them the cruelest blow of all. By the time the superhighway scars were superimposed on the urban landscape, many of the cities were already being abandoned by affluent whites, by their tax resources, and by their leaders, and already they were becoming encampments for little more than poverty, crime, slums, and disease; urban freeway-building sealed that fate. Freeways made the flight from the city the American thing to do, and suburbia became the national way of life. From then on the cities never had a chance: like public health, public schools, public transit, and every other public venture abandoned by those who could afford its upkeep and left only to those who could not, the cities fell into disrepair. It is a natural process. By itself the suburban life style may not be so evil, though it most assuredly sets up a bland and isolationist process of wasteful consumption unparalleled in history; but when used as a retreat from the cities, it leads only to their destruction. Highways, by opening the suburbs to urban dwellers, are destroying the already dying cities. Part of the tragedy is the irony that the highways were so eagerly sought by downtown interests anxious to preserve and build the security of their investments; only belatedly have they learned that superhighways in the city are more bane than boon and begun in earnest to follow their customers out to suburbia and to build there the great new regional shopping centers, which themselves are helping to squeeze the remaining life from our downtowns.

The intolerable financial burden placed on cities by federal highway schemes has also sped urban governments toward poverty and powerlessness in the face of unprecedented need. Most cities, their budgets straining to the breaking point to provide even a bare minimum of social services for their increasingly needy populations, are learning too late that the so-called 10-cent federal highway dollars are considerably more expensive. As in Indianapolis, surface streets need widening, repaving, even rerouting in order to cope with expressway-sized traffic loads, and these surface street "improvements" must be paid for out of local budgets. More than half of the 16 billion dollars in "highway user" taxes collected in 1971 by all levels of government was generated in urban areas, and of the almost 4 billion dollars a year diverted to highways from *non*-user taxes that could well have been spent on more critically needed domestic programs, city treasuries contributed by far the largest chunk—1.7 billion dollars—almost three-fourths again as much as state and federal governments combined. Since 1965 total highway expenditures by cities have jumped 45 percent to an estimated 3 billion dollars in 1971, of which 55 percent is in non-highway-use taxes, and the general tax revenues —usually real estate taxes, the single major source of income allowed most of our beleaguered cities—that cities have poured into highways since 1965 have grown even more wildly, 65 percent by 1971. As Patrick Healy, executive vice-president of the National League of Cities and editor of its *Nations' Cities,* pointed out in the July 1971 issue of the magazine, "Clearly, highway users do not bear the full cost of city highways." He concluded, "It is time for city officials to rethink their position. . . ."

With Uncle Sam offering a dollar's worth of pavement for every 10 cents in state funding and the cities ostensibly asked to contribute nothing but a few headaches and cooperation, few were daring enough to "rethink their position" and turn down such apparent largesse, especially when it seemed to offer *some* kind of hope with *some* kind of public works assistance to cities grasping for hope from almost any quarter. Still, early in the 1960's San Francisco put a stop to highways, in mid-decade Manhattan also put a stop to highways, and in 1971, declaring that the city "does not belong to the automobile," Toronto also rejected urban superhighways and sent a new wave of anti-highway sentiment across the American border to Rochester, New York, and a host of other cities. In the early 1970's urban Americans are growing adamant in their displeasure at highways and their peculiar brand of "progress" and development. Though admittedly still in the minority in most cities, the numbers of urban freeway fighters are growing. It is safe to predict that during the remainder of the 1970's many more cities will join San Francisco, New York, and Toronto in finding superhighways too costly and too impolitic to build.

Perhaps more critical to the city than the direct-dollar costs of "free" ways is the cost reflected in the removal of the urban tax base. On the heels of highway building, each of the five cities reviewed witnessed rapid suburbanization of populations, community facilities, job centers, educational centers, and retailing complexes—each move taking from the city what could have provided vitally needed tax resources. Additionally, as the superhighways have smashed through countless urban neighborhoods like Atlanta's Morningside, they have eliminated hundreds of homes and businesses from tax rolls and have left the communities dismembered and dispirited. As a result, many such communities are becoming blighted, shabby, poverty-stricken, deteriorated, garbage-strewn pockets that pose additional tax burdens on the parent city instead of being preserved as stable, taxpaying members of the urban community. Even the Model Cities programs, launched with such high hopes for revitalizing the urban cores of the nation, have themselves been made the victims of highway havoc.

In "opening" the suburbs, the most dramatic, drastic, and costly change the highways have imposed upon America's cities has been the unplanned and uncoordinated scattering of the "city" over the landscape. What Flint, Michigan, hopes to memorialize in its Automobile Hall of Fame should actually be regarded as a national tragedy. It is an ecological disaster: a rich land being laid waste by the ignorance of too much developmental sprawl and too many unsightly institutions for the care, feeding, and sheltering of man's most voracious beast of burden, the automobile. It is also a sociological disaster: mankind hiding in homogenized island camps, fearful of wayfarers and unlikes, and establishing an amazing number of small governments as jurisdictional barricades from behind which former urban dwellers can do battle against neighbors and those who still remain in the city. Metropolitan regions have become characterized by large arrays of such small overlapping governments, none performing efficiently. This balkanization of the city continues to undermine any rational approach to solutions of urban problems; the additional balkanization of federal programs administered as separate self-protectorates by civil servant bureaucracies only compounds the urban dilemma by increasing the spread of a crazy quilt of patchwork programs and governments working at cross-purposes or on parallel courses but almost never with a comprehensive, coordinated approach to problem-solving.

As happened in Flint, as is happening in Dayton, and as is likely to happen in cities throughout the country if there is no change in transportation policy, public transportation is dying, another victim of suburbanization and the automobile. Hundreds of bus companies, forced by rising labor costs and slumping ridership to raise fares and cut services, have simply gone out of business during the last fifteen years, the years of the Interstate Highway program—most of them leaving the young, the old, the poor and the invalid stranded. Some of the bus companies passed into the hands of local governments to be run as trimmed-down deficit operations, usually with little change in management policies or plunging statistical stairsteps. The reasons were as simple as beginners' math: during the auto-travel-subsidizing years of 1945 to 1970, fare-paying urban transit ridership fell from almost 19 billion a year to just under 6 billion, while costs soared, almost doubling from just over 1 billion dollars to just under 2 billion dollars in 1970.

Public transportation for urban masses needs an *urban* setting—one of densely developed centers of employment and residence. A suburban setting, by definition scattered and sprawled over great acreages of land, fails to provide the common centers of trip origins and destinations that mass public transit requires. Suburbs provide the crowds and jammed traffic patterns, but they are tailored instead to the private automobile service; a common, public carrier would have to match each automobile's trip for its door-to-door service, and that means passenger collection routes that wind their ways through every side street and into and out of every cul-de-sac of every suburban subdivision. Unable to match the door-to-door service convenience of the private car, public transit operators also make the false assumption that they are unable to match the private car's comfort. Because buses *have* not competed, most people—including many bus transit operators themselves—believe they *cannot* compete.

There is evidence, however, that compels quite a different conclusion. The Eagledale experience in Indianapolis, the success of Reston's express, the Shirley "busway" in Washington, the Capital Flyer in Atlanta, and even Flint's Maxi-Cab show that Americans will leave their cars and get on buses when public transportation offers a decent alternative to a traffic jam. Indeed, a 1970 study of public use of and attitudes toward public transportation, conducted by Market Facts, Inc., of Chicago, Illinois, shows that 8 percent of men with family incomes of $15,000 or more a year are likely to use public transportation—comparable to the 6 percent of men with family incomes under $6,000 a year. The fragmentary evidence, the researchers conclude, at least is enough to indicate that American bus service is not aiming at its most likely riders. It is particularly interesting to note that of 5,000 questionnaires sent out by the researchers, 97 percent responded, indicating a considerable reservoir of interest in public transportation that most of its operators probably have no idea exists, judging by many of their informational and promotional performances in recent years.

Not only does public transit suffer ignominiously at the hands of highway building, auto mania, and the resultant widely scattered city, but buses and trains do so despite the fact that they offer the single opportunity most cities have to correct the imbalance. City planners are usually too weak to control the course of urban growth, city zoners seldom use their powers to exercise such control, and little else seems to exist to direct urban growth into logical space-saving patterns; public transit, had it remained a viable and growing service in urban areas, could have helped achieve such a result. The reawakening of interest in public transit at the end of the 1960's and in the early 1970's comes at a time when suburban sprawl via automobile has led Americans where it was eventually bound to lead them—to environmental concern. It could have been expected all along that the primary target of that concern would have been the automobile and its legacy of by-products.

Faced with these transportation realities, the Congress in 1970 took two typically patchwork—and strangely contradictory—actions. It adopted a 3.1-billion-dollar, five-year aid program for public transit (which was subsequently whittled to a pittance in the congressional and White House appropriations and budget processes for the first year or so of the program), and it extended until 1977 the life of the Highway Trust Fund, guaranteeing that about 4 billion dollars a year in federal money will continue to be poured into Interstate pavement during the next five years, much of it for urban freeways to help suburban commuters get into the city in the morning and out in the evening. In addition, the Federal Highway Administration now plans to top off its Interstate program with a scheme to build another 20,000 miles of rural road and urban thoroughfare by 1990 at a total cost of 320 billion dollars—172 billion dollars of it in federal taxes.

Meanwhile, the federal government's Urban Mass Transportation
Administration is using *its* new funding program to fight a rearguard
action and shore up failing bus companies like the one in Dayton. It
is interested in new technologies—small, personal-sized transit cap-
sules, tracked air-cushioned vehicles, and buses controlled by com-
puters for "dial-a-ride" systems—and is making substantial (but still
inadequate and belated) grants to help modernize and expand existing
rail systems in New York, Philadelphia-Camden, Boston, Cleveland,
and Chicago. But in the light of some of its own funded experiments,
it holds to a strangely archaic principle: the administration, in offering
guidelines to those seeking federal aid, specifies that it is most interested in what has been generally conceded to be the three public tasks
assigned to public transit: traffic-jam relief, the spurring of orderly
urban development and efficient and environmentally healthy land use
patterns, and *mobility for nondrivers*. Thus, the United States Government itself proclaims that public transit should be a service for a
special group rather than the considerably wider constituency indicated by the Reston experience, the Shirley "busway" experience, and
the Market Facts study of 1970. What the federal administration and
our cities are left with is a service for the poor—a policy which, as
noted, is sure to see to it that transit remains but a shabby and inefficient tool, deteriorating for lack of resources because its constituency is that part of the population least likely to command such
resources. It is to be hoped that if wiser heads are to prevail anywhere
in the urban problem-solving setting, it would be in the young federal
bureaucracy now growing up to slay the dragon of the freeways with
a new sword of public transportation. The sad fact is that that bureaucracy has demonstrated its weakness and, thus, its primary interest in self-preservation above dynamic resolution of urban problems;
the bureaucracy even fails to understand the full potential of its own
program. Its public transportation sword, on the other hand, is old,
chipped, and, in a shameful number of places, rusty or broken—just
the sort of public tool the nation has customarily reserved for its cities
and their captive populations.

The new rapid transit ventures being opened, built, or planned in
San Francisco, Washington, Atlanta, Baltimore, Seattle, Pittsburgh,
and a score of other cities are considerable improvements, of course,
but the great bulk of public transit in the United States remains a poor
man's service, of hardly any value in attracting great numbers of
affluent whites out of their cars and most definitely of no value in
either attracting new development or controlling the shape of the
city's growth.

Even more important than building sleek new city trains and

stations is the need to put transportation design to work for the total urban environment. The federally aided public transportation effort just beginning on a national scale must also spawn a local and national rethinking of the city's role, its structure, and its goals for itself and its citizens. The question that must be addressed—and one which is not being addressed squarely enough anywhere in urban America— is *not* simply whether sufficient federal funding will be available to salvage dying transit companies for those who, for one reason or another, cannot or will not drive cars, but whether the nation will continue to allow automobiles and highways to dictate the shape of its cities, the quality of the air, and the health of its urban economy and government. Salvaging a few hundred bus companies and building a dozen high-speed transit systems will mean little if the nation continues to pave over its cities with freeways. What is emphatically needed is not only the pumping of more money and technology into rails, rail cars, and buses to make them ride more smoothly, more swiftly, and farther—laudable as such efforts might be—but a new way of looking at and thinking about the city and its parts.

Cities need open spaces, left open not for parking but simply for breezes, trees, flowers, and lunchtime loitering by downtown workers. They need quiet resting places and bustling, active places. They need libraries and health clinics that are neighborhood places, not remote "agencies." They need bicycle paths, bridle trails, and crowded sidewalks and arcades and marketplaces. Cities need wide varieties of homes—new town houses, old row houses, high-rise apartments, and single-family houses. They need decent working environments and shopping environments. They need the excitement of diversity that only humanity can give them. They need these environments clustered in nodes where people are not afraid to be together.

Where modern, swift, comfortable rail rapid transit has gone into service, these kinds of environment have begun to develop—whether by private initiative or under government aegis or control. In this country, only the astounding developmental successes along Market Street in connection with San Francisco's Bay Area Rapid Transit system offers existing evidence of the change rapid transit can effect, but rapid transit and its effects on the urban environment have had considerably more notable success outside the United States. It was little wonder that in 1969 the Undersecretary of Transportation, James M. Beggs, told a press conference, "The foreigners are leading us in this field by a very large margin. . . . Clearly we're lagging the rest of the world. If you want to ride a truly modern transit system, you have to go abroad." Actually you don't have to cross the ocean. On this continent, Mexico City, Toronto, and Montreal have new and excit-

ing rapid transit systems that carry large numbers of commuters to
and from downtown each day in clean and modern subway trains and
stations. Around downtown stations massive new development has
grown up. Other impressively new rail rapid transit systems and lines
have opened or are soon to open in Rotterdam, Oslo, Milan, Stock-
holm, London, Paris, São Paulo, Madrid, Hamburg, Munich, Berlin,
Nuremburg, Vienna, Budapest, Tokyo, Osako, Hong Kong, Moscow,
Leningrad, and Kiev. Even the capital of South Korea will have a
modern, operating rapid transit before the capital of the United States.

But, as Washington is learning from its Transit Development
Team, it takes more than the simple building of a rail transportation
network to redirect the growth patterns of a city; also required are
development incentives, local government initiatives, and a wide range
of coordinated planning and policy decisions. If the score of American
cities preparing to enter the ranks of those with rapid transit are willing to make the difficult but firm commitment to redirected growth
patterns, they can reverse the decay, blight, and deathlike pall that is
reaching across their faces, but it will be no easy chore. It demands a
totally new approach, a new reaction to the private developer's
promises, a new respect for urban planning which separates the
strong plan that would lead a community out of its past from the
weak that would do no more than mirror the past and call it future,
and a new willingness to enforce the plans. The cities *can* be rebuilt
on a public transportation framework; abandonment is *not* their only
option. Indeed, abandonment is unthinkable: it offers no more than a
nation of suburbs and small "new-towns" avoiding at all costs the
festering of urban centers that look like Newarks, havens only for
rats, hate, fear, decay, disease, and the ruins of humanity. Rebuilding
the cities we have, not building "new" ones, alone offers the nation
its second chance of developing an urban society.

The first order of business must be the scrapping of the concept of
a "balanced" transportation system. That any sense of "balance" has
filtered into our ground transportation is a myth that satisfies only the
highway engineers. As has occurred in virtually every American
city, "balance" has meant automobile dominance. Dayton, Indianapolis, Flint, and Atlanta have all thrown their transportation resources
almost entirely into the highway basket, despite federal professions
that dollars will be used only for the balanced transportation systems
drawn up in comprehensive regional plans. Even if those regional
plans and the resulting public works projects for transportation did
produce "balanced" transportation—which they most assuredly do
not, either dollar-wise or potential ridership-wise—it would make
little urban transportation sense. Automobiles simply do not belong

in cities: they pollute the air, they waste energy, resources, and valuable space, they rob tax treasuries, they kill and maim, and they should not be mixed with pedestrian traffic flows. Far from providing a "balance" between cars and buses or trains, the federal government should be concentrating on ways of discouraging (if not altogether banning) automobile travel inside cities. Many cities now find themselves approaching a time when they may have to make decisions on such questions. If they decide to give the cities up to automobiles and private vehicle traffic, we have probably lost the battle to save our cities.

Once an alternative to automobile voraciousness is provided and the cars and highways are stopped at the urban fringe, the unkempt scattering of the city may be brought under control, but the highways' biggest mess, the already scattered urban constituency, still has to be dealt with. That, too, is of top priority if American cities are to be saved.

Only the federal government can make it work. For too long urban areas have been diced into warring fiefs and kept at war by petty officeholders afraid of losing what they are too seldom reminded are positions of public trust. Just as political "leaders" of the old South led an entire white population into racial bigotry through demagogy, so also have local officeholders kept suburbanites angry at city dwellers and their government through hardly less subtle rhetoric. As a result, in two decades only seven cities in the United States (Miami; Nashville; Jacksonville; Columbus, Georgia; Carson City, Nevada; Juneau, Alaska; and Indianapolis) have taken significant steps toward regional government; in many others there were those who advocated such action, but almost invariably their efforts led to failure at the hands of suburban bigotry toward cities. At the rate of seven cities every twenty years, the nation's remaining urban areas can hardly afford to wait so long for a logical framework for local government. It must come more swiftly; and for that, federal initiative—through aid incentives, direct reorganizations, and legislative mandates—will be necessary.

Such federal action, though dramatic on its face, has ample modern precedent. As the city spread itself beyond its corporate borders and new suburbanites refused to recognize any longer their responsibilities to the cities that they had fled, the federal government responded positively in the 1960's with legislation that forced the urban areas to enter into regional planning ventures. The federal government ordered that its planning grants go to specially recognized agencies, one per region, and these most often were regional agencies. The federal government also required that before federal aid could be granted to local public works projects, those projects had to be cleared through a regional "review" agency recognized by the federal government as competent to match the local project against a coordinated plan for regional goals. (The degree of competence among these "review" regional agencies is, naturally, subject to considerable question in some urban areas.) Local councils of governments sprang into being to perform these "review" functions, and in some (admittedly few) instances these councils held a more regional point of view than did the more typical Washington area's council of self-protective local officials. By the mid-1960's the federal government also was insisting on a continuing comprehensive regional transportation study as a prerequisite to continued federal highway aid in urban areas, and completion of such a regional study was a pre-condition to full two-thirds funding of local mass transit projects. In fact, by the 1970's regional planning was a widely accepted fact of urban life and a prerequisite for practically all federal aid—for anything from hospitals to airports, housing to sewers, police services to manpower training. It is now time for the federal government to take the initiative toward the next logical step— regional *government*. If it makes sense to plan regionally, it also makes sense to govern regionally. Washington and any number of other cities offer ample evidence that voluntary regional associations for "cooperation" have little efficacy in the face of large regional problems.

Indianapolis's county-wide consolidated government, Uni-Gov, provides a good model for regional government. It is strong, well organized, and efficiently coordinated. More than merely spreading urban governance over the entire urbanized area, Uni-Gov has brought government structure in line with government programs, in much the same way the mayor of Washington is attempting with his limited powers. Indianapolis, however, has one asset denied to many other local governments—the unification within one department of both planning and zoning. The unusual pairing of the two functions has shown the Indianapolis area especially capable of at least designing the proper tools for controlling growth of the urban area—if it chooses to use the tools. While its planning has had its shortcomings of timidity and is laboring under a peculiarly pro-automobile malady, the city has used its zoning authority to good advantage on some occasions (notable for their fewness as much as for their departures from customary laissez-faire practice). Over the years, however, that city has been as guilty as every other for allowing the random rape of the landscape for suburban development.

The major reason for the ravaging of the land around the nation's cities has been the race for tax revenues. Cities and suburbs alike have been particularly "charitable" in their concessions to developers because state governments have limited them by and large to the property tax as their sole major source of income. As a consequence, city and suburb are in a race for the ad valorem tax dollar and both earnestly believe that the developer is the angel who brings it, like the Tooth Fairy. Thus, in the Atlanta area Fulton County officials are ready to rape a river and large countryside tracts to improve their tax-taking ability, without heed for the fact that the development will require considerably more government-service outlay than that for which the new tax dollars will be able to pay. Similarly, in the Washington area the Maryland suburban counties altered the "wedges and corridors" plan as soon as it was issued by regional planners to assure that maximum development potential is retained over their vast acreages. Thus, also, suburban townships viciously battle Flint, Michigan, in repeated annexation disputes over the right to tax plants, homes, and shopping centers.

States also control cities in other ways. In many cases cities, as state-created corporations subject to state-level whims, are not free to annex, change government structure, set tax rates, reorganize courts, enter into intergovernmental compacts, or perform a whole series of other governmental acts without express permission from the state. Only when cities can free themselves from such outside control (not unlike Congress's control over Washington affairs) can they hope to escape the tax race and the bickering with their suburbs. That leads to the next logical step, a return to an example set in the classical age of Greece—the "city-state" system.

In 1969, when writers Norman Mailer and Jimmy Breslin ran for mayor and city council president of New York and suggested that New York City secede from the state and become a separate city-state in the classical Greek fashion, few took them seriously at first; within another year New York Mayor John Lindsay was seriously talking about the same concept. Under a city-state system urban areas would have the power to decide their own governmental structures, their own tax structures, and their own programmatic structures. They could have their own distinct representation within the federal government and could contract for aid from the federal government free of constraints imposed by rurally dominated state political agencies. Under a city-state system, government of an urban region could be organized to best meet the needs of the region. For instance, a city-state could be a blend of a regional "state" government and a federation of neighborhood councils. At the regional level it would be accorded full state status under the Constitution. Regional guidelines, policies, programs, and financial questions could all be decided at the city-state level as regional matters. The city-state governing body would have to be structured quite differently from a federation, however, since that would produce little more than the indecisiveness so characteristic of today's regional councils of governments. Instead, the city-state governing body could be an elected commission or board, elected from districts (perhaps with cross-jurisdictional lines similar to those mapped for Atlanta's "umbrella" planning council), or at large, or as a mix of both.

The city-state governing board could delegate the administration of programs and the distribution of services to local neighborhood councils to preserve citizen contact with government and, consequently, government responsiveness to its citizenry. Neighborhoods could have "little city halls," community centers, health clinics, libraries, and police precincts—all administered at the neighborhood level in conformity with city-state standards, policies, and directives. Final judgement on regional questions and arbitration of disputes between neighborhoods would have to remain with the city-state, however; only a strong regional government can cope with mounting regional problems—sanitation, housing, education, and pollution abatement, to name a few.

Such a system has yet another advantage: the city-states could be made "organic." That is, they could be permitted to expand or contract as dwelling, employment, and travel patterns altered—just as Standard Metropolitan Statistical Areas grow by Bureau of the Census decision, and the Atlanta "umbrella" agency is to grow with the Atlanta SMSA. As contiguous areas of a city-state became urbanized (according to Census Bureau criteria, for instance) they could automatically be added to the city-state just as they are now added to SMSA's.

The essential element would be a flexibility that would not permit urban residents to flee responsibility for their city and still make use of and demands upon its services, facilities, and employment centers. As populations shifted—suburbanizing further or contracting toward the center of the city again—the boundaries of the city would shift: residents of the city, in fleeing *en masse* to sites outside the city-state, would find the city-state's limits soon expanding to enclose them again. The only escape from responsibility for the city would be to a rural retreat distant enough from the city-state so that its residents could no longer be dependent upon the city-state's services, facilities, employment concentrations, and cultural influence.

As two growing city-states spread toward each other and a geographical area immediately between them in the line of expansion became dependent upon both parent city-states, that area could be allowed to choose between them in a referendum. Two contiguous city-states could also be allowed to form compacts or to merge by referenda if it were determined that by merger still further governmental economies could be effected. The important point is that under an "organic" system of mapping governmental boundaries, the flexibility affords a great variety of choices not now permitted local governments because of the rigidity of jurisdictional boundaries.

The transition to a city-state system, and eventually to an "organic" city-state system, would require dramatic leadership from the national level, both congressional and executive activity, and, more than likely, a major new provision of the Constitution. It is for the nation to decide whether or not the saving of its cities is worth the seemingly drastic action outlined. The action is not as drastic as it appears, however. The city-states would no more be "super-governments" than are the states of Arizona and Utah today. They would, in fact, be states in the full sense of the term as used in American civics; the only difference proposed is that the city-states' boundaries be flexible—contractible and expandable—to meet the needs of shifting populations and to ensure that urban users no longer be permitted and *encouraged* to be urban abusers.

Even such a radical-appearing restructuring of urban government as "organic" city-statism would be but a functional step at best. The problem of the city is much more than one of function; it is one of attitude. That attitude is what has led to the destruction of the city by highways, the flight to suburbia, and an entire range of other phenomena—from racism to our slavery to the automobile. (The two are inseparable parts of the same callousness toward human values that is ruining the city.)

In Washington, where the nation governs *its* city with a heavy hand and thus demonstrates most vividly its urban attitude, the highway-laced suburbs are in the ascendant and the city has become a confinement camp for the poor and the black and the indigent. Washington and the nation's other urban centers are the kinds of places they are because American society became suburbanized before it had a long enough opportunity, in most urban regions, to become urbanized. In its cities America has shown its "urban" policy to be one of freedom for developers, highway builders, and automobiles instead of people. In this way the nation's "urban policy," if it has one, is to use its cities, to meddle in their erratic efforts to improve their environments, but never to cultivate them, nurture them, or pay for their use. Ours has been an anti-urban policy, a suburban policy, designed for and by an anti-urban society. If the effort to save our cities is ever to have a chance of success, the nation must begin to change its attitudes about cities and develop a commitment to their future. The nation must recognize that the city is its "home." We must begin, as a nation, to trust our cities. Too often we regard them as suspicious breeding grounds of revolt rather than as gathering places for ideas.

Only when we begin to think positively about our cities can we hope to start resolving their problems. Those problems were brought on in large measure by callousness, high-handedness, and exploitation on the part of highway builders and their officeholder allies, by indifference toward the cities on the part of those who had once lived in them, and by racial fears that spurred the flight to suburbia. The problems were brought on by fear of the city itself—fear of its crowds, its heights, its age, its differences.

In the suburbs, everything was new, uncrowded (except at rush hour), generally quite flat, and restfully—almost narcotically—the same. The suburbs *looked* more like the rural areas and farms from which Americans had so recently come to the cities. In the suburbs Americans could again begin to farm, even if it were only a 20-by-40-foot plot of crabgrass or a thin row of scraggly rosebushes. In the suburbs the American rancher could again have the freedom of his horse, even if the horse now was 250 horses sheathed in steel and prone to become caught in traffic jams on its way to town. The suburban American of the 1970's is not so far removed from his farming and ranching ancestors. Perhaps they, too, were selfish consumers of machines and land, but they had not been numerous enough to make it show up on a map of the country as great blotches of suburbia's peculiar blight—pavement everywhere, bordered by garish signs, small drive-up commercial establishments, and scented with the exhaust fumes of hundreds of thousands of automobiles.

What is needed now is a new appreciation of urban life and urban styles—high-rise, multiple, heterogeneous, human, exciting, vibrant, and eager for new ideas and new stimuli of ideas—an appreciation that older civilizations developed but that America, regrettably in its passion to place property, profits, and machines above the dignity of man himself, did not have a chance to develop. Great civilizations have forever risen and fallen with their cities. It would be the final irony if that civilization founded on democratic principles failed because, out of its higher regard for property and machines than for men, it failed to build an urban society of urban places and urban men worthy of the term "civilized."

Index

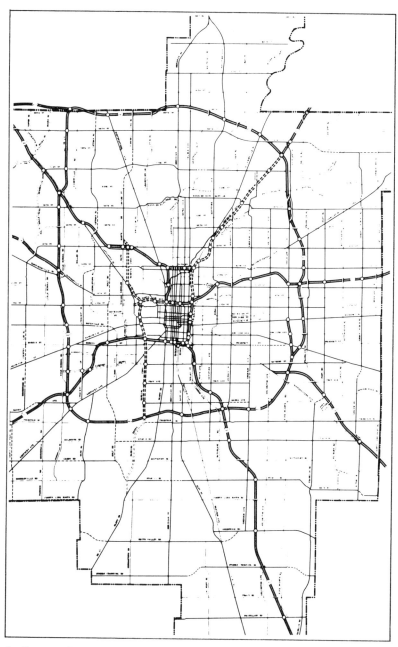

Indianapolis

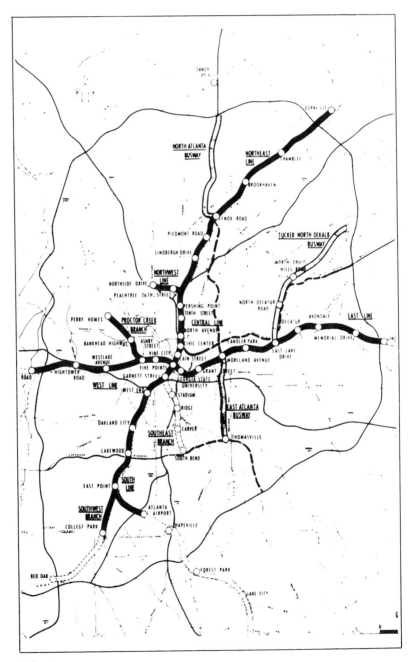

Atlanta Rapid Transit System